Jimmy Carter and the Politics of Frustration

JIMMY CARTER
AND THE POLITICS
OF FRUSTRATION

Garland A. Haas

McFarland & Company, Inc., Publishers
Jefferson, North Carolina, and London

This book is dedicated to that most perceptive observer of the American political scene, Will Rogers, who, when asked about his political party affiliation, explained: "I don't belong to any organized political party. I'm a Democrat."

And to Jimmy Carter, who might be tempted to say, "Amen," if asked to comment.

This book is also dedicated to my father, who was the first (although not the last) person to suggest to me that in American politics there are winners and losers, and sometimes it is difficult to tell which is which.

British Library Cataloguing-in-Publication data are available

Library of Congress Cataloguing-in-Publication Data

Haas, Garland A., 1919–
    Jimmy Carter and the politics of frustration / [by] Garland A. Haas.
    p. cm.
    Includes bibliographical references and index.
    ISBN 0-89950-705-0 (lib. bdg. : 50# alk. paper) ∞
    1. Carter, Jimmy, 1924–   . 2. United States—Politics and
government—1977–1981. I. Title.
E873.H3   1992
973.926'092—dc20   91-51000
                                                    CIP

Manufactured in the United States of America

McFarland & Company, Inc., Publishers
  Box 611, Jefferson, North Carolina 28640

Table of Contents

Prologue

On August 9, 1974, Richard Milhous Nixon flew home to San Clemente, California, a private citizen. The day before he had dramatically announced his resignation as president of the United States.[1] Behind him he left several key members of his administration to go to prison.

The following day, Vice President Gerald Rudolph "Jerry" Ford, the man who had not sought the presidency, took the oath of office as the thirty-eighth president of the United States in the East Room of the White House with his wife Betty holding the Bible. The new president was hailed by his colleagues in both parties as a "decent" and "good" man, who would bind up the wounds inflicted on the nation by the Watergate scandal. As Ford assumed his new duties he promised an administration of "openness and candor." "Our long national nightmare is over," he proclaimed. "Our constitution works. Our great republic is a government of laws and not of men." A relieved people rejoiced with their likeable and attractive new chief executive.

But then, on September 8, 1974, Ford announced that he was granting Richard Nixon "a full, free, and absolute pardon" for all offenses he "committed or may have committed or taken part in" while president. He explained afterwards, "My conscience says it is my duty." He was pardoning Nixon, he said, in part out of compassion and in part "to firmly shut and seal this book" of Watergate. He did it without an admission of guilt from Nixon, and he gave Nixon custody of telltale taped evidence of his crimes.[2]

Ford's action stunned the nation. Some people wondered whether Ford was just gullible or whether he had struck a deal to gain the presidency — whether he had agreed before assuming office to pardon Nixon if he would step aside. There had been no deal, Ford insisted. Others were outraged by the double standard that punished those who had acted on Nixon's behalf but spared Nixon himself. Ford's popularity plummeted. He was "just another politician," a respondent told a *Washington Post* pollster the week after the pardon.[3]

1

More importantly, as a result of the political cynicism revealed by presidents Richard Nixon and Lyndon Johnson, and now Gerald Ford, nearly everyone formed at least a skeptical attitude, or even downright hostility, toward government at all levels and its practitioners. The legacy of the Vietnam War and Watergate, as it affected the American presidency, was a demand on the part of the American people for simple honesty in government, a demand that James Earl "Jimmy" Carter, the honest, truth-telling, anti–Washington outsider, appeared to have made the most of.

The purpose of this book is to describe how it was that Jimmy Carter, a virtually unknown peanut processor from rural Plains, Georgia, finally did end up in the White House, how he comported himself in his new-found role as leader of the most powerful nation in the free world, and why, in the end, he was unable to succeed himself in office. It explores how Carter initially benefited from public demands for accountability created by Vietnam and Watergate, and how his image later suffered at the hands of intractable Congresses created, ironically, by those same scandals. We will also consider the fact that Carter, faced with more volatile issues, more new rules, and more new influences than any of his predecessors, appeared to suffer from an overabundance of simple bad luck. (It almost seems as though Carter used any *good* luck he might have had in getting to the presidency.) It could be argued, of course, that much of his bad luck resulted from the fact that he and his subordinates in the White House were markedly inept in dealing with the members of Congress, even those who belonged to their own party.

Even so, although many observers concluded that Jimmy Carter was at best a very modest success as president of the United States, it is hard to imagine how any president facing the same issues and two Congresses as intractable as the Ninety-fifth and Ninety-sixth could have succeeded.

1. Jimmy Carter's Quest for the Presidency

On a subfreezing January 20, 1977, "Jimmy" Carter[1] was inaugurated as the thirty-ninth president of the United States. A crowd estimated at 150,000 remained hushed as a massed choir of black Atlanta college students sang the "Battle Hymn of the Republic"—the Union's Civil War anthem—and then was moved to cheers as the business-suited and hatless, fifty-two year old "Man from Plains" repeated the presidential oath in the soft-shoe of a South Georgia accent. Following the swearing-in, Carter stated, "I have just taken the oath of office on the Bible my mother gave me just a few years ago open to a timeless admonition from the prophet Micah: 'He has showed thee, O man, what is good; and what doth the Lord require of thee, but to do justly, and to love mercy, and to walk humbly with thy God.'"[2]

His fourteen-minute inaugural address—one of the briefest (and blandest) ever—set a tone of confident but limited expectations. "I have no new dream to set forth today, but rather urge a fresh faith in the old dream.... The American dream endures, we must again have faith in our country—and in one another.... Let our recent mistakes bring a resurgent commitment to the basic principles of our nation, for we know that if we despise our own government we have no future." Human rights, environmental quality, nuclear arms control, and the search for justice and peace were the policy priorities Carter claimed.[3]

In closing, he issued a warning: There would be limits. Americans simply could not afford everything they might want. It was an unpopular idea, he warned—Americans were not accustomed to limits. "We have learned that more is not necessarily better, that even our great nation has its recognized limits, and that we can neither answer all questions nor solve all problems.... We must simply do our best."[4]

After the inaugural ceremonies the proud and smiling new president, breaking a tradition observed by newly-inaugurated presidents since the

3

time of President Jefferson, waved off the official limousine and, with his wife Rosalynn and nine year old daughter Amy, took the cold, mile-and-a-half walk down an avenue of well-wishers from the Capitol to their new home in the White House. The Secret Service men assigned to protect the president were not happy about Carter's decision to walk. Demonstrators along the parade route were carrying various anti–Carter banners including some reading "The Ku Klux Klan Loves Carter" and "Impeach Carter Before It Is Too Late."[5] Nevertheless, Carter had sent his first message to the American public: His administration would be different from that of his predecessors.

In the evening the Carters attended seven inaugural parties[6] where 35,000 guests greeted the new president and his wife. He wore a tuxedo, and the new first lady wore the pale blue satin evening dress she had worn for her husband's inauguration as governor of Georgia.[7] When it was over he told a reporter: "It's been just about a perfect day."[8]

It might have been a perfect day for James Earl Carter, Jr., but it had been a long time in arriving. He had been elected after one of the longest and most arduous campaigns for the presidency in American political history. It had started officially on Thursday, December 12, 1974 — one month after the midterm congressional elections and one month before his term of office as governor of Georgia ended — with an announcement before the National Press Club: "My name is Jimmy Carter, and I am running for president of the United States." The press, and most everyone else, generally greeted his announcement of candidacy with indifference: "Jimmy who?"[9]

It was small wonder that Carter's announcement of candidacy ignited few fireworks. Carter, a Naval Academy–educated nuclear engineer turned peanut farmer, businessman, and politician from Plains, Georgia, was all but unknown. His political experience at the state level was minimal; at the national level, negligible. In 1966 at the age of forty-two, in a lackluster campaign, he had run third in the Georgia Democratic Party primary election for governor, far behind the winner, the arch-segregationist Lester Maddox. In 1970, after serving two terms as a Georgia state senator, he was elected governor, upsetting popular incumbent Carl Sanders in the primary election. For this victory Carter had campaigned for four years, as Jules Witcover put it, "like a migrant worker hustling for harvest work, putting in a regular day at the family's peanut plant, then driving to all corners of Georgia to speak and meet voters."[10]

However, along about 1972, long before his term of office as governor expired, Carter realized that his political options were very limited. He could not succeed himself as governor, since Georgia law limited him to one four-year term. He could try to unseat the well-entrenched Herman Talmadge from the United States Senate, an effort which, even if it succeeded, would leave him a very junior member of that body. Or he could retire, at the age of fifty, to his farm and peanut-processing business in Plains. When his young associates, Dr. Peter Bourne, a British-born psychiatrist, and Hamilton Jordan, urged him to seek the presidency, Carter did not need much persuasion—it was a risk worth taking, he agreed. The way was cleared for two years of quiet but intense preparation.

At best, Carter's chances for the presidential nomination seemed minimal. His list of liabilities seemed endless. Although he was a lifelong Democrat, he was all but unknown in national Democratic Party circles or even among the state leaders of his party. As a Democrat in a one-party state he had had little concern (or need) for the national party organization, having spent most of his political life campaigning in primaries against other Democrats. He had never campaigned against a serious Republican candidate. He was not an incumbent; he was not from the Senate, the traditional breeding ground of American politics; and he was a Southerner and neither party had nominated a nonincumbent Southerner for president since the Civil War (unless Woodrow Wilson can be counted as a Southerner).

Carter also defied ideological categorizing. In fact, he had worked hard to avoid being labeled as either liberal or conservative. In the ensuing campaign for the nomination, when he was pressed to state how he stood in relation to his Democratic rivals for the nomination, he usually replied: "I never characterize myself as a conservative, liberal, or moderate and this is what distinguishes me from them."[11]

Even so, Carter appeared to be clearly liberal in most matters of civil rights. In his inaugural address as governor, he had declared that "the time for racial discrimination is over.... We cannot afford to waste the talents and abilities given by God to one single Georgian." During his administration as governor of Georgia, he had increased the number of black appointees on state boards and agencies from three to fifty-three and the number of black state employees from 4,850 to 6,684.[12] He also placed a portrait of the late civil rights leader Martin Luther King, Jr., in the state capitol building, a move that would have been inconceivable in earlier years. Carter's stand on race relations had secured for him the support of such respected black leaders as Martin Luther King, Sr., and the young three-term Georgia Congressman Andrew Young.

In most matters of economics, however, Carter was clearly conservative, an attitude deeply ingrained in him. (Charles Kirbo, one of his most knowledgeable friends and advisers, characterized Carter as "a little tight" when it came to money.)[13] Because he appeared to be so ambivalent on most non–civil rights issues he was distrusted by many in the New Deal coalition that had dominated the Democratic Party since 1932.[14]

Also, Carter was that frightening political phenomenon – an avowed "born-again" Christian who taught Sunday School, preached and prayed in public. *Time* described him as the "most unabashed moralist" to seek the presidency since William Jennings Bryan (not exactly intended as an endorsement).[15]

Carter was also a stranger to the public. His national claim to fame had been an appearance on the television quiz show "What's My Line" on which the contestants did not know who he was even after the emcee told them. It was clear that, to secure the nomination, Carter would have to overcome odds greater than those overcome by any other major party nominee in recent American history.[16]

After George McGovern's trouncing in 1972, media executives and political observers generally expected that the Democrats would turn to an established leader – former presidential candidate Hubert Humphrey of Minnesota or Massachusetts Senator Edward Kennedy – to be the Democratic standard-bearer. However, Carter correctly sensed that he had a real advantage over Humphrey, a two-time loser whose health was deteriorating, and Kennedy, who was not only still under the shadow of Chappaquiddick but who had official Senate duties to perform which would limit his time available for campaign activities, a real handicap under the new Democratic Party reform rules. (In the race for the presidency in 1976 being unemployed would prove to be an advantage.) And so, along about 1972, long before his term of office as governor expired, Carter began to position himself for the race for the presidency.

CARTER AND THE TRILATERAL COMMISSION. While it was true that Carter came close to being a political unknown in 1974, he was far from being an outsider to the international business community. While still governor of Georgia he had become a member of the new and prestigious Trilateral Commission, an exclusive group of top bankers and businessmen in the United States, Western Europe, and Japan, who met periodically to study their mutual problems.[17]

Carter's appointment to the Trilateral Commission had been arranged by David Rockefeller, the president of Chase Manhattan Bank, who had established the commission in 1972 with the assistance of the Council on Foreign Relations and the Rockefeller Foundation. Carter's membership on the commission had been supported by his longtime friend from Atlanta, J. Paul Austin, chairman of the board of Coca-Cola, who subsequently spent many months introducing Carter to other big businessmen. Other members of the commission were Henry Ford II; Douglas Dillon; Harold Brown, president of California Institute of Technology; Hedley Donovan, a longtime editor of *Time* magazine; Alden Clausen, president of BankAmerica, the nation's largest bank; Leonard Woodcock, president of the United Auto Workers union; W. Michael

Blumenthal, president of the Bendix Corporation; Cyrus Vance, a Wall Street lawyer; and Senator Walter Mondale of Minnesota. The executive director of the commission was Columbia University professor Zbigniew Brzezinski.[18]

Membership in the Trilateral Commission gave Carter valuable foreign policy experience and credentials. It also gave him access to the top corporate elite in America who, as we will see, supported him during and after his quest for the nomination. Also, as we will see, he made many of his key appointments from the membership of the Trilateral Commission.[19]

THE CARTER CAMPAIGN TEAM. As it turned out, Carter's rise from obscurity was phenomenal, thanks in large part to the efforts of one of the most efficient campaign teams in modern politics. They soon provided the answer to the question "Jimmy who?"

As governor, Carter had surrounded himself with a group of savvy young political strategists from Georgia, who, according to chronicler of American presidential elections Theodore H. White, quickly demonstrated that they understood the mass media — especially television — better than any team of troupers who had joined a candidate on the road to the White House before.[20]

The leader of the team was Hamilton McWhorter "Ham" Jordan (pronounced Jerdun), who had been campaign manager of Carter's gubernatorial race in 1970 and had served as executive secretary while he was governor. In 1973 and 1974 he was Carter's aide at the Democratic National Committee when Carter headed the congressional election campaign effort.

When the presidential race started, Jordan ran the campaign in work boots, old pants, no tie, and a windbreaker, with a folksy irreverence that shocked the old-line Democratic Party "regulars" but only partly concealed Jordan's forceful ambition and shrewd political judgment.

Jordan was ably assisted by Joseph Lester "Jody" Powell, Jr., who joined the Carter team in 1969 as a volunteer while a graduate student at Emory University. In the gubernatorial campaign Powell and Carter traveled the length and breadth of Georgia hitting every small town and county courthouse they could find. After speaking, Carter, "grinning and gripping," would work the crowd, while Powell, notebook in hand, carefully jotted down the names and addresses of wellwishers.

After Carter was elected governor, Powell, although he had no journalistic experience, was appointed his press secretary and quickly demonstrated skill in anticipating how the press would respond to Governor Carter's actions and utterances. In the ensuing presidential campaign, the outgoing and irreverent Powell, who appeared to enjoy the give-and-take of the press briefings, brought considerable humor to the otherwise nearly humorless Carter camp, which quickly made him a popular figure with the members of the press who traveled with Carter and covered the campaign. Meanwhile, Jordan, who did not ordinarily travel with Carter, remained something of a mystery to the national press.[21]

There were other important, but less obvious, members of the Carter campaign team. Charles Kirbo, a senior partner in Atlanta's most prestigious law firm and a longtime Carter friend, served as an adviser without portfolio and wielded immense influence. Gerald Rafshoon, a wisecracking New Yorker (one of the non–Georgia natives among Carter's upper echelons), served as the campaign's advertising director and as a member of Carter's inner circle of advisers. Rafshoon had managed the advertising that brought Carter to the governorship in 1970. Patrick "Pat" Caddell came aboard as chief of Carter's polling operations. Caddell had played a prominent role in every Democratic presidential contest since 1972 when, at age twenty-two, he became George McGovern's pollster. Stuart Eizenstadt, an Atlanta lawyer, served as Carter's chief issues adviser. Unlike nearly everyone else, he had experience in the federal government and in national politics, having served in Lyndon Johnson's White House and in Hubert Humphrey's 1968 presidential campaign.[22]

CARTER'S STRATEGY. During the summer and fall of 1972, Jordan outlined in a series of memoranda a strategy by which he believed the Georgia governor could win the Democratic nomination in 1976. In one of his memoranda, Jordan noted that distrust of government was already a national issue of consequence and that it would loom even larger by 1976.[23] The national mood, Jordan concluded, demanded an outsider— "not someone associated with a long series of mistakes made at the White House and on Capitol Hill." If this were true, Jordan concluded, Carter's lack of experience in Washington would be an asset. He also emphasized that the public was more interested in personal qualities—truth-telling, integrity, competence—than in extensive governmental experience (which they had come to distrust).[24] As it turned out, Jordan's diagnosis was right on target. The Carter team also recognized that the Democratic Party leaders would not choose Carter unless they knew him. A first priority, therefore, was to make the governor known better nationally. To this end, the Carters invited political and press luminaries who happened to be in the state to the governor's mansion.[25]

One such invitation brought Carter together with Robert Strauss, the recently appointed chairman of the Democratic National Committee. Strauss agreed to permit Carter to take over as campaign coordinator of the Democratic Party's fund drive for the 1974 congressional and gubernatorial elections. Although this job traditionally was little more than an honorary title, Carter used his assignment to great advantage. He traveled throughout the nation, often at party expense, campaigning for Demo-

cratic candidates in more than sixty congressional races. All the while he
established valuable contacts with state party leaders and local politicians
and with heads of important interest groups representing organized labor,
farmers, and consumers. These contacts would stand him in good stead
when he launched his own drive for the presidency. Meanwhile, Carter's
committee sought out the issues which most concerned the public and
prepared thirty background papers that were mailed to at least a thousand
Democratic candidates.[26]

THE CONGRESSIONAL ELECTIONS OF 1974. Carter's efforts on behalf of
Democratic congressional candidates paid off. Although President Ford
stumped vigorously for Republican congressional candidates and warned
of the dangers of a "veto-proof" Democratic Congress—one in which the
Democrats could recklessly override his efforts to stem their spending
orgies—his campaigning had little effect. The voters responded to Watergate, the Nixon pardon, and increasing inflation by returning a commanding majority of Democrats to Congress. The Democrats would control
two-thirds of the House of Representatives and three-fifths of the Senate
in the Ninety-fourth Congress.

Nearly all the Republican losers were conservatives associated with
President Nixon. Even President Ford's old seat in the Michigan Fifth
Congressional District was captured by a Democrat for the first time in
sixty-four years.[27] Particularly notable was the strong showing the party
made in the South, where many of the GOP gains of previous elections
were wiped out.

Once the congressional elections were out of the way, the Georgians
traveled to forty-six states and the District of Columbia. Everywhere they
went, Carter appeared on local television programs, cultivated political
editors and reporters, and delivered speeches that stressed trustworthi-
ness in government. His message was a simple one. As president he would
eliminate the kind of secrecy in government and diplomacy that had produced the Vietnam War and the Watergate scandal. He would open
government up to the average citizen. If he were president, he told his
growing audiences, he would try to make his administration "as good and
honest and decent and compassionate and filled with love as are the
American people."

Carter knew that he would have to win a lot of primaries to get the
delegates he needed. However, he also recognized that, under the new
Democratic Party reform rules, the vulnerable place in the nomination
process was the primary election system. The point was to enter and win
the early primaries. Even a respectable showing in the early primaries
could produce sufficient momentum for a convention victory. Since
Carter had a name recognition problem, a major objective of his early
campaign was to attract the media. It did not much matter that only a

fraction of the eligible voters voted and that his winning margin was minuscule; the point was to get the headline: "Jimmy Carter Wins (and Wins Again)."[28]

So Carter and his advisers devised a primary election strategy. He would prove himself in the early caucuses and primaries and then use each victory as a stepping stone. A strong showing in the January 1976 precinct caucuses in Iowa, which were usually ignored by the serious candidates because of the small number of delegates selected, and the "first-in-the-nation" primary election in New Hampshire would prove that even though he was a Southerner he could win in the North. This claim would enhance Carter's prospects in the crucial Florida primary against Alabama governor George Wallace, whom he had to defeat in a Southern state in order to establish himself nationally as a Southern alternative to the perennial symbol of discontent.[29]

Carter's strategy was also expected to meet the money problem — winning in Iowa would create media attention, which would produce a flow of funds for campaigning in New Hampshire. Winning in New Hampshire would produce funds for further campaigning, and so on. Federal funds would be used when they became available, and additional money would be raised by direct mail solicitation and other means. Of necessity, it would be a bare-bones campaign, relying heavily on personal organization. The new spending limits and the lack of large contributions meant there could be only a minimal use of high cost campaign literature, buttons, bumper stickers, telephone banks, hired political workers, expensive hotel suites, and luxurious campaign airplanes. On the other hand there should be maximum use (as much as half of the available funds) of television, which should promote "free media" (network evening news, etc.) time.

By early 1975, Carter's team was canvassing the country, state by state, precinct by precinct. Jordan and the headquarters staff, operating from Atlanta rather than an expensive Washington office, conducted the overall campaign. Carter and Powell (and his notebook) traveled the country, taking Carter's "trust me" campaign from one community to another, stirring up interest, recruiting new supporters, and building a grassroots organization in every section of the country. Before they were finished they had raised enough money to qualify Carter for federal matching funds. Eventually, Carter's name appeared on the primary election ballot in twenty-six states, and he campaigned actively in most of them (which was, in fact, a remarkable accomplishment).[30] Local reporters began to write that Carter was an effective face-to-face campaigner, but the national press paid little attention; when they did it was to emphasize the novelty of his campaign.

Indications that Carter was making progress came when a straw poll of 1,094 Iowa Democrats taken by the *Des Moines Register* showed him finishing ahead of the other candidates with 23 percent of the vote. (A good omen for the Iowa caucuses in the spring of 1976.) A Gallup Poll in the same month listed him as the first choice among Democrats for the Democratic nomination.[31] Further encouragement came when Carter won the support of two-thirds of the 1,035 delegates to the Florida Democratic Convention on November 16, 1975, significantly defeating George Wallace.

THE DEMOCRATIC PARTY RULES REFORM. Carter was helped in his quest for the nomination by several important changes made in the rules of the Democratic Party governing the selection of delegates to future presidential nominating conventions.

During the early 1970s the momentum for reform peaked in the Democratic Party. The generally chaotic situation which marked the 1968 Democratic Convention in Chicago led the delegates to that convention to adopt two important reports on future delegate selection. These reports would insure that at the 1972 convention delegates would have to be selected in a way that would permit full and timely opportunities for participation by a broader range of delegates. Furthermore, the newly appointed chairman of the Democratic National Committee, Senator Fred Harris of Oklahoma, was urged to establish special committees to implement the reports. Accordingly, Harris appointed Senator George McGovern to chair a Commission on Delegate Selection and Party Reforms, whose job was to recommend methods for choosing convention delegates "by procedures calculated to promote party unity and head off bitter quarrels over the composition of and procedures at the 1972 Democratic National Convention."

During the spring and summer of 1969, the McGovern Commission held a series of open hearings in seventeen cities and took testimony from over 500 witnesses—many of whom suggested the outright abolition of the convention system.[32] The testimony of these witnesses revealed that in at least twenty states the entire process of national convention delegate selection in the Democratic Party was left to the discretion of a handful of party leaders. In two Southern states, for example, a single governor and the state chairman could name the entire state delegation to the national convention. In some states—as in Massachusetts—the delegation selection process began fully three years before the presidential campaign, before anyone knew what the issues were and who the candidates might be. In New York and Pennsylvania a state committee could name one-third of its state's entire delegation and in Illinois more than one-half.[33] The report added that "secret caucases, closed slate-making, widespread proxy voting[34]—and a host of other procedural irregularities—were common in precinct, county, district, and state conventions."

The report also found representation of minorities far below the proportion of such groups in the population. Blacks comprised only 5 percent of the delegates; women only 13 percent; and a majority of delegations had no more than one delegate under thirty years of age.[35] By September 1970, the McGovern Commission's reform proposals were ready for the Democratic National Committee and were adopted.[36]

The McGovern Commission reforms required that in convention states at least 75 percent of a state's directly elected delegates be chosen from districts not larger than congressional districts and not by the convention at large, to guarantee that a state's delegates were allocated according to the candidate's demonstrated strength in the state. In an even more drastic step the commission required state Democratic parties to set "affirmative action" quotas for the 1972 convention to insure that minorities, women and young people (defined as people not more than thirty years nor less than eighteen years of age), be adequately represented on state delegations.[37]

In a move to take the selection of the party nominees away from the bosses and out of smoke-filled rooms, the new rules stipulated that state parties could not appoint public or party officials as delegates merely because of their official positions. As a result, many regular party functionaries and leaders were shut out of the 1972 convention.[38] It proved to be a drastic change. By breaking the control of party leaders over the selection of convention delegates and turning the process over to the masses, the Democrats opened the way for special interest groups to assume the role the party organization had previously played in the selection of delegates and candidates.[39] The party convention was virtually stripped of power. As it turned out, the nominees would be chosen by direct primaries, which favored image makers and not coalition builders.

In the short run, the changes did, of course, help outsiders like Jimmy Carter who had little appeal to the Democratic Party to secure the nomination. In the long run, as we will see, the destruction of party consensus which resulted would make it very difficult for Jimmy Carter to govern.[40]

Not surprisingly, the changes brought about by the McGovern reforms led to the nomination of the senator himself as the Democratic candidate in 1972 and, many thought, the humiliating defeat which McGovern subsequently suffered at the hands of Richard Nixon.[41]

THE DEMOCRAT'S 1974 MINI-CONVENTION. Their successes in the November congressional elections of 1974, the continuing economic downturn, and encouraging early polls indicating that the Democrats stood a good chance of victory in the 1976 election put the Democrats in a jubilant mood when they convened their first midterm party conference on December 6, 1974, at Kansas City.[42] The 2,035 delegates from every state and territory came to hear, debate, and approve a new party charter.[43] But mostly they came to extrude from the party's delegate selection process several of the more "suicidal" 1972 reforms.[44]

When they were finished, mandatory quotas were repudiated. Instead the delegates were to be selected according to "affirmative action programs" under which state party officials were required actively to recruit minority group members, women, and young people into the party. Further, delegates were to be chosen in the same calendar year as the national convention, and no party or public officials could be delegates *ex officio*. Finally, anyone who aspired to be a Democratic convention delegate, whether via primaries or caucuses, would have to declare his or her presidential preference.[45]

The new rules banned open crossover primaries. Also winner-take-all primaries were eliminated to prevent a repetition of the 1972 California primary outcome in which George McGovern won a narrow victory over Hubert Humphrey, yet received California's entire bloc of 271 delegates, the largest of the 1972 Democratic Convention. Instead, states were to apportion delegate votes, whether selected in caucuses, primaries, or conventions, according to the popular preference for rival candidates. Party activists returned from Kansas City bathed in good feelings.

THE FEDERAL ELECTION CAMPAIGN ACT AMENDMENTS OF 1974. Late in 1974, Congress, pressured by the public outrage against the excesses of Watergate,[46] acted to control campaign financing by passing the Federal Election Campaign Act of 1974. Passed after prolonged debate, the act constituted the most sweeping campaign reform measure in American political history.

From the standpoint of political unknowns like Jimmy Carter, who are usually severely handicapped by a lack of campaign funds, the most important provision of this act is that candidates may now receive partial funding of their nomination and election campaigns from the government. Specifically, the government will match the money raised by a candidate up to a limit of $5 million in the primary and $20 million for a major party candidate in the geneal election with proportional amounts for minor party candidates who received 5 percent or more of the total vote in the previous presidential election (or available retroactively if 5 percent were obtained in the current election). To obtain these funds a presidential candidate need only accept the spending limitations and raise an initial sum of at least $5,000 in each of twenty states with no single contribution to exceed $250. A prospective candidate thus had to demonstrate more than just regional support. Finally, the act created an eight-member, bipartisan Federal Elections Commission to supervise and monitor its provisions.

GROWTH OF POLITICAL ACTION COMMITTEES (PAC's). Paradoxically, although the reformers intended by their reforms to secure "public financing" of political campaigns — that is, public subsidies from the government to major candidates to eliminate private financing by individual "fat cats" and secret corporate slush funds which bankrolled pet legislators and covertly bought influence — the campaign finance reforms of 1974, by granting legitimacy to organized fund-raising, gave a green light to businesses to become aggressively involved in financing political campaigns. Although the reformers achieved public financing for the general election campaign for the presidency in 1974, Congress blocked such taxpayer subsidies for congressional races — leaving that arena open to individual contributions and to the formation of political action committees (PACs) to raise and spend money.

Almost overnight, PACs became the major new money channel. Business- and labor-oriented PACs, each of which concentrated on the issues and candidates of its choice, quickly proliferated. These political action groups soon became an effective electoral rival to political parties.[47] In 1974, there were 608 PACs of all kinds including eighty-nine corporate PACs. In 1976 labor PACs, including teacher associations, raised and spent $8.1 million, much of which was on behalf of Jimmy Carter.[48]

The Other Democratic Candidates

In all, fourteen Democrats announced that they would challenge Carter for the Democratic nomination for the presidency in 1976. The superabundance of candidates was almost certainly one of the first fruits of the 1974 Federal Election Campaign Act — for the first time the federal treasury was picking up roughly half the cost of running.

Also, the significant increase in the number of primaries had an impact. By 1976, some thirty states and the District of Columbia had passed some kind of presidential primary law, and nearly three-fourths of the 3,008 delegates to the 1976 Democratic National Convention would be chosen or bound by these primaries. In several states, the Democratic state party organization had simply concluded that the complex Democratic reform rules — especially the requirement of "affirmative action" to insure minority representation in their convention delegations — demanded too much of the state party organization. Rather than maneuver in state caucuses and conventions and risk challenges on grounds of discrimination later, they simply surrendered national nominating politics to the new activists by establishing a presidential primary. In many cases, these "new style primaries" would produce delegates and candidates who had never served an apprenticeship in the party.[49]

SENATOR EDWARD M. KENNEDY. Most people, including Carter, assumed that the young and attractive junior senator from Massachusetts, Edward M. "Ted" Kennedy, would be the Democratic front-runner for the nomination in 1976. National polls showed him far ahead of all prospective contenders. Local and state Democratic politicians shared doubts about his electability, but accepted the inevitability of his nomination if he wanted it. In 1968 and 1972 liberals in the Democratic Party had pressed Kennedy to seek the nomination, but he had held back. Now, he was being pressured again to run.

It had long been assumed that Kennedy would make his bid for the presidency at the first logical opportunity. After his brother Robert's death in 1968, Kennedy had spoken of his determination to "pick up a fallen standard," and although he declined to do so as a presidential candidate in 1968 and 1972, the expectation was that a third bid for the White House was only a matter of time. Nineteen-seventy-six appeared to be that time. The Republicans were extremely vulnerable. Watergate, the low state of the economy, President Ford's poor showing in the early polls, and the rather obvious disunity in the GOP provided the Democrats with an excellent opportunity to wrest the White House from the Republicans.

There was hanging over Kennedy, of course, the question of the now-famous 1969 incident at Chappaquiddick Island, Massachusetts, in which a young woman drowned when an automobile driven by Kennedy plunged off a narrow bridge into a tidal pool late at night. At the time questions were raised by reporters and politicians not only about the circumstances of her death, but about Kennedy's handling of the incident. Among other things he failed to report the accident for almost ten hours. The senator pleaded guilty to the minor charge of leaving the scene of an accident. It was an open wound into which the press intermittently poked and prodded. Kennedy recovered quickly in public opinion polls, however, and by mid–1974 he generally led all other Democrats in presidential preference polling. However, on September 23, 1974, Kennedy unexpectedly and dramatically announced that because of his obligations to his family he was removing himself from the race. "I will not accept the nomination . . . at the national convention, and I will oppose any effort to promote my candidacy in any other way." The decision, he said, was "firm, final, and unconditional." Some inevitably viewed his withdrawal with skepticism.[50]

Carter and his team were dismayed over Kennedy's decision not to run. With Kennedy in the race, they reasoned, the other liberal Democrats would stay out. With Kennedy out of the race it was hard to tell who would finally emerge as the competition. As it turned out, however, the proliferation of liberal candidates Kennedy's withdrawal set loose was more beneficial to Carter than Kennedy's presence in the field.

SENATOR WALTER FREDERICK MONDALE. An early announced candidate for the 1976 nomination was Minnesota senator Walter "Fritz" Mondale. Mondale had established a strong record in the Senate as a bona fide liberal. He was the moving force behind passage of the landmark open housing provisions of the Civil Rights Act of 1968, and he was a firm supporter of the use of busing to help speed school desegregation. Although he had initially supported the American presence in Vietnam, by 1968, after a visit to Vietnam, he had reversed his position and had urged Humphrey, then tied to the Johnson administration war policy, to do likewise. After 1968, he supported all Senate efforts to limit fighting or military expenditures in Southeast Asia. He was also co-chairman (with Fred Harris) of Hubert Humphrey's 1968 presidential campaign.

Unexpectedly, after more than a year of traveling the country and speaking to Democratic groups "exploring his chances" for a 1976 bid (and being unable to raise much money), Mondale quit the race two weeks after the 1974 fall elections. "Basically," he explained, "I found I did not have the overwhelming desire to be president which is essential for the kind of campaign that is required." He added: "I don't think anyone should be president who is not willing to go through fire." He couldn't face, he said subsequently, spending another whole year "sleeping in Holiday Inns."[51]

REPRESENTATIVE MORRIS K. UDALL. Kennedy's and Mondale's withdrawals produced a rush to enter the race. Among the liberals the first to announce was Representative Morris K. "Mo" Udall of Arizona, a former professional basketball player. Udall, a forthright liberal, was fifty-two years old, six feet, five inches tall, affable and witty (and probably the most intelligent Democratic candidate in 1976). He hoped to inherit the McGovern support among Democratic liberals. The Arizonan began his quest for the nomination with little public recognition.[52] Although the House of Representatives had never been a propitious place from which to start a race for the presidency,[53] Udall hoped that the new esteem generated by the Nixon impeachment hearings had created a new public acceptability for a congressional candidate. He offered himself as a candidate who could "bring the Democratic Party together again" after the McGovern fiasco of 1972. He also hoped, as had McGovern in 1972, to become the candidate of the left. Udall was helped in his search for the nomination when Tip O'Neill, the majority leader of the House of Representatives and certain to be the next speaker, threw his rather considerable influence and prestige behind his candidacy.

SENATOR HUBERT HORATIO HUMPHREY. A real but unannounced candidate was former Minnesota senator and Vice President Hubert H. Humphrey, the hyper-energetic practitioner of the politics of "Zest and Joy."[54] As a senator and vice president, Humphrey's name had been attached to every cause labeled "liberal" — civil rights, Food for Peace, nuclear disarmament, student loans, Social Security, rural electrification, and more — but running for President in 1968, he had supported the Johnson Vietnam War policy until a month before election day, for which the Vietnam era liberals had never forgiven him.

In 1976, now a two-time loser (the election in 1968 and the nomination in 1972), Humphrey did not delude himself about his chances. In the current battle, if all the active combatants managed to do each other in, he hoped that the Democrats would again turn to him, the acceptable elder statesman of the party. "If that happened to me," he said, "I wouldn't say no. I'd say, 'Let's go boys. Let's get this show on the road.'" Many of the older liberals were looking at Humphrey with a kind of nostalgic fondness: "We could do worse than old Hubert." By December 1975 Humphrey had moved ahead of Wallace (30 percent to 20 percent) in the Gallup Poll as the first choice among members of his party.[55]

As 1975 progressed, others joined the fray.

SENATOR HENRY M. JACKSON. Senator Henry "Scoop" Jackson of Washington State, a veteran of twelve years in the House of Representatives and twenty-two years in the Senate, delared on February 6, 1975.

The sixty-two year old Jackson, a recognized expert in the fields of energy, national defense, and conservation, was widely considered the Hill's most effective senator. In 1972 he made a brief run for the presidency. However, his support of the Vietnam War, and a growing reputation as a conservative, had hurt his chances and forced his withdrawal. He had come out of the 1972 campaign with the reputation that he couldn't win.

Nevertheless, Jackson had vigorous backing from influential Jewish leaders because of his long-held and vigorously expressed support of Israel, organized labor, and the defense establishment, which gave him a presidential consituency willing to fund his campaign. (Jackson was widely known as the "senator from Boeing" because he openly pushed the interest of Boeing Aircraft, the biggest military contractor from the state of Washington.)[56]

GOVERNOR EDMUND G. BROWN, JR. In 1974, Edmund G. "Jerry" Brown, Jr., won the California Democratic gubernatorial primary, and went on to capture the governorship by a modest margin. In office he set an example of fiscal austerity by such gestures as grounding the gubernatorial airplane, replacing the gubernatorial limousine with a modest Plymouth, living in a $275 a month apartment instead of the new $1.3 million gubernatorial mansion, and walking to work. As governor, he demonstrated that he was liberal on many social issues — supporting, for example, job training for the hard-core unemployed, and environmental conservation. Although the news reporters soon dubbed him "Governor Moonbeam" because of his eccentricities, he became phenomenally popular with the people.

Brown claimed to be the voice of "the new generation in politics." As he put it to students at Towson State University in Baltimore: "I started in politics in the 1960s, in the civil rights movement, in the antiwar movement. I marched with Cesar Chavez." To those attending the May 1976 Black Delegates' Congress in Charlotte, he said: "I represented the generation that came of age in the civil rights movement, in the anti–Vietnam war movement..."[57]

SENATOR FRED R. HARRIS. Senator Fred Harris of Oklahoma announced himself as the "new populist" (pronouncing it "popolist") candidate who could strip George Wallace's constituency away. Harris was an outspoken radical, supporting radical tax reform, all-out war on privilege for the rich and big business, massive public service employment. His slogans, "Take the rich off welfare" and "No More Bullshit," delighted campus youths radicalized by the Vietnam War and by dislike of the glaring economic inequalities in American society. Harris conducted a "people's campaign"—low budget, high enthusiasm, living off the land guerrilla-style. He stayed in private homes, used borrowed cars, and eschewed high-priced media experts and paid television.[58]

SENATOR LLOYD M. BENTSEN. Senator Lloyd M. Bentsen, a Texas insurance millionaire with a hankering to be president, was widely perceived to be running for president in the hope of being nominated for the vice presidency. Bentsen was an authentic war hero, having flown thirty-seven missions over Europe as a bomber pilot in World War II. He would be competing with "Scoop" Jackson for the political middle. Of some interest was the fact that Bentsen had defeated George Bush for the Senate seat from Texas in 1970.[59]

GOVERNOR TERRY SANFORD. Terry Sanford, the fifty-seven year old former governor of North Carolina and president of Duke University, presented himself as the liberal Southern candidate who would persuade George Wallace's supporters to his side. He had been severely beaten by Wallace in 1972 in the North Carolina primary and so, in 1976, it was critical that he beat Wallace in the Tarheel State. To establish his credentials as the better Southern alternative to George Wallace, he planned to compare his record on civil rights in the same time and place with Wallace's facing the same problems and atmosphere.[60]

R. SARGENT SHRIVER. Sargent Shriver, the fifty-nine year old former Peace Corps and anti-poverty director and ambassador to France, had been a stand-in in 1972 for Thomas Eagleton as the Democratic vice-presidential nominee. Shriver, a brother-in-law of Ted Kennedy, was considered by many to be a stalking horse for a Kennedy candidacy.

GOVERNOR MILTON SHAPP. Milton Shapp, sixty-two, a mild, soft-spoken man, had compiled a liberal record in two terms as governor of Pennsylvania (a major industrial state). He also enjoyed an excellent record as a self-made businessman in the emerging cable television business. Shapp was not taken seriously by the media, however, and as a Jew, he was bucking one of the great remaining political bugaboos for the presidency.

SENATOR BIRCH E. BAYH, JR. Birch Bayh, a forty-six year old, three term senator from Indiana, had strong labor support. Also as a chief sponsor of the Equal Rights Amendment, he would also have the support of women's groups the country over. Bayh emphasized his "electability" and the theme that he could unite the party as the candidate on whom Democrats would agree. His motto: "Birch Bayh: The One Candidate for President Who Can Put It All Together."

SENATOR FRANK CHURCH. Idaho Senator Frank Church, fifty, was a foreign-policy specialist and an early critic of the Vietnam War. He was now engaged in an investigation of the nation's intelligence community. A late entrant into the race (on March 18), Church declined to enter the competition personally until he had completed his investigative responsibilities. He thus undercut his chances by limiting his opportunities for public exposure.[61]

GOVERNOR GEORGE CORLEY WALLACE. Off to the right of the Democratic Party by himself was fifty-five year old George Corley Wallace. Although crippled and confined to a wheelchair because of the paralyzing effects of a would-be assassin's bullet during the 1972 campaign, he had not surrendered his presidential ambitions to his infirmity. Wallace was trying desperately to convince voters that he could physically handle the presidency. Well supplied with funds (some $7 million) raised through direct mail from millions of small contributors, Wallace again expected a mass revolt to bring him dollars—now matched by the federal government—as well as primary votes, delegates, and a major voice in the convention maneuvering, if not the Democratic Party nomination itself.[62]

The candidacy of Wallace presented a serious dilemma to the Democratic Party. The party leaders recognized the necessity of regaining the South lost to the Republicans in the election of 1968 if they were to regain the White House in 1976. However, winning the presidency through the selection of Wallace as the party's presidential nominee would carry, several thought, a prohibitive price—the projected loss of 29 percent of the Democrats and 27 percent of the Independents who would likely support any other candidate than Wallace—as well as a drastic reordering of the party's priorities. The dilemma was how to regain the South without alienating the supporters of Wallace.

The Alabama governor had become a national figure in June of 1963 when national television had shown him standing in the door of the

University of Alabama adminstration building, defying the United States government's order to admit blacks as students. After an abortive try for the presidency in 1964, in the summer of 1968 he formed the American Independent Party, which obligingly nominated him for the presidency. He then led a revolt of conservative Southern whites outraged over the liberal civil rights policies of the national Democratic Party. His was a demagogic and sarcastic campaign in which he appealed to America's darker side of fear, prejudice, intolerance, and hate. Nevertheless, he was able to achieve the remarkable feat of getting his name on the ballot in all fifty states, usually under the rubric of the American Independent Party, and to persuade ten million voters to vote for him.[63]

With this encouragement, Wallace ran again in 1972, and in that year's Democratic primaries he collected nearly four million primary votes — the largest popular vote in the pre-convention period up to the time of the attempt on his life. In 1974 his campaign also raised more than $2 million in campaign contributions from over 300,000 hard-core followers. In 1976, although Wallace was no longer (at least outwardly) a snarling segregationist, he still stood firmly and solidly for white supremacy. New York Times correspondent James Wooten suggests that, although the years had taught "the little judge" to conceal cleverly what he was really selling with the accepted and familiar code words of the era, he was still the white man's candidate in 1976.[64]

Wallace's candidacy was a problem for all of the Democrats who feared his real or potential stength.[65] How to woo Wallace supporters without directly attacking Wallace, even though he was clearly disregarding the progressive objectives that had marked the history of the Democratic Party? Fortunately for Carter, he did not have this problem. Since he was running clearly as a Southern alternative to Wallace, the Alabaman was an opportunity for Carter.

As he campaigned, Wallace pledged that he would wrest the Democratic Party from the "ultra-liberal, exotic left-wing few" who had seized it. The prime issue, he said, was "the survival and salvation" of what he called "average Americans." He was the only candidate, he told audiences, who gave a damn about the white working people whose lives were being constantly disrupted by an uncaring, unfeeling federal bureaucracy. He told them that they were the backbone of the land; that they were the ones who "paid their taxes, obeyed the laws, loved their families, respected their religious traditions, served their land — and always wound up getting it in the neck."[66] Enough was enough, he said. And the people loved it. Wallace's campaign slogan: "Trust the People." Almost unrecognized, Wallace was sparking a tradition (or revival) of right-wing populism in American politics which in four years would sweep another unknown conservative populist, Ronald Reagan, into the White House.

Among the many Democratic hopefuls, a free-for-all seemed in the making, with several candidates hoping to play either a dark-horse role or become a member of a new Democratic coalition.

The Republican Candidates

On the Republican side, President Ford would most likely receive the nomination for a full term even though he was an accidental president. Republican tradition was on his side. No Republican president since Chester Arthur in 1884 had been denied renomination (provided he wanted to be renominated). Ford's record was apparently acceptable to much of the electorate, for he was close to or ahead of potential Democratic opponents in the polls. Among the members of his own party, he also seemed secure, winning the support of up to 61 percent of party identifiers in 1975 (even after the Nixon pardon).[67] Moreover, since the polls estimated that in 1976 only a fifth of the nation identified with the GOP, a contest in the Republican Party seemed not only unwise but unlikely.

Unfortunately, Ford had a problem with the press. After his pardon of Nixon, the media dumped on him. He had, after all, deprived them of a state trial of a president that would have been one of the really big shows in American political history. Reporters appeared to go out of their way to report his verbal lapses (he frequently mispronounced words) and his physical stumbling. The public saw pictures of the president tripping as he descended from Air Force One, falling down on skis, or hitting his head on a helicopter. An image emerged of him as a well-meaning bumbler. Some in the White House Press Corps dubbed him "President Turkey" and accused him of "trying to sew up the klutz vote."[68]

The Republicans also had to consider Ford's "Nixon Connection." Ford was widely viewed as Nixon's choice,[69] not the choice of the party around the country, and though Ford had not been involved in the Watergate scandal, the Nixon pardon had roused suspicion and hurt him with many voters. Also, for all his conservative rhetoric, he was presiding over a federal budget out of balance by a colossal $66.5 billion, and he had just appointed several liberal Republicans to high office — most notably Los Angeles lawyer Carla A. Hills as Secretary of Housing and Urban Development.

Moreover, Watergate had damaged the prestige and authority of the presidency, making incumbency of less value for Ford. Further, the new financial laws removed one of the greatest advantages of an incumbent president: his access to large financial contributions.[70]

Ford's political qualifications were none too strong. Following service with the navy in World War II in the South Pacific, Ford returned home to Grand Rapids, Michigan, and won election to the national House of Representatives in 1948 as a Republican. In that body he won recognition for his integrity, sincerity, and common sense rather than his intelligence, initiative, or imagination.

In 1965, the House Republicans selected Ford to replace the aging Charles Halleck as House minority leader. In that role he proved to be an excellent leader through his engaging personality, honesty, and ability to establish close personal relationships with both allies and opponents. His voting record was moderately conservative. He voted for the Civil Rights Act of 1964, the Voting Rights Act of 1965, and the Fair Housing Act of 1968; however, he opposed many aspects of Lyndon Johnson's "War on Poverty" and other social welfare spending measures. He supported defense spending and supported both Johnson and Nixon in their conduct of the Vietnam War. As we have seen, the selection of Ford to be Vice President was widely applauded in Congress and the news media, and Ford was quickly confirmed by the Democratic-controlled Congress. After the years of Watergate, and a notable absence of candor in the White House, Ford's open sincerity appealed to the Congress, the news media, and the general public.

FORD'S "NELSON ROCKEFELLER PROBLEM." In 1976, although he was an incumbent president, Ford expected that he would be challenged for the nomination by his vice president, Nelson Rockefeller, who had "Potomac Fever" of the most virulent type, and Ronald Reagan, the former two-term governor of California, who was being pushed by the conservatives in the GOP. As we have seen, one of Ford's first acts as president had been to nominate Rockefeller, former governor of New York, as his replacement as vice president. Rockefeller had for many years been one of the few liberal Republicans who could attract Democratic and Independent voters.

But the New Yorker was anathema to the Republican conservatives. Ford hoped that the appointment of Rockefeller would heal the breach in the Republican Party between the conservatives and the liberals. However, it actually exacerbated the unity problem. The Southern conservatives in the GOP had been irreconcilable to Rockefeller since at least 1964 when he had turned his back on their beloved Barry Goldwater. The governor was, in the view of many conservatives, a rich and arrogant New Yorker who thought he knew more than the rest of them, who thought he could buy anything he wanted.[71]

Then Rockefeller unexpectedly announced that he did not want to be considered for the vice-presidential slot on the Ford/Rockefeller ticket in 1976. Some hearers, ever mindful of Rockefeller's unquenchable presidential ambition, suspected that he might be making a tactical withdrawal so as to position himself for a possible later reentry as a full-blown presidential candidate. They remembered his divisive, all-out drive in 1964 and how in 1960 and 1968 he had conducted on-again, off-again flirtations with the Republican nomination process. Moreover, when asked specifically if he was withdrawing himself categorically from the race for the presidency he refused to give a categorical answer.[72]

Once Rockefeller announced his withdrawal, Ford's candidacy moved quickly. Unfortunately for Ford, much precious time had been spent in trying to discourage Ronald Reagan from challenging him for the GOP nomination, as well as in finessing the presidential bid by Rockefeller. Ford's time would have been better spent raising money and organizing. Consequently, the Ford campaign was never able to gain the offensive. In June, Ford selected Secretary of the Army Howard "Bo" Calloway, a former Georgia congressman and a card-carrying conservative, to take over as his campaign manager. Ford's appointment of Calloway was greeted with considerable dismay since the Georgian had never organized a national campaign and would be working with a candidate who had never run in one.

On July 8, President Ford, speaking from the Oval Office, declared his candidacy. He would run, he pledged, "an open and aboveboard" campaign in compliance with the "letter and spirit" of the new campaign reform law. Then, on November 7, 1975, he unexpectedly announced that he would enter every 1976 primary. He considered himself obliged to campaign actively in the primaries, he said, even though no recent sitting president had felt compelled do do so.[73] The next day, his campaign headquarters issued statements saying that the president did not mean that he would *campaign* in every primary, only that he would *enter* them.[74]

Despite his incumbency, President Ford was challenged for the nomination.

JOHN CONNALLY. On CBS News's "Face the Nation" in mid–October, former Texas governor John Connally, from the right side of the Republican Party, suggested that he might run as a favorite-son candidate in Texas. If Ford slipped in the early primaries, he suggested, he would be available to challenge Reagan.

However, Connally was tainted by his peripheral association with Watergate. In 1974, he had been indicted by a federal grand jury for having taken $10,000 from the American Milk Producers, Inc., in exchange for persuading President Nixon to support a hike in milk price supports. Although the trial jury cleared him in 1975, the smear stuck.

SENATOR CHARLES MATHIAS. From the left (or what passes for the left in the Republican Party) Ford was challenged by Senator Charles "Mac" Mathias of Maryland. In late October in a speech at the National Press Club, Mathias had expressed deep concern that "President Ford's fascination with a very real threat on his right is limiting debate among Republicans," and he had suggested that he himself might seek the party's presidential nomination.

RONALD WILSON REAGAN. As Ford feared would happen, his serious challenge came from Ronald Reagan. Reagan had enormous political assets. He had the support of the growing conservative wing of the Republican Party and widespread organizational support in the GOP.[75] He had never held office in Washington and had no ties to the discredited Nixon administration.

Reagan had moved to the center of the political stage after a speech ("The Time for Choosing") he had made on October 27, 1964, on national television on behalf of Senator Barry Goldwater, the conservative Republican presidential candidate who was opposing Lyndon B. Johnson, the incumbent president. "You and I have a rendezvous with destiny," he told the audience. "We can preserve for our children this, the last, best hope for man on earth, or we can sentence them to take the first step into a thousand years of darkness." America, Reagan said, had come to "a time for choosing" between free enterprise and big government, between individual liberty and the "ant heap of totalitarianism."

The speech, which *Time* magazine said was the one bright spot in the dismal Goldwater campaign, catapulted Reagan into national political prominence and won him the hearts of the right-wing faction of the GOP. The following Tuesday, when the American voters buried Goldwater under what was up to that time the greatest landslide in presidential election history, the mantle of conservative political leadership in the United States passed from Goldwater to Reagan.[76] No longer was he looked upon as a Hollywood actor whose career was fast fading. Now he was the most talked-about prospective conservative leader in America.

Within months, a group of wealthy California businessmen had established a well-financed committee, "Friends of Ronald Reagan," to launch Reagan's candidacy for governor of California in 1966.[77] His campaign shocked the Republican moderates. He came out in opposition to a state fair housing law, called for an investigation of the University of California, endorsed an antipornography initiative, emphasized the reduction of the role of government and resisted upward pressure on taxes — drastic departures both from California's recent past and from the nation's present.[78] Even so, he easily won the Republican gubernatorial nomination with almost 65 percent of the vote in a five-candidate race.

In the fall campaign against the genial free-spending Governor Edmund G. "Pat" Brown, Sr., the Democratic incumbent, Reagan charged that, under the Democrats, big government had become the master instead of the servant. High taxes, excessive government, and skyrocketing state aid to minorities had devoured the hard-earned wages of working men and women. At the same time, it made life easy for welfare cheats—lazy people, freeloaders. It choked free enterprise with regulations and red tape. The state's problems, Reagan said, grew out of a lack of will; they stemmed from morally lax leaders who allowed convicts to go free. He condemned "campus radicals" at the University of California at Berkeley and other universities who were demonstrating against the Vietnam War.

Brown later admitted that he did not take Reagan seriously as a challenger until it was too late. However, the Californians did, and Reagan was swept to victory by nearly one million votes, the largest plurality by which a sitting governor had ever before been defeated throughout American history. Reagan's ability as a vote-getter had been dramatically established. Four years later, he was overwhelmingly reelected with a vote total of 3,742,913—more than any previous California gubernatorial candidate had received up to that time—despite his strong support for the Vietnam War and his hard-line handling of campus disruptions.

About the middle of his second term as governor, Reagan's thoughts turned toward the White House. He had halfheartedly sought the Republican nomination in 1968. He had not campaigned and had not shifted from a favorite-son status to a full-fledged candidate until two days before the Republican balloting in Miami Beach. At the convention, despite Reagan's obvious popularity with the delegates, leading conservatives, including Senators Barry Goldwater, Strom Thurmond, and John Tower, decided that Nixon was a better choice to face Lyndon Johnson, and Reagan was defeated for the nomination.[79] When Reagan left the office of governor at the end of his second term in 1974, he was replaced by Jerry Brown, the son of the man he had defeated to become governor in 1966.

When Nixon was elected in 1968, Reagan's presidential prospects in 1972 were forestalled because Nixon's claim, as the incumbent president, on the 1972 nomination would be unassailable. Thus Reagan had to lift his sights to 1976. Nixon was reelected in 1972, but then the Watergate scandal intervened, Nixon resigned, Ford messed up, and the 1976 political scenario was drastically changed. Reagan and his advisors were ready to go. There was, however, an ominous sign: Reagan would be sixty-five years old in 1976.

Reagan officially declared his candidacy for the 1976 presidential race at a press conference at the National Press Club in Washington. He said that he was running against "evil incarnate in the buddy system in Washington."[80] The capitol, he said, "has become the seat of a buddy system that functions for its own benefit—increasingly insensitive to the needs of the American worker who supports it with his taxes. Today it is difficult to find leaders who are independent of the forces that have brought us our problems—the Congress, the bureaucracy, the lobbyists, big business and big labor."[81] Reagan billed himself as the outsider with clean hands, the savior come to Washington to purify the waters.

When pressed by the reporters, Reagan refused to identify Gerald Ford as part of the Washington "buddy system." He also refused to lash out at Ford, saying that he was running on the issues and not because of any personal animosity for Jerry Ford. He was invoking, he said, the Eleventh Commandment: "Thou shalt not speak ill of any fellow Republican."[82]

James Reston, the venerable political observer, wrote in the *New York Times*: "The astonishing thing is that this amusing but frivolous Reagan fantasy is taken so seriously by the news media and particularly by the President. It makes a lot of news, but it doesn't make much sense."[83]

However, it did make sense to the conservatives in the Republican Party. A Ford-Reagan contest assured that the Republicans would be nominating a conservative to head their 1976 ticket.

THE REAGAN CAMPAIGN TEAM. To head his campaign team, Reagan selected John Sears, a non-ideological political tactician. The urbane and articulate Sears ingratiated himself with Ron and Nancy Reagan. However, from the start, he was on a collision course with Lyn Nofziger and the other hard-line conservative aides dedicated to an ideological confrontation with Ford. Nofziger felt that Reagan's great chance for the nomination was mass support from the grass-roots conservatives who nominated Goldwater in 1964; therefore Reagan must maintain a high rightist ideological tone. Sears, on the other hand, was determined to avoid Goldwater's experience of 1964 when he roughhoused his way to the nomination and alienated half the party in the process. Sears wanted to snatch the nomination from Ford, but he also wanted to end up with a unified party. To do so, in his view, it would be necessary to rub off some of the hard-right ideological edges from Reagan's reputation to make him acceptable to Republicans of all varieties and indeed to the electorate in general. This conflict undercut Reagan's 1976 campaign and carried into his campaign of 1980 as well.

The Democratic Primaries

IOWA. The first major battlegrounds for the Democratic Party nomination were the Iowa precinct caucuses, where the process to select delegates to the Democratic National Convention would begin on January 19, 1976.

In the Iowa caucus system, the Democrats met in caucuses in their neighborhood schools, church social halls, etc., to choose delegates to later meetings in congressional districts and the state convention. Because in the precinct caucuses the participants were required to announce their candidate preference, it was possible to project the final outcome of the state. Although the delegates to the national convention were selected at the state convention, the attention of the candidates was inevitably focused on the local caucuses. Because of the few delegates chosen in Iowa, most candidates had previously ignored what was in reality a system unlikely to produce much in the way of delegate support or media attention.[84]

In line with his game plan, Carter began his delegate-seeking activities in Iowa early in 1975. He spent a great deal of time in the state, mooching rides, staying in homes of volunteers and making his own bed, dropping in on farmers in the field for a talk, and, at least once, appearing on television from a studio kitchen demonstrating one of his favorite camping recipes.[85]

His hard work paid off. When the Iowa ballots were counted Carter had corralled 28 percent of the vote—twice as much as Birch Bayh, his closest rival.[86] Despite the fact that all the candidates ran far behind the uncommitted vote, which stood at 37 percent, the press commentators hailed the outcome as a Carter victory in the first "official" test of voter support in 1976.[87] Nobody really cared about the numbers, and before long the face of "Jimmy Who?" from Georgia was appearing on the cover of *Time* and *Newsweek*.[88] Critics were quick to point out, however, that Carter's success depended on weeks of personal contact which would be impossible in larger states once the primaries began.

NEW HAMPSHIRE. An optimistic Jimmy Carter came into the New Hampshire primary intent on maintaining the momentum he had generated in the Iowa caucuses. During frequent campaign visits to the state he talked of America's basic goodness, a decency only temporarily obscured by the debasement perpetrated by Nixon, Agnew, *et al.* The voters liked it. Carter's "peanut brigade," a group of middle-aged Georgians, black and white, who followed their candidate from state to state at their own expense, doorbelled the Granite State as no one had before. By election day, February 24, there were few in New Hampshire who had not heard the name of Jimmy Carter.[89]

Once again, Carter's efforts paid off. He led the field with nearly 30 percent of the Democratic primary vote (including write-ins), beating such Washington "insiders" as Bayh, Harris, and Udall, and thereby winning fifteen of the seventeen delegate votes. Although only 23,000 persons had opted for him, Carter promptly announced that his victory proved that "a progressive Southerner can win in the North." The television networks dutifully proclaimed Carter the winner. As in Iowa, his triumph was exaggerated by the mass media. However, his victory, narrow as it was, ended skepticism about the seriousness of his effort. Suddenly the peanut farmer was the Democrat to beat in 1976.[90]

MASSACHUSETTS. Carter received a temporary setback in Massachusetts the following week, where he finished a disappointing fourth behind "Scoop" Jackson, Morris Udall, and George Wallace. Jackson had skipped New Hampshire (where he had little chance of winning) to run in Massachusetts, widely regarded as the most liberal state in the Union (where his chances figured to be even slimmer). In Massachusetts Jackson pitched his campaign against Wallace, presenting himself as a more reasonable alternative, especially among the thousands of Bostonians who felt caught in the middle of that city's festering school-busing controversy. Wallace, too, had decided to stay out of New Hampshire and to enter Massachusetts. As Jules Witcover puts it: "The Alabamian liked the idea of going up North and sticking it to the Yankees in their own back yard."[91]

Although Jackson polled 164,393 votes in Massachusetts (more than the total cast in New Hampshire), his win garnered little media attention, for national television had moved its cameras southward to follow the Florida primary and the far more interesting match-up between Carter and Wallace.[92]

Running in Massachusetts, Carter made a major tactical error regarding Tip O'Neill, the liberal majority leader of the House of Representatives and certain to be the Speaker of the House Carter would have to deal with if he should become president. Carter made O'Neill a prime target after the congressman threw his influence and prestige behind the candidacy of his House colleague, Morris Udall. It was not until much later in the spring, after Carter's nomination had become inevitable, that O'Neill publicly gave him his blessing and support. But O'Neill's support was never enthusiastic, even after Carter received the nomination, or indeed even after Carter became president. It was an ill omen for the future, when Carter would need the help of the Democratic House.

VERMONT. Carter was able to salvage some momentum because he won the primary in Vermont (on the same night as the Massachusetts contest) with more than 42 percent against three other candidates. Shriver lagged far behind in second place with 27.6 percent. Although the Vermont primary was merely advisory (a "beauty contest"—no delegates selected), Carter's win was a psychologically important offset to his loss in Massachusetts.

FLORIDA. Carter's major test in the primaries, however, was certain to be in Florida. A confrontation with Wallace in the Sunshine State, where Wallace was considered to be unbeatable after his huge win (42 percent of the primary vote) in the Florida primary in 1972, had been projected by Carter as the critical make-or-break exercise. He had to draw away some of Wallace's strength in the South to show that he was a national contender. Also, if he could rid the Democratic Party of the pesky Wallace, then liberals, blacks, and other Southern Democrats weary of being perceived in the Wallace image would be in his debt.[93] Carter repeatedly went back to Florida — twenty-five times before 1976. Wallace told Floridians that a vote for him would "send a message to Washington." Carter told them that a vote for *him* would send a president to Washington. Then Carter extended an invitation to come visit once he got there.[94]

In Florida Carter received crucial support from Martin Luther King, Sr., Representative Andrew Young, and Leonard Woodcock, president of the United Auto Workers. Young, a young and articulate black former minister and three-term congressman from Georgia (the first black man since Reconstruction elected to Congress from the Old Confederacy),[95] had been a key lieutenant of the Reverend Martin Luther King, Jr., and executive director of the Southern Christian Leadership Conference during the civil rights struggles of the 1960s. Young first met Carter in 1970, when Carter was running for governor of Georgia. Though not close then, their mutual respect grew over the years, and by 1976 Young was ready to support Carter in the Florida primary, largely because he thought his fellow Georgian had the best chance of knocking off super-segregationist Wallace. Young's support, coupled with his unquestioned status among black voters, is credited with turning out more than 75,000 crucial black votes for Carter in the Florida contest. On March 9 Carter won Florida with 35 percent of the vote to 31 percent for George Wallace. Jackson was third with 23.9.

Although Udall was uneasy about the support that Carter was getting from liberals determined to knock Wallace out of the race (and eliminate him as a major force in the Democratic Party), he stayed out of the Florida primary and advised his supporters there to back Carter. He warned Leonard Woodcock, "If Jimmy wins Florida, he doesn't expect to go back to raising peanuts."[96] In the end, only Henry Jackson, among Carter's major rivals for the nomination, joined the Florida competition between Carter and Wallace, and Jackson was not strong enough to prevent Carter's victory.

Winning the Florida primary gave Carter first claim on all the Southern delegations. Coming on the heels of his victory in New Hampshire, it also made him the acknowledged front-runner for the nomination among the Democratic candidates. On March 15, 1976, the Gallup Poll showed Carter leading President Ford 47 percent to 42 percent among nationwide voters surveyed.

ILLINOIS. The next week Carter went to Illinois, where he surprised nearly everyone on March 16 by winning 48 percent of the popular vote — more than twenty points ahead of Wallace. Wallace's low vote was a serious blow to his campaign. Shriver, who had expected to score well in the contest, finished a distant third with 16.3 percent of the vote. On March 22 he withdrew from the presidential race and released his eleven delegates.

NORTH CAROLINA. On March 23, Carter followed his Florida and Illinois victories with an easy win in North Carolina — 53.6 percent against 34.7 percent for Wallace, who had received a majority there in the 1972 primary. Carter's win made him the first Democrat to receive a majority of votes in any primary. Carter demonstrated strength in all parts of the state, but ran especially strong among blacks and in urban areas.

Needless to say, North Carolina was an important state for Carter. His triumphs over Wallace in Florida and North Carolina effectively ended the right-wing threat to the Democratic Party and indicated that if there were to be a Southern candidate, it would be Carter, not Wallace.

THE ETHNIC PURITY GAFFE. Carter's campaign was interrupted in early April (April 4) when he got into trouble with blacks and Northern liberals over a response he made to a reporter for the New York Daily News when he was asked about subsidized low-income housing in the suburbs. He replied: "I see nothing wrong with ethnic purity being maintained. I would not force racial integration of a neighborhood by government action. But I would not permit discrimination against a family moving into the neighborhood."[97]

Andrew Young publicly termed the statement a "disaster" and insisted that Carter apologize — which he did, quickly and repeatedly. After a couple of weeks the furor died down — ironically, largely because of the support of Young, who had apparently convinced himself that he could trust the white Southerner.

WISCONSIN. On April 6, in the midst of the "ethnic purity" turmoil, Carter came from behind in Wisconsin to squeak past Udall by 1 percent after Udall had claimed victory based on projections by two television networks. Carter's come-from-behind win boosted his campaign and sustained him through the "ethnic purity" controversy.

NEW YORK. Meanwhile, Carter was picking up delegates. In New York's complicated April 6 primary he finished third behind Jackson, who won a plurality of delegates (38 percent); Udall placed second with 25.5 percent. Carter ran third with 12.8 percent (and thirty-five delegates). Uncommitted delegates received 23.7 percent of the vote. Though Jackson won more delegates than any other candidate, his total fell short of the majority he had anticipated.

PENNSYLVANIA. With Pennsylvania, on April 27 the big industrial states began to fall. In an effort to prove that Carter could not win in a Northern industrial state, Jackson, who had the support of the labor bosses and Philadelphia mayor Frank Rizzo (one of the few remaining big-city bosses with real power), mounted an all-out effort in the Keystone State. But Carter saturated the state with a classic TV blitz in which he reminded the voters that Mayor Rizzo had backed Richard Nixon in the 1972 presidential campaign. In response, the voters gave Carter a decisive victory over Jackson — 37 percent to 24.6 percent.[98]

In winning the Pennsylvania primary, Carter had demonstrated that he could win in a Northern industrial state over labor and the "special interests." Jackson's all-out effort in the Pennsylvania primary was the last hurrah for the ABC (Anybody But Carter) crowd, a temporary coalition who hoped to undercut Carter's momentum. Jackson quit the race early the next month.

But it was good-news-and-bad-news time for Carter. The good news came on May 1 when he unexpectedly won ninety-two of ninety-eight Texas delegates, defeating favorite-son Lloyd Bentsen as well as George Wallace. He also easily won the May 4 primaries in the District of Columbia, Indiana, and Georgia. By early May, Carter had more than a third of the 1,505 delegate votes needed for the nomination.

The bad news came as he faced the two late-entering challengers, Frank Church and Jerry Brown. On May 11, he was upset by Church in the Nebraska preference primary. Then, on May 18, Brown, on his first foray into national politics, beat Carter badly in Maryland (48.4 to 37.1).[99] The news from Oregon on May 25 was even worse as Church won again. This time Church's margin of victory was 35 percent to only 28 for Carter. However, the really big news from Oregon was the remarkable 24 percent recorded for Brown, all on write-ins. The same day Carter also lost to Church in Idaho and to Brown in Nevada.

Six days later, on June 1, Carter's delegates in Rhode Island placed second to an uncommitted slate backed by Brown, and Church beat him by more than two to one in the Montana primary. In California on June 8, Carter took another drubbing (by a three-to-one margin), this time at the hands of Brown. The Californian was even more spectacular in New Jersey, booting home a makeshift uncommitted slate with 42 percent to 25 percent for Carter. Carter's momentum was fading visibly.

OHIO. All eyes were now on Ohio, the last primary, and Carter came through impressively, winning with more than 52 percent of the vote and picking up 126 (of 152) delegates, which pushed his delegate total over 1,200.

After Ohio, the party leaders acknowledged that Carter had the nomination sewed up, and a stampede of party elders into his camp soon followed. Within hours Carter had received pledges of support from several big-city mayors including Frank Rizzo of Philadelphia, Richard Daley of Chicago, Abraham Beame of New York City, and Walter Washington of Washington, D.C., as well as New York governor Hugh L.

Carey. Two especially important endorsements were those of Senator Abraham Ribicoff of Connecticut, one of four Jewish Democratic senators (many Jewish voters had expressed concern about Carter's Southern Baptist beliefs), and Tip O'Neill. He also won the public support of most of his opponents in the primaries, including Wallace, Jackson, Shapp, Bentsen, Church, and Udall.

Carter's defeats in the late primaries did not prove as damaging as they at first seemed. For one thing, the proportional division of delegates in most primaries allowed Carter to increase his convention support even in states where he was beaten. Also, his base of support in the South absorbed the losses elsewhere. In the end, Carter ended the longest primary season ever with 39 percent of all votes cast. In the twenty-six presidential preference primaries he entered, Carter finished first in seventeen and second in eight.

Even so, Brown still refused to jump on the ever-accelerating Carter bandwagon. He continued to travel the country, needling Carter and picking up a few loose delegates here and there.

The Republican Primaries

NEW HAMPSHIRE. The first confrontation between Ford and Reagan was in the heavily publicized New Hampshire primary. In this state, which many regarded as the fountainhead for a do-less government, Ford pounded away at Reagan's "$90 billion boondoggle"[100] and his tinkering with the social security system. His opponent's position on the issues, Ford charged repeatedly, put him too far to the right to be president. Reagan countered by doing his "arithmetic thing," in which he quoted questionable statistics for the first (but not the last) time. He told audiences that the taxpayers of New Hampshire sent $115 million annually to Washington and got back only $100 million in services, so why wouldn't it be better just to keep the money at home and save $15 million? He was genuinely surprised when someone pointed out the illogic of his conclusion since it ignored the value of the army, navy, air force, highways, etc., to the people of the state.[101]

The outcome was a very, very close call for the president—he won by a mere 1,317 votes out of a total of a little over 108,000 cast for both candidates in the Republican primary. Even so, Ford, for the first time, had demonstrated that he could appeal to voters outside of his home district, and he proclaimed the New Hampshire victory over Reagan a "great springboard to success in the forthcoming national convention."[102] Depite the narrowness of the outcome, the press also played New Hampshire as a Ford victory and a Reagan defeat.

As Reagan left New Hampshire he was on the defensive and display-ing little contrast with Ford on the issues, which made it extremely difficult to mount an attack, even against a less-than-popular incumbent. The president went on to win the Massachusetts and Vermont primaries handily the following week without active competition from Reagan. Hindsight was to reveal that Reagan's defeat in New Hampshire ruined Sears's strategy and would prevent Reagan's nomination.

FLORIDA. On March 4, five days before the Florida primary, Reagan shifted his attack to Ford's foreign affairs performance. He charged that President Ford had shown "neither the vision nor the leadership neces-sary to halt and reverse the diplomatic and military decline of the United States." Under Kissinger and Ford, said Reagan, the country had "become Number Two in military power in a world where it is dangerous—if not fatal—to be second best..." Even so, Ford won the Florida primary on the strength of the "Social Security" vote (Reagan's "anti" views on Social Security were well known) by a 53 to 47 percent margin.

ILLINOIS. On March 16, Reagan lost the primary in Illinois (his home state) to Ford, who received 49 percent of the Republican vote. Reagan had now lost five straight primaries to the president and trailed him fifty-four to 166 in delegate strength. Republican officeholders were beginning to openly urge the discouraged Reagan to quit the race in the interests of "party unity."[103] However, Reagan declared that he was going all the way to Kansas City.

NORTH CAROLINA. In North Carolina Reagan, with the assistance of a very efficient organization forged by Senator Jesse Helms, mounted an all-out effort. He fired at Ford with every gun in his arsenal—the perils of detente, the "giveaway" of the Panama Canal, and the awful mess in Washington. On the eve of the election he appeared on television screens throughout North Carolina with a prime-time, thirty-minute attack on Ford's policies (despite Sears's advice). When the voters went to the polls on March 23, to the amazement of the Ford professionals, Reagan won his first primary victory with 52 percent of the vote to 46 percent and twenty-eight of the fifty-four delegates.[104]

The North Carolina victory was an important one for Reagan and proved to be the turning point of his political career.[105] It kept him in the 1976 race and preserved him as a legitimate presidential candidate. Lou Cannon, a Reagan biographer, suggests that without his win in North Carolina, Ronald Reagan at age sixty-five would surely have drifted into political oblivion.[106]

Even with the victory in North Carolina, Reagan was still a long way from the nomination. A nationwide Gallup Poll taken after the North Carolina contest showed that Ford retained a commanding 56 percent to 32 percent lead over Reagan among all Republican voters.

TEXAS. In Texas, a crossover state where Democrats could vote in the GOP primary, Reagan openly appealed (as did Carter) to the former followers of George Wallace and other disaffected Democrats. "I've been a Democrat all my life," a Reagan commercial began. "A conservative Democrat. As much as I hate to admit it, George Wallace can't be nominated. Ronald Reagan can. He's right on the issues. So for the first time in my life I'm gonna vote in the Republican primary. I'm gonna vote for Ronald Reagan." The ploy paid off. On May 1, Reagan, with lots of Democratic help, swept all ninety-six of the Texas delegates at stake. Ford had suffered the worst primary defeat ever experienced by an incumbent president, and Reagan had moved ahead of Ford in the delegate count for the first time.

Three days later Ford received more bad news when Reagan swamped him in three more conservative states: Indiana, Alabama, and Georgia. In Indiana Reagan had come from behind (closing a gap of twenty-four percentage points) to win by 17,000 votes and capture forty-five of Indiana's fifty-four delegates. On May 11, after Reagan won Nebraska, the perception began to spread that the President Ford Committee was a sinking ship. As the halfway point in the process approached, Reagan had 468 committed delegates to Ford's 318, as well as a good share of the 354 who said they were uncommitted. If he continued his winning pace, Reagan had the nomination secured.

MICHIGAN. In Michigan, once again, Ford and Reagan confronted each other in a crossover primary in a state with a large number of disaffected Democrats. In 1972, Michigan had handed a Democratic primary victory to George Wallace (running as an independent) with 51 percent of the vote. More than 800,000 Michigan voters, including many Republicans, had cast their ballots for him. Now that Wallace was no longer a viable candidate, where would those Wallace supporters go? If they supported Reagan it would be an extremely embarrassing (probably fatal) defeat for Ford. If they supported Ford it would likely be the end of Reagan's chances. Needless to say, both candidates went after the Democratic crossover voters.

On May 18 President Ford won decisively, garnering fifty-five delegates to twenty-nine for the Californian. The same day, he had also won all of Maryland's forty-three delegates. Ford was now back to neck-and-neck with Reagan.

CALIFORNIA. In the winner-take-all California primary Ford's strategists attempted to tap the fear of having Reagan's finger on the nuclear button by running a television ad that observed: "When you vote on Tuesday, remember: Governor Ronald Reagan couldn't start a war. President Ronald Reagan could." But the scare tactic didn't work. In fact, it actually inspired sympathy and support for the former governor, and on June 8

Reagan clobbered Ford 66 to 34 percent, winning 167 delegates to his side. Reagan's sweep of California, however, was balanced by Ford victories in Ohio and New Jersey, where the president captured a majority of the vote and most of the delegates.

With the end of the primary season (and with 90 percent of the delegates chosen), each candidate had gained the once-magic 40 percent that had historically led to nomination bandwagons. The *New York Times* gave Reagan 1,063 delegates, or sixty-seven short, with ninety-four uncommitted. Private counts on both sides differed on specific numbers, but all agreed that Ford was ahead.[107]

THE SELECTION OF SCHWEIKER. To buy time, and to keep the Republican convention from being a cut-and-dried coronation of Ford, on July 26 Reagan announced that he would select Richard Schweiker, a liberal Republican senator from Pennsylvania, as his running mate if he were nominated for president. The rationale for the selection of the little-known and essentially colorless Schweiker was that this would attract liberals to Reagan's banner and bring him a sizable bloc of convention votes from Pennsylvania, which has the third largest number of delegates.

However, the choice of Schweiker, although arguably a pragmatic masterpiece, proved to be an ideological disaster which created widespread disarray among conservatives in the Republican Party. Schweiker's pro-labor record was reflected in the 89 percent favorable rating of the Americans for Democratic Action and 100 percent favorable rating of the AFL-CIO, two of the more conventionally liberal political groupings in the country.[108] Congressman John Ashbrook, an Ohio conservative, labeled the selection of Schweiker "the dumbest thing I ever heard of." And Illinois congressman Henry Hyde, another staunch conservative, said it was like "a farmer selling his last cow to buy a milking machine."[109]

The selection of Schweiker was, in fact, a serious tactical error and may have cost Reagan the nomination. He received only a handful of Pennsylvania's votes when Drew Lewis held Pennsylvania's delegation in line for Ford. Nor did Schweiker unlock any big state delegations to Reagan. Further, by selecting a liberal to be his running mate, Reagan damaged his conservative credentials in a party that increasingly placed ideological purity above pragmatic considerations of electoral success.[110] Also, Reagan was embarrassed repeatedly when he was unable to get the pronunciation of his running mate's name right.

The Democratic Convention

The thirty-seventh quadrennial Democratic National Convention opened on July 12 of the nation's bicentennial year in New York's Madison Square Garden—a sports palace converted to a convention center.[111] It was the first Democratic convention held in New York since the famous (or infamous) "bloodletting" convention of 1924, when the McAdoo (dry) and Smith (wet) forces chopped each other up for sixteen days and 105 ballots. Among the 3,353 delegates assembled was a good representation of women, blacks, and young people.[112]

The convention was the party's most peaceful and harmonious in twelve years—a stark contrast to the bitter and divisive conventions of 1968 and 1972. There were no significant disagreements. No credentials challenges were carried to the convention floor, and just one minority plank to the platform was offered.[113]

Representative Barbara Jordan of Texas, the first black woman to give a Democratic keynote address, set the tone: "There is something different and special about this opening night," she began. "I am a keynote speaker. ... The past notwithstanding, a Barbara Jordan is before you tonight. This is one additional bit of evidence that the American Dream need not forever be deferred."[114] The delegates responded with a standing ovation.

THE PLATFORM. The ninety-page party platform, which was written by the Carter forces, contained few surprises. In an effort to make the platform process more open to the people, prior to the convention the Platform Committee, chaired by Minnesota governor Wendell Anderson, had held thirteen public hearings in all parts of the country and had heard more than 500 witnesses. The platform was adopted by voice vote after only twenty minutes of debate.

The platform stressed unemployment rather than inflation as the country's main problem. "The Democratic Party," it said, "is committed to the *right* of all adult Americans willing, able and seeking work to have opportunities for useful jobs, at living wages. To make that commitment meaningful, we pledge ourselves to the support of legislation that will make every responsible effort to reduce adult unemployment to three percent within four years."

It also called for tax reform "to ease the burden for the poor and increase it for the rich" and for a reduction in the defense budget, though maintaining parity with the Soviet Union on strategic weapons. And pledges were included to grant "full and complete" pardons for Vietnam War resisters, and to support the Equal Rights Amendment, the Supreme Court's *Roe vs. Wade* ruling, and a national health insurance system to be funded through payroll deductions and other federal tax revenues.

THE NOMINATION OF CARTER. Carter was the first candidate nominated for president. "With honest talk and plain talk," said New Jersey congressman Peter Rodino, who had become a celebrity during the

Nixon impeachment hearings, "Jimmy Carter has appealed to the American people. . . . As he has brought a united South back into the Democratic Party, he will bring a united America back to a position of respect and esteem in the eyes of the world."[115]

Also placed in nomination were Morris Udall, Jerry Brown, and Ellen McCormick, a housewife from Long Island who had collected 238,862 votes in seventeen primaries as an anti-abortion candidate.[116] However, before the balloting started, Udall withdrew his name from nomination and urged his delegates to get one of those green[117] Carter/Mondale buttons that dogged him all over America and to join him as "a soldier in the Carter campaign."[118] However, Udall's supporters voted for him on the roll call even though he had freed them to do otherwise. Governor Brown's name was placed in nomination by Cesar Chavez, leader of the United Farm Workers, who used the time to argue for social justice and equal rights and barely mentioned Brown's name or his position on issues or record.

On the roll call California's 205 votes gave Brown a momentary lead, but the District of Columbia put Carter ahead. The Georgian received the nomination when Ohio, the state where he had won his crucial primary victory on June 8, cast 132 votes for him, giving him nearly three-fourths of the total votes, and far exceeding the needed majority.[119] A handful of votes were cast for Hubert Humphrey, Henry Jackson, and George Wallace. After all the balloting was completed, Carter had received 2,238½ of the convention's 3,008 votes — the largest percentage of any non-incumbent Democratic candidate since 1908. A motion to make the vote unanimous was approved by voice vote. As the orchestra struck up "Happy Days Are Here Again," the song that had been Franklin Roosevelt's song and had become a Democratic trademark, the delegates clapped and cheered. One delegate paraded with a sign that said, "Peanut Butter is Love. Spread Some Around Today." The conventioneers were well aware that not since Wendell Willkie, thirty-six years before, had anyone so politically unknown captured the nomination of his party.[120]

Carter engaged in a well-publicized deliberative process before recommending Minnesota senator Walter Mondale to be his ticket mate.[121] Carter's first inclination for vice president had been Frank Church or "Scoop" Jackson. Both had been opponents in the primaries, and he was familiar with their general political philosophies, their stands on particular issues, and their campaign strengths and weaknesses.[122] However, he finally concluded that Mondale, who unlike Carter was an insider, would provide some balance of experience to the ticket. Since Carter had never served in Washington, he needed someone who was familiar with the federal government and particularly with Congress.[123] The selection of Mondale also strengthened his candidacy by cementing relations with

Northern liberals, blacks, union members, and political bosses, which Church and Jackson could not do. Also, the deliberate pattern of selection further aided Carter's election effort by presenting a public image of a careful but decisive leader.[124]

Senator Hubert Humphrey placed Mondale's name in nomination, calling him "my colleague in the Senate, my personal friend and a truly good and great American." Following his one-sided approval by the convention,[125] Mondale delivered a rousing acceptance speech. He welcomed the return of the South to the Democratic Party. "For well over a century," he declared, "our nation had been divided North against South and South against North. . . . But tonight we stand together. . . . Our days of discontent are over." This was followed by a vigorous recital of the glories and programs of the Democratic Party. Mondale then brought the delegates to their feet with a rousing indictment of the opposition. "We have just lived through the worst scandal in American history," he declared, "and we are now led by a president who pardoned the person who did it. . . . They have asked us to accept high unemployment," Mondale said of the Republicans, "and cruel inflation, high interest rates, a housing depression and a massive increase in welfare. . . . They have used the power and prestige of the White House to try to persuade America to abandon its most cherished objective: that special American notion of fairness and compassion."

CARTER'S ACCEPTANCE SPEECH. Just before 11:00 p.m. on Thursday, July 15, Jimmy Carter entered Madison Square Garden to present his acceptance speech in the prime-time television slot which the campaign managers had so carefully protected. As he made his way to the podium he paused to greet party greats—Hubert Humphrey, Robert Wagner, Averell Harriman—paying his dues to the past. Then he proceeded to acknowledge his debt to the future.

The Georgian smiled his famous full-tooth smile and began with the line he had used time and again during his primary contest: "My name is Jimmy Carter, and I'm running for president. It's been a long time since I've said those words for the first time. And now, I'm standing here . . . to accept your nomination. . . . Nineteen seventy-six will not be a year of politics as usual. It can be a year of inspiration and hope. . . . We felt that moral decay has weakened our country, that it's crippled by a lack of goals and values and that our public officials have lost faith in us. It's now a time for healing. We want to have faith again."[126] In his most provocative passage he charged that "too many have had to suffer at the hands of a political and economic elite who have shaped decisions and never had to account for mistakes nor to suffer injustice. Too often unholy, self-perpetuating alliances have been formed between money and politics, and the average citizen has been held at arm's length."

The convention closed with a tableau of unity. Leaders of every democratic faction—George McGovern and George Wallace, Hubert Humphrey and Edmund Muskie—crowded onto the stage to receive a fiery benediction delivered by the Reverend Martin Luther King, Sr. In closing the delegates joined hands to sing "We Shall Overcome"—the hymn of civil rights protest that had become an anthem for the whites and blacks, Northerners and Southerners.[127]

Although it was raining as the delegates left town on Friday (munching "big apples" distributed by the city), they were in a jubilant mood. In 1976, for the first time in a long time, unity was evident in the Democratic Party.

The Democratic prospects were brightened four days after the close of the Democratic convention when George Meany announced the AFL-CIO endorsement of Carter and pledged "all-out support" of labor's extensive political organization, which had sat out the 1972 McGovern campaign. Carter also received a second significant boost with the endorsement of the 1.47 million–member National Education Association which, in 1976, endorsed a presidential candidate for the first time. The NEA's prime objective in 1976 was the formation of a Department of Education (which Carter had promised to work for if elected).

A Louis Harris Poll conducted immediately following the close of the Democratic convention (on July 26) showed Carter leading Ford by a margin of 66 to 27 percent and Reagan by a margin of 68 to 26 percent. The Harris organization said Carter's lead was "one of the most substantial" it had ever recorded. A Gallup Poll, released August 1, on the eve of the Republican convention, also showed Carter with huge leads over Ford and Reagan. He led Ford 62 to 29 percent and Reagan 63 to 28 percent. Unfortunately for Carter, his early, overwhelming lead in the polls made complacency a problem.

The Republican Convention

When the badly divided Republicans met in Kansas City on August 16 for their thirty-first convention it was generally assumed that President Ford would be renominated, but it was not a happy thought with many of the delegates who preferred a more "electable" candidate. The polls consistently indicated that most Americans thought Ford was "a nice guy," but that "he does not seem to be very smart about the issues the country is facing." Ronald Reagan was the sentimental favorite of the convention. Former president Nixon was not invited to the convention, was not celebrated, was not even mentioned. He had twice won the White House for the GOP; but the party was obliged to disown him.

In reality, the crucial vote of the convention came on the evening of August 16, just before the nominations were made. As we have seen, three weeks before the convention opened, Reagan announced that he had selected Richard Schweiker of Pennsylvania to be his running mate. He had then challenged President Ford to make his preference known before the first nomination tally. When the president declined, the Reagan forces attempted to write this new procedure into the party rules (to become known as Rule 16C). On the roll call on the rule change, the Reagan-sponsored amendment was defeated by the narrow margin of 111 votes (1068-1180)—signaling to everyone that Ford had enough votes to win.

On the nomination roll call on the evening of August 18, Reagan, bolstered by the votes in California and some deep south states, took an early lead. But as everyone expected, Ford's strength in the big north-eastern states proved decisive. West Virginia's twenty delegates provided the razor-thin winning margin for the president: 1,187 delegates to 1,070 for Reagan.[128]

As it turned out, the nomination of the vice-presidential candidate provided most of the pyrotechnics and interest of the convention. After discarding Senator Howard Baker, William Ruckleshaus, and William Scranton (and being turned down by Reagan), the President selected an old congressional friend, Senator Robert Dole of Kansas, as his running mate—a choice which satisfied just about everyone except the extreme conservatives. Dole, a sharp-tongued, conservative former chairman of the Republican National Committee, was known as an effective gut-fighter possessed of a biting wit and sarcasm that approached, at times, insult.

THE REPUBLICAN PLATFORM. Although the conservative element of the Republican Party had not succeeded in winning the nomination, they nevertheless effectively dominated the platform's framing. The platform emphatically rejected the Democratic Party's call for wage and price con-trols to curb inflation, saying that such controls had proven to be a "dismal failure." In the long run, the platform argued, they served to create "short-ages, black markets and higher prices." On the issue of busing of school children to achieve racial integration, the platform warned, "If Congress continues to fail to act, we would favor consideration of an amendment to the Constitution forbidding the assignment of children to schools on the basis of race." President Ford was embarrassed by a floor-added plank critical of his adminstration's policy of detente with the Soviet Union. Ford would be running on a platform that found his conduct in office par-tially flawed.[129]

On the final night, the president accepted the nomination with a speech which was, most observers agreed, the best of his long political career. He took credit for cutting inflation in half, increasing employment to a record level, and bringing the country to peace. "For two years, I have stood for all the people against the vote-hungry, free spending congressional majority on Capitol Hill. .... I am against the big tax spenders and for the little tax payer."[130] The speech was highlighted by an unexpected challenge to the Democratic candidate, Jimmy Carter, to debate the campaign's real issues "face-to-face" on national television—a proposal the convention noisily approved. Speaking directly to the millions of citizens watching on television, the president reminded them, "You are the people who make our system work. You are the people who make America what it is. It is from your ranks that I come, and on your side that I stand."[131] When he finished his speech he turned to the gallery where Nancy and Ronald Reagan were seated and invited them to join him on the dais. As he closed, the delegates joined in singing "God Bless America," the unofficial theme song of the convention.

The day following the convention, Reagan said a lyrical goodbye to his campaign workers with a few lines from an ancient Scottish ballad:

> I'll lay me down and bleed awhile;
> Though I am wounded, I am not slain.
> I shall rise and fight again.[132]

After his defeat at the convention, Reagan resumed his radio broadcasts, his newspaper column, and his speech-making. Although he made appearances for Ford in twenty states, he made sure to stress the conservative aspects of the Republican program. He was really marking time. He was still determined to be president.

The Carter Campaign

CARTER'S CAMPAIGN STRATEGY. Since Carter did not owe his 1976 nomination to party regulars, a decision was made at the outset of his campaign not to turn the running of it over to state parties. It would be centrally directed from Atlanta to underscore the outsider image Carter desired to project, even though that would create some tension with state party leaders. Operating from Atlanta would also make it much more difficult for Washington-based Democrats to interfere with the conduct of the campaign. Carter himself withdrew to his home in Plains, 140 miles away, where he and Mondale hosted gatherings of experts on the economy, foreign policy, and defense, held press conferences, and pondered strategy.[133]

As Robert Shogan points out, in defining the approach to the nation which he would take, Carter was faced with several agonizing political and ethical decisions. Although he had won the nomination by emphasizing that he was not beloved by Democratic Party regulars, and had tried to put some distance between himself and the party's liberal ideology, he had, nevertheless, accepted the nomination of the Democratic Party. In so doing he had inherited the Democratic Party, with its pronounced liberal bent, whether he wanted it or not. To accomodate the liberalism and to help unite the party, he had selected Walter Mondale, perhaps the best and the brightest of its liberal leaders, as his running mate. He had also accepted in broad outline the party's platform, which embodied most of the principles of traditional Democratic liberalism.[134] From a pragmatic point of view, it would not be an easy matter for Carter to disown the traditional liberal philosophy of his party and expect to retain the support of labor unions, blacks, and other groups whose effective cooperation was vital to his candidacy.[135]

On the other hand, if Carter too eagerly and openly embraced Democratic liberalism, he risked the loss of the conservatives whose support had helped him gain the nomination. He could be charged with having shifted from his support base on the nonideological center into a corner on the left.

In the end, it was decided that Carter would follow the strategy that had been so successful in securing the nomination for him. He would emphasize his own personal attributes—his versatility, decisiveness, sincerity, and responsiveness. He would not evade issues, but he would not emphasize them in his campaign. He was, he would say, a fiscal conservative who would restrain government spending and a social liberal who would fight for the poor, the aged, nonwhites, workers, urban dwellers, and farmers. Beyond that he would stress his basic themes of balanced budget, strengthened local government, a maximum of personal privacy and a minimum of governmental secrecy. He failed, it would appear, to recognize what others quickly and clearly saw as a paradox inherent in his position.

Mainly he would capitalize on the "anti–Washington" sentiment that pervaded the country in the aftermath of Watergate by making a virtue out of being an outsider. As far as Washington was concerned, he would stress, most Americans were "also outsiders." "It's like a wall has been built around Washington," Carter would say. "A lot of us are outsiders. We don't see why these strange things happen in Washington." His slogan, "A Leader for a Change," would suggest how different he was from the old-style Washington establishment politicians and the two recent Republican presidents. In the South, he would emphasize his distance from Washington by stressing his Southern origins: "Isn't it time," he asked, "that we had a President without an accent?"[136]

THE CAMPAIGN. Carter launched his official campaign for the presidency on Labor Day morning (September 6) from the steps of Franklin D. Roosevelt's summer retreat at Warm Springs, Georgia. The selection of Roosevelt's "Little White House" was a sharp break from party tradition. For decades Democratic standard-bearers had begun their fall campaigns in Detroit's Cadillac Square, in symbolic salute to the American working man in the automobile capital of the nation and the world.[137]

In his kickoff speech, Carter evoked memories of FDR, Harry Truman, and John Kennedy as he compared Ford with the Republican president Herbert Hoover in 1932. "This year, as in 1932, our nation is divided, our people are out of work and our national leaders do not lead," he said. "Our nation is drifting without inspiration, without vision and without purpose. ... When Truman was in the White House, there was never any doubt who was captain of the ship. ... Now, every time another ship runs aground — CIA, FBI, Panama, unemployment, deficits, welfare, Medicaid — the Captain hides in his stateroom and the crew argues about who is to blame." Slightly modifying the Kennedy slogan of sixteen years earlier, Carter said that it was time "to get our country on the move again."[138]

THE FAILURE-OF-GOVERNMENT ISSUE. As he campaigned, Carter returned again and again to the theme of the loss of faith in government. He talked of Watergate and the president who had lied and subverted federal agencies. He contended that respect for government could be reestablished only if that government could be made as good as the American people — honest, compassionate, and even filled with love. If elected, he promised "to make the government work," efficiently and economically. He promised a government that would be "decent and honest and trustworthy, a source of pride instead of shame." Not many politicians could have made that pledge sound credible, but Carter did.

However, even before the 1976 campaign officially got under way, Carter, because of his considerable courage (or political naivete) and candor, succeeded in antagonizing several rather large and influential groups of potential voters.

THE DRAFT EVADER ISSUE. Early on, Carter got himself into trouble with the nation's veterans when, in an address to the national American Legion Convention in Seattle, he reiterated his determination if elected to grant a "blanket pardon" to all Vietnam War draft resisters. He had been careful to use the word "pardon" — which implied wrong had been done but it had been forgiven — to the word "amnesty," which implied the opposite. However, the 15,000 or so veterans and their wives in the audience (who may have missed the significance of the distinction) engulfed Carter in a flood of booing. Jules Witcover, a reporter of the incident, suggests that it was a calculated move on Carter's part to demonstrate to the wider national audience his courage and candor as a campaigner.[139]

Predictably, Robert Dole, the Republican vice-presidential candidate and an authentic hero of World War II, hurried to Seattle and told the legionnaires that Ford's position on Vietnam War draft evaders was "unequivocal." There would be, he said, "no blanket pardon, no blanket amnesty, no blanket clemency." This time the veterans cheered.[140]

THE GRAIN EMBARGO ISSUE. Likewise as a result of his candor, Carter succeeded in antagonizing the nation's farmers. In Des Moines, Iowa, Carter attacked the farm and export policies of "Nixon, Ford, and Butz," and especially the unpopular grain embargo of 1975. He pledged that if elected he would "stop embargoes once and for all." But then, when pressed in an interview with the Des Moines Register, he said that in times of national emergency, which he did not foresee, he might have to resort to an embargo. Not surprisingly, Dole followed Carter to Des Moines, where he attacked the Georgian as inconsistent on the critical farm-belt issue of grain embargoes.

THE RELIGION ISSUE. Carter, of course, was well aware that he would have to meet the religion issue head on. No presidential candidate in modern times has placed such stress on his religion. His avowals of trust in God greatly reinforced his efforts to convince voters that they could trust him. In his early campaigning, he was careful to emphasize that, as a professing born-again Christian, he was not some kind of a religious weirdo who considered himself to be better than other people. Nevertheless he was well aware that his frequent proclamation of his faith caused acute discomfort among Catholics and Jews, whose perceptions of Southern Baptists were influenced by old stories of night riders and burning crosses. These groups had to be assured of the candidate's aversion to bigotry and his belief in separation of church and state.[141]

The religious issue created a number of awkward situations for Carter. In August he met with a group of Catholic bishops, hoping to placate traditionally Democratic Catholic voters who were disturbed by his unwillingness to support a constitutional ban on abortions. For his trouble he was publicly rebuked by the bishops and picketed by right-to-life groups.

However, the most potentially embarrassing situation involving his religiosity developed after an interview appeared in Playboy magazine in which Carter attempted to persuade people that, although he was a devout Baptist, he was no hard-nosed, narrow-minded, self-righteous fundamentalist.[142] After the interview appeared, many evangelical Christians, who had been strong Carter supporters, were deeply offended. The Ford people, of course, made the most of the Playboy article. Carter admitted later that he deeply regretted the day he had agreed to the interview. Ultimately, as his campaign progressed, Carter decided on the prudent and simple course of talking less about his religion.[143]

The Ford Campaign

FORD'S CAMPAIGN STRATEGY. To defeat Jimmy Carter and win the presidency, Ford was confronted with several difficult tasks. For one thing, he faced the problem of unifying the Republican Party after an especially divisive selection process. Secondly, he would have to broaden his popular appeal, and that would require overcoming the effect of his "Watergate connection" and his pardon of Richard M. Nixon. Thirdly, since there were fewer Republicans in the electorate than Democrats, he would have to broaden the base of the Republican Party itself by cutting into the Democratic coalition and appealing to Independents—a task which, as it turned out, required Ford to deemphasize his Republican affiliation. (Much of his campaign materials contained only his picture, without indicating his Republican Party affiliation.)

The president's political advisers suggested that since he was not a terribly effective campaigner (news of his appearances seemed to be associated with declines in his popularity at the polls) he would be better off with what they called a "no-campaign campaign" strategy. He should stay as close as possible to the White House "looking presidential"—a hard-working and competent president performing his executive duties and holding press conferences from time to time to demonstrate that he was on top of things. Should his opponent claim that he could do a better job, the president's obvious response was that he was the only candidate with experience in a job for which there existed no other completely appropriate training. The strategy soon came to be known as the "Rose Garden Strategy."[144] Meanwhile, Ford would rely on sophisticated television advertising to project his strengths—a good family man trying sincerely to do his best in difficult times, running against an unsophisticated and inexperienced opponent.[145] Also emphasized would be how far he had brought the country to believing in its president again after Nixon. The slogan for Ford would be "The Man Who Made Us Proud Again."[146]

The main thrust of Ford's campaign, however, was the need for reduction in federal spending. According to the president, business was not responsible for the current economic slump. The real villain was the federal government, whose fiscal policies were controlled by the Democratic Congress.[147]

President Ford finally left the White House on September 15 to launch his election campaign before a largely student audience at his alma mater, the University of Michigan, where he had starred in football four decades ago. In a strong attack on his Democratic opponent, he promised "specifics, not smiles, performances, not promises." He stressed Republican claims that Carter flip-flopped on issues and experience. "The question in this campaign of 1976," he said, "is not who has the better vision of America. The question is who will act to make that vision a reality."[148]

The Television Debates

THE FIRST DEBATE. During September and October Ford and Carter engaged in a series of three nationally televised debates (the first ever to include an incumbent president). Ford agreed to participate in the debates, although he was less articulate and had more to lose from debating than Carter. However, he saw them as an opportunity to appear presidential and to chip away at his Democratic rival's "soft backing."[149]

The debate format and style, however, lacked the fire of the 1960 exchanges between Richard Nixon and John Kennedy. In the ninety-minute first debate in Philadelphia's historic Walnut Street Theatre on September 23, Ford was calm and self-assured throughout and looked like a president who was very much in charge, whereas Carter seemed nervous and uncertain.

On the issue of inflation and unemployment, after charging that the president was insensitive to the jobless, Carter emphasized the need to create government service jobs to cut the unemployment rolls. Ford, in his turn, stressed orthodox fiscal conservatism and argued for stimulating the private sector with tax incentives to create productive employment. He asked the nation to accept what he called the "new realism," which meant reliance on private business, not the government, to make jobs.

After the debate was over, Ford was acknowledged as the "winner." The Gallup Poll conducted immediately after the first debate showed Carter's lead over Ford was evaporating. Just before the debate Carter had led Ford by 18 percent — 54 percent to 36 percent. But afterwards his lead dropped to eight percentage points: 50 to 42.[150]

THE SECOND DEBATE. Thirteen days later, the second debate was held in the Palace of Fine Arts Theatre in San Francisco. Carter took the offensive by charging the President with weak leadership, a secretive style, and a lack of moral principles. In response, the visibly irritated Ford opened up an unanticipated issue when, in defending his record of negotiating with the Soviet Union in regard to Eastern Europe, he asserted that "there is no Soviet domination of Eastern Europe and there never will be under a Ford administration." The obvious error was quickly picked up by Carter when he retorted: "I would like to see Mr. Ford convince the Polish-Americans and Hungarian-Americans . . . that those countries don't live under the domination and supervision of the Soviet Union behind the Iron Curtain."[151]

This exchange clearly hurt the president with voters of East European descent. It also raised grave doubts about whether Ford really understood the complexities of international politics or fully appreciated the Soviet Union's influence in Eastern Europe. The Ford effort was stalled for two weeks as he attempted to explain away his comment. By contrast, Carter now appeared relatively competent in foreign affairs.[152] Most polls conducted after the debate indicated that the president's gaffe probably had limited impact on the final vote.

THE VICE-PRESIDENTIAL DEBATE. The vice-presidential nominees, Robert Dole and Walter Mondale, confronted each other in a debate on national television on October 22 from the Alley Theatre in Houston, Texas. Unfortunately for Dole, he played to the live audience—a mixed group of savvy politicos who enjoyed his partisan one-liners—and forgot that his main impression, the one that counted, would be made on the relatively unsophisticated television audience. He also infuriated the Democrats when he said: "I figured up the other day, if we added up the killed and wounded in Democrat Wars in this century, it would be about 1.6 million Americans, enough to fill the city of Detroit." Dole's poor performance was later thought to be critically helpful to the Carter-Mondale ticket.

THE THIRD DEBATE. In contrast to the first two debates, the last of the televised confrontations, held on October 22 at the College of William and Mary in Williamsburg, Virginia, covered a wide range of issues starting with a question on the economy and ending with one on election prospects. Both candidates proceeded cautiously. Each had been declared the unofficial "winner" in one of the first two debates, and neither wanted to commit a fatal blunder that would lose him the debate and possibly the election. In consequence, the viewing public gleaned few new facts. Nearly all the positions taken by both men had been laid out earlier in the campaign.

In their closing statements assessing their electoral chances, Ford charged Carter with being "inconsistent in many of the positions that he takes. He tends to distort on a number of occasions." There was, the president said, a "new spirit in America" with which Carter was not in step. The people, he said, "are healed, are working together." He asked the voters to support him on election day and say, "Jerry Ford, you've done a good job. Keep on doing it."

Carter in his turn, acknowledging that Ford was "a good and decent man," asked his listeners to consider what had been accomplished during the president's two years in office. "A lot remains to be done," he said, listing his opponent's failures. "I believe the American people are ready for a change in Washington."[153]

Telephone surveys conducted immediately after the debate indicated that public opinion was split on the outcome. Ford, most observers felt, had just about held his own. However, later polls indicated that he never really recovered from his image as "a mistake-prone, inept bumbler."

THE MEANNESS ISSUE. Inevitably, Carter's unusual emphasis on the importance of character as the principal issue of the election led the press and his rivals to focus attention to an extraordinary degree on *his* character. In consequence, Carter was subjected to an examination so intense that any candidate would have had difficulty escaping without injury or embarrassment.

Unfortunately, as he campaigned in 1976, Carter turned nasty on occasion. In the primaries, when Hubert Humphrey finally said that he would not enter the race, Carter commented that he would have liked to show that he could beat him. After the *Playboy* interview, Carter was quoted as saying that his religious beliefs would prevent him from ever taking on "the same frame of mind that former Presidents Nixon or Johnson did — lying or cheating and distorting the truth."[154]

Then, campaigning against Ford, Carter became strident and personal in his attacks on the president. Following Ford's assertion in the second television debate that Eastern Europe was free from Soviet domination, Carter punished the president mercilessly. He suggested that Ford had been "brainwashed" and asserted that Ford had been more secretive, less informed, and generally worse as president than Richard Nixon.[155]

In commenting on the challenger's performance, columnist Joseph Kraft said Carter had "a streak of ugly meanness — an egotistical disposition to run right over people — a disposition to be a sorehead." The syndicated columnist team of Evans and Novak concluded: "He has a vein of vindictiveness." The "mean incidents" put a serious strain on Carter's credibility.[156]

In the closing days of the campaign, a grim-faced Carter, facing the possibility of defeat, attempted to rally his followers: "I want to talk to you in a quiet, very sober way."[157] But it appeared to have little effect. The polls continued to reveal that Ford, having recovered from the furor over Eastern Europe, was pressing ever closer on the heels of his challenger. However, Ford suffered a second setback when, five days before the election, the Commerce Department Index of Leading Indicators fell for the second straight month, by seven-tenths of 1 percent, with farm prices dipping 5 percent from mid–September to mid–October. Unemployment was reported at almost 8 percent. Carter, campaigning in Philadelphia, argued that the figures made a "mockery of Ford administration predictions" of economic recovery. The prospect, he warned his urban audience, was for "a further decline in the standard of living for the average worker." The country "simply cannot depend on those who created this economic mess to clean it up," he said.

THE 1976 OUTCOME. By election eve Ford had made a remarkable recovery, and the race between Ford and Carter had again become a race too close to call.[158] The Gallup Poll showed Ford ahead by one percentage point, 47 to 46, and the Harris Poll found Carter leading 46 to 45. No polling organization (and few political analysts) would forecast the outcome. In the last week of the campaign a fifth of the electorate were still responding "undecided."

When the people voted in record numbers[159] on November 2, 1976, Jimmy Carter, the classic "outsider," won. Close it was: Approximately forty-one million voters (50.1 percent) cast ballots for Carter and just over thirty-nine million (47.9 percent) for Ford.[160]

The Georgian's popular vote produced 297 votes in the Electoral College, where 270 were needed to elect. Carter had brought together just enough of the old New Deal Coalition—the poor, blacks, union families, Catholics, Southerners, and city dwellers—and New Liberals to do the job. Since it was such a close election it was difficult to determine which group, if any, provided the margin of victory. It could have been the support of labor. Although only one major union, the United Auto Workers, supported Carter in the primaries, the AFL-CIO's enthusiastic endorsement and COPE campaign helped bring back large numbers of blue collar workers.[161] It might also have been that Carter would not have won without black support. Too, Carter ran much stronger among Southern white Protestants than any Democratic nominee since 1960.

THE 1976 CONGRESSIONAL ELECTIONS. The Democrats also swept Congress. Trooping in with Carter, House Democrats outnumbered Republicans 292–143, establishing a two-thirds majority in the House of Representatives and a nearly two-to-one margin in the Senate. The Senate had unusually high turnover. Fewer senators than usual sought reelection, and of this group only 64 percent kept their seats. Congress thus had more new members than at any time since 1948. In their victory the Democrats regained many seats once regarded as forever lost to the Republicans.[162]

Ford took his narrow defeat with good grace, remarking that he had lost a "close one." He conceded defeat in a telephone call to Carter shortly after 11:00 a.m. on November 3. Carter's victory remarks to the American people were brief: "I'm not afraid to take on the responsibilities of the president of the United States because my strength and my courage and my advice and my counsel and my criticism come from you." He offered a traditional plea for unity "of all those in the United States whether they, like you, supported me or supported Mr. Ford or someone else." He closed on a characteristically personal note: "I want to thank all of you. I love everybody here. You've been great to me."[163]

After the 1976 election the Republican Party appeared to be worse than decimated. The *New York Times* headlined, "POLITICIANS FIND GOP FIGHTING FOR ITS SURVIVAL," and the *Wall Street Journal* opined, "Ailing GOP May Not Recover." John Deardourff, a manager of the Ford campaign, expressed the plight of the GOP well when he said in a *Wall Street Journal* interview: "It takes a long time for a party to die or be killed, and I assume there will be a lot of ferment for a couple of years. But the Party's prospects certainly are not very bright."[164]

On November 4, president-elect Carter [165] held his first news conference in his home town of Plains, Georgia. He said his narrow popular vote margin did not deny him a "mandate" for vigorous pursuit of his goals as president. "I feel deeply obligated to people, but I'll do what I think is best for the country. I don't have any strings on me." The key question facing Carter was whether he could convert his electoral coalition into a governing coalition.

2. President Carter and the Congress

During his campaign Carter promised to bring "new faces and new ideas" to Washington. Shortly before his nomination, he told the *National Journal*: "I can't say I would never use somebody who has served in the previous administration. Obviously I will use some. But my inclination would be to go to a new generation."[1] Generally, he kept his promise to appoint unknowns — often to his political detriment. When he made his cabinet appointments he generally ignored the major interest groups that make up the Democratic Party — blue collar labor unions, city leaders, and white ethnic groups. Many of the people he appointed to cabinet posts were drawn from the Trilateral Commission, the Brookings Institution, and other institutions championing an open world economy.[2]

For his secretary of state the new president selected Cyrus Vance, a lawyer and diplomat who had previously served as secretary of the army and deputy secretary of defense during the Kennedy and Johnson administrations. The fifty-nine year old West Virginian was also an experienced negotiator who had served as special trouble-shooter for more than one president when there were crises in Cyprus, Korea, and Vietnam.

Carter's selection of Vance was intended to convey a message of continuity in foreign policy to the allies of the country, to the communist world, and to the American people. Vance, in contrast to his colorful predecessor, Henry Kissinger, preferred to conduct diplomacy with as little fanfare as possible. As Hamilton Jordan put it: "With Vance ... no diplomatic hocus-pocus, shuttles, or sleight-of-hand were needed to pursue America's interests. Just hard work and a steady course would get the job done."[3]

Werner Michael "Mike" Blumenthal came from the presidency of the Bendix Corporation to be secretary of the treasury. Charles Schultze, who had been Lyndon Johnson's budget director, had the support of Democratic liberals in addition to the strong endorsement of many of his fellow economists. However, Blumenthal, an expert in international economics, had served as the United States representative at international trade negotiations in the Kennedy administration, and that was an area about which Carter was especially concerned, particularly the need for better coordination of United States economic and foreign policy. In addition, Blumenthal was a liberal Democrat committed to social causes who had enjoyed great success in the corporate world. His no-nonsense management style had led Bendix to record earnings for the past four years despite the nation's economic difficulties. Even so, Carter's selection of Blumenthal was regarded as somewhat unusual since treasury heads usually come from Wall Street or the banking world.[4]

The selection of a secretary of defense was a little more difficult for Carter as he came under severe pressure from the two fiercely competing groups in the long-standing debate of United States military strength. The hard-liners urged the appointment of James Schlesinger, President Ford's former defense secretary, to the Pentagon post. Paul Warnke, former assistant secretary of defense and adviser to George McGovern, was the favorite of the doves.

As a compromise of sorts, Carter settled on Dr. Harold Brown, the forty-nine year old president of the California Institute of Technology. Brown had been in and out of government since 1961, when he joined the band of relatively young economists and systems analysts with whom Robert S. McNamara set out to manage the Defense Department. The "Whiz Kids," as they came to be called, quickly earned the profound enmity of senior military officers and their congressional allies for killing several weapons proposals wanted by the high military brass on what were essentially nonmilitary considerations. At the age of thirty-three, Brown was named Pentagon director of research by McNamara and subsequently became secretary of the air force under Lyndon Johnson in 1965. In 1969, after Brown had become president of Cal Tech, President Nixon appointed him to the United States delegation to the SALT negotiations with the Soviet Union. He was still a member of the United States team seeking an agreement on SALT II at the time of his appointment by Carter.[5]

As his attorney general, Carter appointed Griffin B. Bell, a boyhood chum and former United States Circuit Court of Appeals judge and law partner of Charles Kirbo. Bell had resigned from the bench early in 1976 and had not taken a prominent role in Carter's presidential campaign. He had, however, quietly helped raise money and had given advice.

Judge Bell's appointment stirred a wave of protests from several civil rights groups, black organizations and public interest advocates, as well as several senators, including Ted Kennedy.[6] These protesters were angered by Bell's attitudes on race. Many of the black leaders who had backed

Carter's candidacy also complained about Bell's memberships in three Atlanta clubs that excluded Jews and blacks.

Carter's naming of Bell also struck Republicans and many Democrats as inconsistent with Carter's pledge to take politics out of the Justice Department. He had criticized Richard Nixon's naming of his political supporter and friend John N. Mitchell as his first attorney general. Early in his campaign, Carter had said it was "a disgrace" that during the Watergate era the public had come to believe that "the Attorney General was not fair enough and objective enough and nonpolitical enough to pursue the enforcement of the law." In appointing Bell, the president said, the promise to remove the attorney general from politics had not been broken, only postponed.[7]

Joseph A. Califano, Jr., selected to head the Department of Health, Education, and Welfare, probably had the longest period of service with the federal government. Califano had been assistant to Cyrus Vance when Vance had served as general counsel for the Department of Defense. When Vance became secretary of the army, Califano became general counsel for the Department of the Army and later special assistant to the secretary of defense. In 1965, President Johnson chose Califano as special assistant to the president for domestic affairs, in which capacity he shepherded much of the Great Society legislation through Congress. Thus, Califano helped to create the giant bureaucracy at HEW that he would be administering for Jimmy Carter. Because of his extensive experience in the White House, Califano was considered a master of the Washington bureaucracy. It was assumed this quality would be a help to Carter, but it really wasn't.

For secretary of the interior he selected Governor Cecil Andrus of Idaho, a close personal friend. The choice of Andrus helped him keep a promise to Democratic governors that one of their number would be in his cabinet. Bob Bergland, a Congressman from Mondale's home state of Minnesota and a longtime friend, was chosen secretary of agriculture. In another bow to Capitol Hill, Carter selected Representative Brock Adams of Washington State, the former chairman of the House Budget Committee, as transportation secretary. Adams had campaigned hard for the transportation post.

The process of picking a labor secretary embroiled Carter in a bitter dispute among important supporters of Carter's candidacy. The AFL-CIO strongly backed John Dunlop, who had been President Ford's labor secretary. However, feminist and black groups opposed Dunlop because of what they contended was his poor record in combating job discrimination. Irritated by the public pressure from labor leaders, Carter bypassed the controversial Dunlop and instead chose F. Ray Marshall, a University of Texas economics professor who got along well with the unions.[8]

As a candidate, Carter had pledged to give "heavy representation" to minority groups and women in his cabinet; his stated goal was to place two women and two blacks in cabinet-level jobs. However, in actual practice, he found that it was much more difficult to match slots to people than he had anticipated. Still, he was able to appoint two women (both Democrats) to his cabinet—the first time that two women had ever served in cabinet posts at the same time.

Juanita Morris Kreps, an economics professor and vice president for academic affairs at Duke University, a director of several large corporations (J.C. Penney, Western Electric, Eastman Kodak), and a public member of the governing board of the New York Stock Exchange, was selected to head the Department of Commerce (the first woman to head the department since it was created in 1913). Kreps accepted the job but gave the president-elect a piece of her mind. She suggested that he could have done more to recuit women for his cabinet. "In the case of the search for women, it was the men who did the searching," she said. "And I do think that we simply have to do a better job of searching in the case of both women and minorities."[9]

Patricia Roberts Harris was chosen to direct the Department of Housing and Urban Development (HUD). She was a lawyer, the ambassador to Luxembourg under President Johnson, a civil rights activist, and a director of IBM, Chase Manhattan Bank, and Scott Paper Company. Mrs. Harris was the first black woman appointed to a cabinet post. Several black leaders advised Mrs. Harris to decline the appointment, arguing (correctly, as it developed) that she would be caught between the pressures of urban needs and the limitations of the economy and the federal budget. Many blacks disapproved of the choice of Harris to head HUD, complaining that she was too close to the white community. Also, the United States Conference of Mayors complained that Harris had virtually no experience in housing or urban affairs and had shown "a striking insensitivity to the problems of the cities."

The highly strategic post of ambassador to the United Nations, with cabinet rank, was given to Representative Andrew Young of Georgia.[10] As we have seen, Young's support was considered a major factor in helping Carter win black votes in the 1976 presidential election. In announcing the appointment of Young, Carter praised him: "Of all the people I have ever known in public service, Andy Young is the best. . . . His status will be equal to that of the Secretary of State or the Secretary of the Treasury or anyone else."[11]

The appointment of Young to the United Nations post signaled a clear change in the style of United States foreign policy. Young had openly deplored the politics of confrontation that repeatedly split the international forum. He called for a moral dimension to United States alliances. "Once we get on the right side of moral issues in this world," he said, "then we can have an orderly approach to the problems of the Middle East and a genuine dialogue on the international economic order." Referring to South Africa, Young said that the United States had "unwittingly supported the worst leadership groups and as a consequence we have become party to a vast network of oppression. We have ignored the real human needs."[12]

Carter's essentially conservative economic views were clearly indicated by his appointment of Thomas Bertram "Bert" Lance to be the director of the Office of Management and Budget, a critical post in any adminstration. The appointment of Lance, a tall, hard-driving former bank president from rural Georgia (who described himself as a "fiscal conservative"), was designed to assure the nation's business leaders that basic tax and spending priorities would be guided by a levelheaded business executive rather than someone inimical to the interests of American business.

Lance and Carter were long-time friends. Lance had served as Carter's transportation commissioner in Georgia and also as his banker. When Carter was elected president, his peanut business had loans from Lance's bank totaling $4.7 million. Because of his banking background, Lance was initially considered for secretary of the treasury, but he preferred OMB because that would place him close to the power center in the White House. Carter made communication easier for Lance by granting the OMB post cabinet status. Lance soon became, as expected, the president's most influential advisor. Lance also became a favorite of the press, who loved to quote his numerous rural aphorisms: "You can't hoot with the owls and soar with the eagles," and, "If it ain't broke—don't fix it."

Carter and His Advisers

ZBIGNIEW BRZEZINSKI. Probably the most controversial selection made by President Carter was that of Dr. Zbigniew "Zbig" Brzezinski, a forty-eight year old East European scholar and former State Department policy planner, to serve as his adviser on foreign policy matters with the title of assistant to the president for national security affairs. Brzezinski also served as director of the National Security Council. He was accorded the same rank as cabinet secretaries.[13] Brzezinski had a "hawkish" reputation on U.S.–Soviet relations.

Carter met Brzezinski through David Rockefeller and the Trilateral Commission. During the campaign, Carter, who himself had no experience in international diplomacy, had found himself relying heavily on Brzezinski's counsel in developing his positions on world affairs. As the campaign had progressed, demanding more thoughtful decisions and statements on defense and foreign policy, the word had gone out to the campaign staff: "Clear it with Zbig."[14]

Dr. Brzezinski generally agreed with Henry Kissinger, his predecessor as national security adviser, that United States power had waned in the world and that America must seek a new world order—including detente with the Soviet Union (but with more of a tilt toward the United States), normalization of relations with China, and greater interdependence with the industrialized nations of Western Europe and Japan. He did, however, fault Kissinger on several counts, including his alleged neglect of the nation's "traditional" ties with less powerful but natural allies. (Pressed to comment on Brzezinski, Kissinger summed him up as "smart but not wise.")[15]

Carter's trust in and dependence on Brzezinski grew as the months of his administration passed. The notion soon spread outside the White House that Brzezinski had the president's mind as well as his ear. Since Brzezinski was known not to be deferential to secretaries of state, who were the traditional foreign policy advisers to presidents, many observers wondered how long it would be before the outspoken and ambitious Brzezinski came into conflict with Secretary of State Vance, and who would prevail. Most money was on "soon" and "Zbig." When conflict came after the seizure of the hostages in Iran, Brzezinski explained that there was a generational gap between himself (then fifty-one) and Vance (sixty-three). Vance, thought Brzezinski, still lived with the memory of Vietnam and feared the use of force. He himself feared more the show of weakness.[16] As for Carter, he soon found that he was less supported than immobilized by the conflicting counsel coming from his foreign policy experts. The perception was soon widespread that there were two voices in foreign policy—a perception that hurt the president with those who believe that there can be only one spokesman in foreign policy and that spokesman has to be the secretary of state.

THE SORENSON EMBARRASSMENT. President Carter was seriously embarrassed by only one proposed appointment—that of Theodore C. Sorenson, a New York lawyer and former assistant to President Kennedy, to serve as director of the Central Intelligence Agency. A large part of the problem was that the CIA had become a subject of increased public and congressional concern as a result of a series of newspaper disclosures and government investigations, including a Senate inquiry which had revealed "the use of bribery, corruption, and violence in almost every corner of the world . . . aimed at our friends as well as our foes."[17]

Another part of the problem was that Sorenson, who was well enough known on Capitol Hill and was politically acceptable to the liberals in the Senate, was, like Carter, an outsider so far as the intelligence community was concerned — which was not what many insiders wanted. It was, however, exactly what Carter believed the intelligence community needed. Critics of the appointment charged that Sorenson had no direct experience in intelligence and pointed to his criticism of intelligence operations — especially the use of covert operations — to indicate a basic failure to understand the role of the intelligence agency. On a more personal level, they argued that Sorenson had demonstrated a causal attitude toward the use of classified information while serving as special assistant to President John F. Kennedy.[18]

Although he was warned that the nomination was in serious trouble, Carter publicly reiterated his confidence in the nominee. However, when Democrat Robert C. Byrd, the newly elected Senate majority leader, informed the president that he could not commit himself to voting for confirmation of Sorenson to head the CIA, Sorenson asked Carter to withdraw the nomination — which he did, three days before the inauguration. It was the first time since the Coolidge administration that a president had been rebuffed on a nomination by a Senate controlled by his own party.[19] Several of the president's critics suggested that if Carter had fought a little more vigorously for Sorenson he could have saved the nomination. Shortly after Sorenson's withdrawal, Carter submitted a much safer choice for the CIA: an Annapolis classmate, Admiral Stansfield Turner, who had been serving as NATO commander in Southern Europe. Turner was easily confirmed.[20]

Another controversial appointment was that of James R. Schlesinger, a Republican economist and former Nixon and Ford cabinet officer, to be presidential assistant in coordinating energy policy. Since Schlesinger had been head of the Atomic Energy Commission under Nixon, he seemed a logical choice to head the new Department of Energy whose creation Carter was to recommend. Carter made it clear that he was, in effect, appointing Schlesinger to what he envisioned as an expanded cabinet.

Additional key appointments were Charles Schultze to be chairman of the Council of Economic Advisers, and Stuart Eizenstadt to advise on domestic policy and to direct the Domestic Policy Staff (DPS).

VICE PRESIDENT MONDALE. President Carter, in contrast to his predecessors, relied heavily on Vice President Walter Mondale for advice and assistance in governing. He was anxious, he said, "to free the vice president from the institutional and ceremonial duties that had occupied his predecessors" in order to leave him free to advise on a wide range of issues and handle special assignments. In a sharp break with precedent, the vice president was given an office in the White House — vice presidents usually have an office in the Executive Office Building next door — and his staff was integrated with the president's. Mondale was also given unprecedented access to information. He received the same security briefings as the president and saw the same messages he received. He was automatically invited to participate in all official meetings, and helped to plan strategy for domestic programs, diplomacy, and defense.

Although he was never a member of the inner group of Georgians, the vice president was given practically unlimited opportunity to comment on decisions while they were in the making, and he frequently expressed disagreement with Carter's proposals if he thought the president was making a mistake, wasn't getting good advice, or didn't have all the facts. Yet he was a good team player, and although behind the scenes he fought hard for what he believed in, he would accept the president's decisions and defend them publicly.[21]

Mondale also made important trips abroad on behalf of the president. On these trips he sought to reassure possibly apprehensive heads of state that Carter would not cut American commitments to traditional allies.

ROSALYNN. However, by far the closest confidante, and most influential adviser, of the president was his wife of thirty-four years, Rosalynn (whom he frequently called "Rosie"). Carter's dependence on his wife's political judgment began even before his election as governor of Georgia. She had been a skilled and tireless campaigner for him in that race and also in his quest for the presidency.[22] She and the president discussed most important issues (except highly secret and sensitive security matters) so she knew pretty well all that was going on. She received detailed briefings from members of Carter's domestic and national security staffs and occasionally sat in on cabinet meetings, taking notes and later discussing issues with her husband. She also represented the president at such occasions as inaugurations of foreign leaders, funerals, or commemorations of important state holidays.[23]

Most observers agreed that Rosalynn projected a good image as first lady. She involved herself intensely in serious projects that helped both her husband and the country. As honorary chair of the President's Commission on Mental Health, she presided over a series of hearings in United States cities and worked with the commission to draw up recommendations aimed at improving mental health services.

Carter's detractors soon learned that Rosalynn, despite her soft Southern drawl and smile, could be tough as nails in the defense of her husband—which happened often enough to eventually earn her the nickname "the Steel Magnolia."

CARTER AND HIS CABINET. Throughout the transition period between the Ford and Carter administrations, Carter never left any doubt that he planned to rely heavily on his cabinet officers—that he would, in fact, institute genuine cabinet government, with policy development in the departments rather than in the White House. Possibly this government would include a parliamentary "question time" where his cabinet members would appear before the houses of Congress to answer questions. Cabinet meetings would be open to the press.[24]

Professor Erwin Hargrove concludes that as President Carter was not at all interested in the incremental development of policy which his predecessors had favored (and which Congress quickly revealed that it also favored). He had strong views that policy should be developed in the department concerned, with the emphasis in the departments on developing broad-based comprehensive programs dealing with national problems. Essentially, since the departments were dealing with national problems requiring comprehensive solutions, there was no need for the departments to compromise or consult. Carter's approach to policy development guaranteed that he would not take congressional opinion into account at the outset but would hold out for the "right" solution. There would not even be a strong White House coordinating role. The cabinet officers were charged with the responsibility for policy development; beyond that, Carter did not have in mind a well-developed model for the relations of his staffs to the departments should the need for central coordination of policy development appear. As such problems emerged, he basically would leave it up to his chief lieutenants in the White House to work out their relations with cabinet officers and departments.[25]

Eventually, those ideas all fell victim to political reality. At the beginning Carter met frequently with his entire cabinet, and in the first year Carter had thirty-six sessions with the full cabinet. In short order, however, the cabinet members rebelled at the idea of having the members of the press sit in on cabinet meetings, and the president was forced to back down. Nevertheless, even though cabinet meetings were closed to the press, there were "leaks," and most of the deliberations reached the press after each meeting.

Also, once his cabinet was assembled, Carter found that the members were far more diverse in background and interest than he had realized. With little in common to tie them together, they spent much too much valuable time sparring for recognition and approval of their pet projects. In addition, the size of the group — sixteen people — made decision-making almost impossible. Discussing routine matters that could be covered in memoranda left too little time for important matters such as foreign policy, the minimum wage, unemployment, and inflation. The number of full cabinet meetings dwindled and during the three succeeding years, only twenty-three, then nine, then six such meetings were held.

Carter and the Public

President Carter moved quickly to deflate the atmosphere that during the Nixon and Johnson years had been described by critics as the "imperial presidency." He banned the playing of "Hail to the Chief." He wore blue jeans around the White House. He put the mammoth presidential limousine in mothballs and rode in a more modest sedan. White House staffers, who had expected to have door-to-door limousine privileges, were told to use their own cars or cabs.[26] Carter also liked to be seen carrying his own bags from the presidential helicopter.

He also initiated a number of highly publicized ventures which brought him into direct contact with citizens. He attended an old-fashioned "town hall meeting" in Clinton, Massachusetts,[27] a solidly Democratic, small industrial city of about 13,000 people fifty miles west of Boston. There he answered the questions of about 700 people selected by lottery who had gathered in a local auditorium, and spent the night at the home of a Massachusetts beer distributor, where he made his own bed. He also held a two-hour question-and-answer call-in radio show over CBS Radio, with Walter Cronkite moderating the questions for the president (who often called the questioners by their first names).[28]

Carter's stress on openness and honesty in government apparently struck a responsive chord in the American people. After his first six months in office, a Gallup Poll revealed that the public approved of his overall performance, with 66 percent voting favorably.

Carter and the Press

Before taking office, Carter promised he would hold news conferences every two weeks, which he did during the first weeks of his administration. Eventually, however, Carter became convinced that his decline in popularity ratings was the result of the bad press coverage he was receiving, and like other recent presidents, he became remote from the press. He was also well aware that he had gained office despite the fact that a vast majority of the national press had been editorially against him.[29]

In mid-1979 Carter changed his strategy for dealing with the media. He announced that in the future he would largely abandon the formal Washington press conference format and instead talk to local reporters on trips around the country and to columnists and news executives in private meetings. Shortly thereafter, he took his wife and daughter on a week-long, 659-mile trip on the Mississippi River aboard the riverboat *Delta Queen*, where he made a point of talking to local reporters but gave little attention to the national press corps that accompanied him.

In reality, Carter and his advisers did not make much of an effort to understand or appreciate the media. Consequently they were unable to deal with the extent to which Watergate and the resignation of a president, as well as Vietnam, the nation's first military defeat, had pushed the Washington press corps from skepticism and doubt into out-and-out cynicism about the American political process generally and the presidency specifically. The coverage of both Vietnam and Watergate had taken on the air of a struggle between the press and the president.

Nor, for that matter, did the media make much of an effort to understand Carter. An obscure Georgian before he became president, he was not easy to get to know after he became president. Carter, for his part, failed to grasp the opportunity to educate the press, and to the end of his administration he remained an enigma to those who reported the comings and goings at the White House and on the Hill. In consequence, there were no long-established friends in the press corps who would naturally come to Carter's defense in a public debate on a controversial issue.

Probably the major irritant in the relationship between Carter and the journalists who covered him was that the president appeared to regard himself as superior to the reporters in intellect and moral goodness. The news media, the president frequently implied, were superficial in their treatment of national and international events and tended to trivialize the most serious problems with a cynical approach which did not present the public with a faithful picture of events in the nation's capital. Predictably, the reporters came to regard Carter as mean-spirited and self-righteous and treated him accordingly. Sam Donaldson, who covered the White House during the Carter years for ABC-TV, points out that although most presidents conduct a running battle with Washington journalists, the antagonism of the Carter administration toward the media beggared comparison.[30]

For another thing, Carter suffered from a pronounced lack of humor in his relations with the press. He preferred to project the image of a very serious, straightforward person. The American people, he was convinced, were not looking for a particularly urbane, sophisticated, witty type. In consequence, many of the correspondents covering the presidential campaign concluded that Carter lacked any ability to laugh at himself — preferring to laugh at the other fellow.

As Charles Mohr of the *New York Times* put it: "A little [humor], he seems to believe, goes a long way." Consequently, on the rare occasion when he engaged in self-deprecating humor he didn't manage to sound convincing.[31] Unfortunately for Carter, the Washington press corps was accustomed to the idea that Democratic presidents were supposed to be witty. John Kennedy had been — and they had transferred their affection for John Kennedy to his brother Ted, resulting in a cozy relationship which Carter resented.[32]

THE BERT LANCE AFFAIR. Carter was especially frustrated by the media handling of three scandals early in his administration. The first came in the summer of 1977 when it was revealed by the media that Bert Lance, his director of the Office of Management and Budget, was under investigation by the Office of the Controller of the Currency (the agency that regulates national banks) because of questionable banking and campaign practices which he had engaged in, first as president of the National Bank in Calhoun, Georgia, and then as president of Atlanta's National Bank of Georgia. It was charged that Lance had loaned money to family members without adequate collateral; that he had made unsafe loans; and that he had violated banking and securities laws or regulations, or had at least observed them carelessly.

The "Lance Affair" became, and remained for several weeks, the number one news story in the national capital. Congress and other sources demanded an investigation, and Lance was forced to undergo three days of televised hearings conducted by the Senate Governmental Affairs Committee in mid–September. Although Lance adroitly defended himself against the charges, his image was damaged in the eyes of many members of the administration, as well as several key members of the congressional Democratic leadership. Many reached the conclusion that Lance, although probably not a criminal in the strict sense of the term, was not the kind of man who ought to be the chief financial adviser of a president who had placed such public emphasis on ethics and morality (and who people would hold to higher standards of public and private morality than they had expected from some previous presidents). Carter had been elected as someone who would never lie to the American people, but it was now suspected that some of his associates might tell something less than the whole truth.

The president's frustration and bitterness grew as it became increasingly clear that Lance would not survive the controversy. When Senate majority leader Robert Byrd told Carter that Lance should go, he resigned. The president announced Lance's resignation with obvious sorrow.[33]

Lance's financial difficulties were also an embarrassment for the Senate, which had confirmed the Georgia banker after only a cursory examination of his banking background. It was obvious that the senators had not been very diligent in their probing of Lance's qualifications for the office of budget director. The whole affair provided one of the most damaging episodes for the Carter administration and Congress, and understandably, it increased the tension between Capitol Hill and the White House.[34]

THE MARSTON AFFAIR. A second media bashing of the Carter administration occurred as a result of the firing of David Marston, the United

States attorney for Philadelphia who had been appointed by President Ford. In the summer of 1977, Marston's office launched an investigation into the roles played by two Pennsylvania Democratic representatives, Joshua Eilberg and Daniel Flood, in the financing of a $65 million addition to Philadelphia's Hahnemann Hospital. In November 1977, after Eilberg demanded that the president remove Marston from office, Carter instructed Attorney General Griffin Bell to find a replacement for Marston.

The press quickly reminded the president of his campaign pledge that "all federal judges and prosecutors should be appointed strictly on the basis of merit without any consideration of political aspects or influence." Even so, Marston was dismissed on January 20, 1978. Attorney General Bell subsequently admitted that the firing was "politically motivated." There was an immediate uproar. Carter found it difficult to explain why he would remove a United States attorney doing his job reasonably well in response to the entreaties of a Democratic congressman who had been touched by that attorney's investigation.[35]

THE PETER BOURNE AFFAIR. President Carter also suffered an acute embarrassment when Dr. Peter Bourne, his assistant for health affairs, admitted that he had written a prescription for a controlled drug for an aide using a false name. Bourne resigned the next day but unfortunately was quoted by the *New York Times* as saying there was a "high incidence" of marijuana use and some use of cocaine among junior White House staff members. Although Bourne later denied making the statement, the impression remained of drug use close to the White House.

Carter and the Ninety-fifth Congress

Considerable harmony was expected between the president and the Ninety-fifth Congress, the first Congress with which Carter would have to deal. The heavy Democratic congressional majorities — 291 in the house and sixty-one in the Senate — were expected to feel a sense of relief, after eight long Republican years, on being able to deal at last with a president of their own party.[36]

The congressional leadership appeared to be ready to assist the president in carrying through his program. Thomas P. "Tip" O'Neill, the newly elected speaker of the House of Representatives, promised his full support. Congress, said O'Neill, would meet the President's goals.[37]

It did not work out that way, however, and Carter endured endless frustrations in his attempts to lead the Democrats — many more frustrations, it would appear, than a president whose party controlled two-thirds of the membership of Congress should reasonably be expected to encounter.[38]

Ironically, Carter's frustrations with the Ninety-fifth Congress really had their roots in the congressional elections of 1974, which he had worked so hard to win for the Democrats and which had produced seventy-five new Democrats for the House of Representatives—the biggest Democratic freshman class in recent years. However, they were also the most independent-minded freshman class ever elected, at least in modern times. Most of the newly elected members were not inclined to submit to party discipline. They had raised their own money and run their own campaigns, and they felt little debt to the national Democratic Party, its congressional leadership, or its president.

Soon after they convened as the Ninety-fourth Congress, the House Democrats radically altered the power structure in the House of Representatives. Taking power that largely rested with the chairmen of the twenty-two House standing committees, they parceled it out to the 172 subcommittees. Now, suddenly, relatively junior Democrats could be elected subcommittee chairs, from which position they could become policy entrepreneurs, hector the administration, bargain with high officials, or simply grab publicity. Since they were no longer under the thumb of full committee chairs, several of them became aggressive and freewheeling. The resultant proliferation of power in Congress loosened discipline and made it hard, first for Jerry Ford and then for Jimmy Carter, to put together a clear political agenda or develop a congressional coalition to pass major legislation.

By the time the Ninety-fifth Congress convened, two groups had emerged in Congress which were highly destructive of party unity and which became especially hard for Carter to deal with once he became president.

The first consisted of about fifty conservative Southern Democrats who styled themselves the "Boll Weevils" because they were boring from within the Democratic Party, just as insect weevils bore from inside the cotton boll. These Democrats had clashed for years with their national party leaders on several key issues, including defense spending and budget deficits. They were in a renegade mood and had no intention of supporting Jimmy Carter just because he was a Southern Democrat.

The second group, the "Gypsy Moths," were some fifteen to twenty liberal Republicans from the Northeast and Midwest. Habitual defectors from the Republican ranks, they joined centrist and liberal Democrats in legislative coalitions. But like the "Weevils" whose name they parodied,[39] they did not plan to support Carter.

The lessening of unity in the Democratic Party resulting from these developments made it virtually impossible for President Carter to establish a governing coalition based on the party. Theoretically his Democratic Party ties should have helped him, but the climate of independence in Congress was at its peak in the late 1970s.[40] It didn't help matters that he had won both his nomination and his election as the "outsider" who had campaigned against Washington and its insiders—including, of course, members of Congress. Moreover, congressional Democrats felt no political debt to Carter. Many pointed out that they had run independently of Carter in the 1976 campaign, and polled larger votes in their districts than he had. In addition, because of his narrow victory over Ford, many members doubted that he had a broad public mandate to carry out the program he was pressing on them. Carter thus had less leverage to exert for his legislative program than would a president who led the ticket.[41] As Hamilton Jordan put it: "There was a subtle but strong feeling when we arrived in Washington that 'Well OK, you Georgians won the big prize through gimmicks, good fortune, and by running against Washington. But now we are going to show you who's boss in this town.'"[42]

Also many Democrats, especially the liberals, were against Carter because they were convinced that he was trying to lead the party and the nation in the wrong direction. His election, they argued, had won him no mandate to abandon the party's traditional approach. Inevitably, several of Carter's decisions that he believed to be in the best interests of the country were made at the expense of a consensus of his own party.[43]

Despite the organizational and philosophical difficulties Carter faced in dealing with a Congress in turmoil, there is little doubt that many of his problems in dealing with the Ninety-fifth Congress stemmed from his, and his aides', lack of understanding that the Democratic (and Republican) members of Congress were important people in their own right (more than one of whom thought that he himself, rather than Carter, should be president). These members had political concerns beyond passing the extremely long legislative agenda of the president,[44] which included such highly controversial (and best avoided) subjects as the Panama Canal, stringent budgets, government reorganization, deregulation of major industries, civil service reform, tax reform, energy conservation, Social Security reform, welfare reform—much more than Congress could handle even with the best of relations between the White House and Capitol Hill. Unfortunately for Carter, when offers of help came from older Washington hands whose support would be critical to his programs, he spurned it.

Then, to make matters worse, Carter and his aides appeared to be determined repeatedly to rub congressional fur the wrong way. Carter staffers frequently failed to return members' telephone calls. Legislative packages were announced by the White House without prior consultation with members, and Hill people complained thay had no clear sense of priorities—what was most important and what was least important, and which policies would be compromised to ensure the adoption of which other policies.[45] As far as Congress could tell the administration thought *everything* was important. Often, presidential priorities were changed without warning, leaving members who had supported the president out on a limb. The official line was often unclear as cabinet officers endorsed positions independently of the White House. Also, the president took trips without informing the member of Congress whose district he was visiting.

Members of Congress also frequently complained that Carter and his Georgians made no attempt to understand the "congressional view" of the nature of policy formation in American politics. Rather, the president frequently dismissed the members of Congress as bothersome claimants for presidential attention and resources, rather than seeing them as instruments of political action. Also, Congress resented the president's complaints that some members wasted his "extremely valuable time" because they were not as well prepared as he was on the occasions when they discussed pending legislation. As Hedrick Smith, the *New York Times* bureau chief, put it: "Carter did not understand that Congressmen did not come to the White House to hear a logical argument from the President. They came down to swap stories and go back up to the Hill and brag to the others, 'I told the President . . . and he told me.'"[46]

The perception began to grow among his fellow Democrats that Carter, and his aides, viewed Congress and the Democratic Party with a "thumb-to-the nose" attitude.[47] By the fall of 1977, the new president's presumed ineptness (in party and policy leadership) was being discussed openly and joked about in Washington. In December 1977, Russell Baker writing in the *New York Times* observed that "if the Carter administration were a television show it would have been canceled months ago."

However, probably the most politically significant cause of Carter's inability to work effectively with Congress was the long-simmering tension between presidents and Congress in the making and executing of public policy which the Johnson and Nixon administrations had brought to the fore. Following the Vietnam War and Watergate, an assertive Congress rose up to challenge not just Nixon but the presidency as an institution. As the *Wall Street Journal* observed in 1973, Nixon "aroused a snoozing Congress and made it mad."[48] The Ninety-third and Ninety-fourth congresses subsequently passed a series of executive branch–curbing measures designed to enable Congress to have what it considered its proper role in running the government. Thus, Carter's election as president brought him into confrontation with a Congress arrogantly asserting its own powers and prerogatives and determined to restrict presidential authority in both the domestic and foreign arenas. As Tip O'Neill, the Democratic speaker of the house, firmly put it: "We are a coequal branch

of government."[49] The message was clear: Congress had its own requirements, and they could not be altered merely to satisfy the requirements of a president—especially an "outsider" president who, the
members of Congress were convinced, had no intention of becoming an
"insider."

Carter was thus projected into a conflict which he had no role in making and could do very little to resolve. By 1976 presidency-curbing statutes
and extralegal changes in institutions and practices had so sapped the
ability of the chief executive to exercise leadership that it was a fight
Carter, even in the best of circumstances, could not win.[50]

PARDON FOR DRAFT EVADERS. Unfortunately for Carter, the frustrations with Capitol Hill emerged early. On January 21, his first day in office,
he issued his first executive order. Using the same presidential authority
by which Gerald Ford had pardoned Richard Nixon, he granted a "full,
complete, and unconditional pardon" to all draft violators of the Vietnam
War. It was a symbolic act (and many presidents have opened their administrations with a symbolic act) that should not have come as a surprise to
the members of Congress, since he had made the promise of a blanket pardon during his campaign for election.

However, Carter's act evoked immediate, strong criticism. Peace
groups said the president had not gone far enough (most wanted amnesty). Veterans' groups called the pardon an insult to the millions who
had served. Four days later the Senate narrowly defeated (forty-eight to
forty-six) a resolution expressing the sense of the Senate that Carter
should not have issued his unconditional pardon to persons who violated
the draft laws in the 1960s and early 1970s.[51]

Carter's National Energy Plan

When he became president, Jimmy Carter inherited an energy shortage which neither President Nixon nor President Ford had been able to
solve and which was becoming increasingly severe. Solving the energy
crisis, he concluded, had to be on the top of his agenda, and he gave
establishing a comprehensive national energy program the highest initial
priority.[52]

The energy shortage had been building since 1973, when the Arab
states, embittered by President Nixon's support of Israel, imposed severe
limitations on the shipment of oil to the West and began a systematic raising of prices on the world market through their oil cartel, the Organization of Petroleum Exporting Countries (OPEC).[53] The federal government continued after 1973 to keep the price of oil artificially low through
modified price controls but did little to penalize excessive domestic

consumption through taxation. By the winter of 1974, however, the cost of energy, whether for heating oil in New England winters or for gasoline all over the country, could no longer be controlled by either normal commerce or the American government. In turn, the energy scarcity fed inflation, and deficits in the balance of payments to the oil-producing nations were beginning to produce extensive unemployment in energy-related industries.

Although the Arab oil embargo produced considerable fear and even panic, at its conclusion toward the end of 1974 energy consumers returned to their wasteful ways, refusing to believe that there was an energy problem as long as gasoline was flowing out of pumps at the service stations. By the time Carter took office the country was importing more than half of the oil it consumed—about nine billion barrels a day.

Professor Erwin Hargrove suggests that this was the kind of issue Carter liked, as it pitted the national interest, and a public good, against regional and economic interests. It also required comprehensive treatment, joining conservation and production, oil, gas, coal, nuclear power, and taxes. Carter felt a moral obligation to exercise stewardship in regard to national resources. Furthermore, he was critical of the manner in which politicians had failed to face the hard questions. As Hargrove notes, "he has little patience with the normal political tendency toward a policy of drift, opportunism and irresponsibility."[54]

THE "FIRESIDE CHAT." On February 2, 1977 (a record cold day in a record cold winter), the new, self-assured president gave his first nationally televised "fireside chat" sitting before a roaring three-log fire in the White House library (the fire went out before he finished speaking). He wore a heavy cardigan sweater to underline his message that the nation needed to conserve energy. He spoke of harsh realities. "We must face the fact that the energy shortage is permanent," he said. "There is no way we can solve it quickly." By the time the talk was completed, millions of viewers had gained the impression of a president who was confident and realistic and in command of his job.

On April 8, 1977, Carter opened his energy campaign with a nationally televised address in which he sought to shock the nation into an awareness of the seriousness of the problem, which he said was "unprecedented in our history," and "except for preventing war," was "the greatest challenge that our country will face during our lifetime." The nation, he somberly warned, faced the possibility of nothing less than a "national catastrophe" unless it responded to its energy problems with "the moral equivalent of war." Two days later he went before a joint session of Congress to disclose his specific proposals and to urge congressional support of his energy program. Action was needed, he said, "to cope with a crisis that otherwise could overwhelm us."

He then outlined a full-scale energy conservation program designed to decrease oil imports by encouraging Americans to conserve oil and gas, to switch to other fuels such as coal when possible, and to produce more oil and gas from domestic reservoirs. The program involved a variety of new taxes, incentives, and controls, including taxing gas-guzzling automobiles (that is, those that did not meet the federal fuel efficiency standards) and raising the price of all domestic oil to the price level of foreign oil to encourage domestic oil and gas production. Also proposed was a standby gasoline tax (from five to fifty cents per gallon), which would go into effect if total gasoline consumption exceeded stated annual targets.[55]

The president's program came under immediate criticism. The oil and gas companies said it put too much emphasis on reducing consumption and far too little on developing incentives for more production. Many members of Congress of both parties were greatly aroused by the fact that the program had been developed almost entirely in secret by James Schlesinger and his technocrats. Congress was not consulted or even informed about what to expect. Also, except for a series of leaks to the press, the public was kept in the dark, as were, for the most part, the members of the cabinet and the White House staff.

DEREGULATION OF NATURAL GAS. One of the most controversial elements of Carter's National Energy Plan was a proposal to continue federal price controls on natural gas. Initially, as a candidate for president, Carter seemed to favor deregulation of natural gas prices. He had written a letter to Texas governor Dolph Briscoe pledging that he would work with the Congress, as the Ford administration had been unable to do, to establish a phased-in deregulation of newly discovered natural gas. So it was a surprise and a shock to the lobbyists for the oil and gas industry and the members of Congress from the oil and gas states when he called for continuing federal price controls on natural gas.

Over the intervening months, Carter had become convinced that there was enough domestically produced natural gas to meet the needs of the nation, but it was not going to the right places. In the severe winter of 1976–1977, the northeastern parts of the country had suffered from a shortage of gas, and many schools and factories had to be shut down. The problem, as Carter saw it, was that in 1954 Congress had placed a very low ceiling on the price that could be charged when natural gas was transported across a state line. The oil and gas companies were therefore eager to sell as much as possible within the producing states, where the ceiling did not apply, and as little as possible anywhere else. The non-producing states were always last on the priority list for new gas deliveries.[56]

And so, when Carter stated at a press conference of September 29,

1977, that he did not "support complete deregulation of natural gas prices" because it would provide windfall profits without increasing supply, he was accused of waffling on the issue. Many democrats denounced the president's action as the Carter administration's great double cross.[57]

THE DEPARTMENT OF ENERGY. By midsummer of 1977 Congress had approved the first of Carter's energy goals, the creation of a Department of Energy. On August 5, 1977, James R. Schlesinger, the White House energy advisor, was confirmed as the first secretary of the new department.

THE NATIONAL ENERGY ACT. Also on August 5, 1977, the National Energy Act cleared the House of Representatives virtually intact, largely because Speaker O'Neill made an all-out effort for it. In the Senate, however, the program encountered extensive opposition. The energy industry — especially the automobile and oil lobbies — launched a media campaign to convince the public that all energy problems could be overcome if only the oil producers, public utility companies, and nuclear power industry were relieved of government interference and left to run their own businesses. The problem, they said, was not a shortage of fuel but a shortage of free enterprise.[58]

However, the Senate Finance Committee would not budge on what Carter was convinced was the most important part of the original bill, a proposal to decontrol domestic oil prices (to raise them to the world level) and to tax the oil companies' resulting windfall profits.[59] Carter proposed to rebate the additional cost to consumers through a crude oil equalization tax, but Senator Long, a Democrat of Louisiana and the chair of the Senate Finance Committee, wanted the oil industry to get the extra revenues.[60]

Although Congress appeared to be dragging its heels on the president's energy program, the country did not seem to mind, for despite Carter's efforts, half of the nation refused to believe that there was an energy problem at all — which probably increased the program's vulnerability to opposition lobbyists (of which there were many).[61] At home, because of his apparent lack of public and congressional support, confidence in Carter as a leader was undermined. Abroad, America's NATO allies were distressed by the president's obvious inability to lead Congress effectively.

In the meantime, largely due to dependence on high-priced foreign oil, double-digit inflation reared its ugly head, creating another unanticipated problem for Carter. Simultaneously the United States balance-of-trade deficit soared to an unprecedented $26 billion, and the once dominant dollar suffered a dismaying drop in relation to other major currencies on the exchanges of Europe and Asia.

During early 1978, the energy measure was bogged down as the conference committee tried to resolve differences over the natural gas pricing section. Finally, a compromise was passed by the Senate on September 27 and then by the House of Representatives on October 15, 1978, the last day of the second session of the Ninety-fifth Congress (nearly eighteen months after the measure was first introduced). The natural gas deregulation incorporated in the final bill aimed only at deregulating new natural gas — although "new" gas was liberally defined.

The energy bill that Congress passed and that went to the president for his signature was vastly different from the measure that Carter had said was necessary for the nation's survival. The tax on domestic crude oil was not included. It was more important, Congress decided, to encourage energy production than to discourage use as the president had requested. Also missing was the proposed tax on businesses and utilities that did not convert to alternative fuels. In fact, the only tax that ultimately remained in the bill was a watered-down charge on "gas guzzler" cars. The Japanese automobile industry got the message and went into high gear producing smaller, more fuel-efficient cars to sell to Americans as they switched from these same old-fashioned gas guzzlers.[62]

Senator Kennedy and other members of Congress, consumer organizations and labor unions urged a veto — denouncing the decontrol decision as an invitation to the oil companies to gouge the public. Nevertheless, President Carter, eager for some sort of energy legislation, signed the measure. Passage of the bill, he said, was a victory. "We have declared to ourselves and the world our intent to control our use of energy and thereby control our own destiny as a nation."[63]

Carter's critics were quick to point out that the energy bill had consumed far too much of Congress's time, largely because the bill was so flawed with technical errors which the members of Congress had to unknot that they found themselves tangled with every lobby in the nation. "The energy bill," said a White House staff member, "was the single greatest mistake we made in our first six months. When we couldn't pass it, people got the impression that the President just couldn't manage the government. We never recovered from that impression."

Other Legislation

Airline Industry Deregulation. A top Carter priority was an airline deregulation bill. He expected to score an early and easy victory in Congress because airline deregulation legislation already had been the subject of extensive congressional hearings on a bill proposed by President Ford in 1975, during the previous Congress. Ironically, many airline companies opposed airline deregulation in the Ninety-fourth Congress. Over the years government regulators and the industries they regulate have woven close relationships in which an industry agrees to follow certain rules in return for a reprieve from the rigors of the free marketplace. In many cases, federal regulations have relieved private firms of worry over new market entry, price competition, safety standards, technological obsolescence, and inefficient management — a situation which the airlines could appreciate.

An airline deregulation bill was passed by both houses of the Ninety-fifth Congress with large margins on the last day of the session. President Carter, who viewed airline deregulation as a consumer issue, signed the bill on October 24, 1978. By unleashing the airlines the bill promised to increase free-market competition in the commercial passenger industry, which Carter hoped would result in lower air fares.

The legislation did, in fact, bring about dramatic reductions in some air fares as several airlines introduced unprecedented discounts. Even so, some airlines predicted dire results. Scheduled service to many small communities, which was generally unprofitable, would be cut. The airline trade unions complained that deregulation would mean large-scale layoffs.

The drop in air fares and the increase in airline profits were expected to pave the way for other transportation deregulation measures in the next Congress. Despite the success of the airline deregulation measure, however, transportation industry deregulation remained a controversial issue in some quarters. In railroads and trucking, both Congress and the administration put off major policy decisions until 1979 or later.

TRUCKING INDUSTRY DEREGULATION. Federal regulation of the trucking industry, Carter had said as a candidate, was a source of inflation, energy waste, and above all, unnecessarily high costs for consumers. Therefore, in March 1977, the president announced that his administration would seek legislation to deregulate the trucking industry. Within months, however, Carter was forced to confront an uncomfortable truth: The group most opposed to his regulatory reform plan turned out to be the trucking industry itself.[64] At the close of 1978, legislation to reform the trucking industry remained stalled in the Office of Management and Budget, bitterly opposed by the American Trucking Associations and the Teamsters Union, the nation's largest labor union. Deregulation, they argued, would lead to excessive competition, lower profits, bankrupt trucking firms, and unemployment.

However, Carter found support in an unexpected place: the Senate, where Massachusetts Senator Ted Kennedy had been holding hearings since October on a similar bill. Kennedy's staff had worked with the White House on the bill. Trucking deregulation, they said, would save consumers $5 billion a year by reducing shipping costs, and would result in energy savings by allowing truckers to operate more efficiently. By January 1979 the senator had assembled a coalition of industry-associated groups to support deregulation. He sponsored the administration's bill and testified on its behalf. The bill passed the Senate in April 1980, and the House approved a slightly different version of the legislation in June. In July 1980 Carter signed the bill. The final bill did not go as far as the version he and Kennedy had originally proposed, but they embraced it as providing substantial regulatory relief.

CIVIL SERVICE REFORM. Another significant achievement was the Civil Service Reform Act of 1978, which terminated the Civil Service Commission and called for the creation of a Senior Executive Service — the first major change in the federal civil service system in nearly a century. Despite resistance from the labor unions that represented most of the 2.1 million federal employees, Carter got much of what he wanted, including more freedom for managers to fire workers for cause. At the same time the bill strengthened government labor unions. It attempted to establish a genuine merit system and discontinued automatic promotions.

SOCIAL SECURITY REFORM. By the time Carter took office as president, the Social Security system was rapidly running out of funds. Congress responded to this danger in 1977, and after much debate, the Social Security Bill (PL95-216), which was designed to keep the Social Security Trust Fund solvent for the next twenty-five years, was signed by Carter on December 20, 1977. Included in the bill was an increase in payroll taxes over a period of ten years by the astronomical sum of $227 billion. The bill came under repeated attacks during the year 1978. Criticism centered on the cost to employees and employers and on the growing proportion of beneficiaries to workers. In 1978, efforts to change the tax rate and the wage base to find alternate funding sources were defeated, but only after extended, acrimonious debate in Congress.

HOUSING AND COMMUNITY DEVELOPMENT BILL. A $14.7 billion housing and community development bill, signed into law by President Carter in October 1977, was designed to provide housing for low-income families and to improve slum areas, especially in such large northern cities as New York, Detroit, and Baltimore.

MINIMUM WAGE LAW. Congress also enacted a new minimum wage law in 1977, boosting the figure in stages from $2.30 an hour to $3.25 by 1981. Unfortunately, this time Carter antagonized the AFL-CIO, one of his major support groups, by not consulting them (they had to read about it in the newspapers). Even worse, he had asked Congress for an increase of only twenty cents (from $2.30 to $2.50). Predictably, George Meany, the head of the AFL-CIO (who wanted $3.00), denounced the president's $2.50 proposal. It was, he said, "shameful" and a "bitter disappointment to everyone who looked to the administration for economic justice." He demanded more—which Congress gave him. Carter was concerned, however, that even this modest upgrading would increase unemployment, especially among young blacks, eliminating many low-paying jobs entirely.[65]

Carter's Failures with the Ninety-fifth Congress

President Carter suffered several painful defeats at the hands of the Ninety-fifth Congress.

CONSUMER PROTECTION AGENCY. One of Carter's most significant defeats was the surprise rejection by the House of Representatives of his proposed Consumer Protection Agency. The proposal was never even sent to the Senate.

The bill would have centralized consumer protection in a federal agency that would represent consumer interests before federal agencies and courts, support research and testing on products and services, and recommend to Congress and the president how they could improve protection of consumers from shoddy and dangerous products.

It was an especially embarrassing defeat for the president, who had pledged in his campaign that the establishment of a consumer protection agency would be one of his highest priorities. Consumer groups also ranked it as their top legislative priority. Carter had no doubt that it would be easily done. A bill to establish such an independent agency came close to becoming law under President Ford. Carter, with a two-to-one Democratic margin in the Congress, did not expect to have any difficulty getting it past both houses.

Lobbying on both sides of Carter's bill was intense and wide-ranging. In support, among others, were the Consumer Federation of America, Ralph Nader's Public Citizen, Friends of the Earth, and the United Auto Workers. Opponents included Exxon, the Business Roundtable, General Motors, and the United States Chamber of Commerce. Even an eloquent last-minute plea by House Speaker O'Neill was not enough to save the measure. "Never mind the commitment that you may have made to a businessman along the line," he told the members. "You have only one commitment, that commitment is to the public, to the person who has a family . . . to the housewife, to the consumer."

After the bill's defeat, consumer organizations complained that Carter had done almost no lobbying on its behalf. In any case, after its defeat, Carter stopped mentioning the Consumer Protection Agency as one of his legislative goals.

LABOR LAW REFORM. Carter's relations with organized labor were further chilled when he failed to secure passage of the AFL-CIO–backed common-site picketing bill which he had promised as a candidate. The bill, which would make union organizing easier (and which organized labor called "labor reform"), was drowned under a tidal wave of business opposition.[66] After the bill's defeat, many labor leaders accused Carter of only halfhearted support. It appeared to organized labor that Carter was giving too little attention to labor's substantive positions. They threatened to support another candidate for the Democratic presidential nomination in 1980, or to sit the election out. Several unions, as we will see, switched their support to Ronald Reagan.

Carter's Vetoes

Many of President Carter's frustrations with the Ninety-fifth Congress stemmed from what the Democratic congressional leadership regarded as his overzealousness in vetoing some of the Democrats' most cherished measures. Before the Ninety-fifth Congress adjourned in October 1978, Carter vetoed nineteen measures (including five pocket vetoes) — a rather large number for a president with a Congress of his own party. Although all of his vetoes were sustained, in several cases it was only after the administration had suffered considerable political damage.

Three of the vetoes — the Clinch River breeder reactor, the water development projects, and defense spending — produced especially bitter confrontations between the White House and Capitol Hill, since they suggested the president was more determined to do what he considered right for the "national interest" (as distinguished from "special interest") than to support the priorities of the congressional Democrats. According to Carter's congressional critics, the president did not understand that the bills he vetoed were the kinds of pork-barrel projects that members of Congress of both parties count on to demonstrate tangibly their influence in Washington — the kinds of measures that a president who wants to get along with Congress goes along with.

THE BREEDER REACTOR VETO. Carter used his first veto (on November 5, 1977) against the fiscal 1978 Energy Research and Development Administration appropriations bill, which included a $6 billion authorization for energy research. Included in that amount was $80 million for commencing construction of a plutonium-powered nuclear breeder reactor on the Clinch River near Oak Ridge, Tennessee. In vetoing the measure, the president, a nuclear engineer by training, said that the proposed plant was obsolete and overpriced and would open up a new and very dangerous plutonium industry in the United States.[67] The president's veto was not challenged in 1978.

WATER DEVELOPMENT PROJECTS. The confrontation with the Democratic leadership which probably best illustrates the divergence between Carter and Congress came in February 1977 over the president's decision to cut the water project funds from the federal budget.

The fiscal 1978 budget previously submitted by the Ford administration (which Carter inherited) contained several water projects in various states. On February 18, without consulting any congressional leaders, Carter picked out eighteen of these projects and announced publicly that he had decided to cut off their federal funding, although they had been previously approved by Congress. The president then added to the original eighteen projects the $248 million Richard Russell Dam back home in Georgia. The savings from the cuts on what came to be called the White House "hit list" would come to $268 million in fiscal 1978 alone, and would reach about $5 billion in the long run.[68]

The president's action in cutting out the water projects quickly produced a bitter confrontation between Carter and some powerful senators and congressmen in whose states the projects were located, including such influential Democrats as Russell Long, chairman of the Senate Finance Committee (whose state would lose five of the nineteen projects), House majority leader Jim Wright, House Interior Committee chairman Morris Udall, and Senate Armed Services Committee chairman John Stennis. They had labored for years, persuading and finagling, to get their projects approved and funded, and they were not about to give them up.

The word came back from the White House that the president was hanging tough on the dams. "The dams are non-negotiable," he said—and threatened to take his case over the heads of Congress to the people. The angry senators quickly handed Carter the first serious legislative defeat of his new presidency by simply adding the water projects as an amendment to the public works job bill, which the Congress expected the president` to sign. Despite a threat by the president to veto the bill, the amendment swept through the Senate by a vote of sixty-five to twenty-four, with thirty-five Democrats among the ayes, while only twenty-five were opposed.[69]

On October 5, 1978, Carter carried out his threat to veto the public works appropriation bill—because, he said, it would hamper the nation's ability to eliminate waste and make the government more efficient. He also said that funding of the projects would be inflationary and could not be economically justified.[70] Despite strenuous efforts by Democratic leaders to override the veto, the House vote was fifty-three votes short of the two-thirds needed. Almost every Democratic leader had voted to override the president's veto.

Ironically, the victory in the fight over the water projects turned out to be a political disaster for Carter as the injured congressmen took their revenge on his major legislative proposals—including his energy conservation program. His announcement of the proposed cuts also set off a firestorm of protest in the western states, where water subsidies and funds for road construction are as important as urban development aid or welfare are in the East. In the end, Carter was forced to back down, but by then he had hastened the departure of several key western states from the Democratic Party.

THE B-1 BOMBER DECISION. During his campaign Carter promised to cut the defense budget by some $5 billion, provided there was no fundamental change in international conditions. Despite his promises, Carter's first budget provided for an increase in defense spending. However, as inflation reached double-digit proportions and as the size of the federal budget deficit grew, the president came under increasing pressure to fulfill his promise to cut the budget as a whole and defense in particular.

Under President Ford, four B-1 prototypes had been built, and the defense establishment was putting tremendous pressure on Congress to go ahead with plans for an entire fleet. However, with the end of the Vietnam War, the B-1 had become the target for the defense budget cutters in and out of Congress, and they pressed hard for its elimination from the defense arsenal. The members of Congress, in the election year of 1976, finally came to a conclusion: Let the next president decide. However, they reserved to themselves the right to reverse the newly elected president's decision once it was made.

On June 30, 1977, Carter announced that he had decided against spending money for production of the B-1 bombers, although the money had been authorized by President Ford. The national defense would instead be strengthened by the cruise missile then in development, which, he said, was a more cost-effective alternative.[71]

The president's decision was widely acclaimed by liberals. However, it sent shock waves throughout the American aerospace industry. The United States Air Force had planned to procure 244 of the expensive supersonic bombers (estimated to have reached a cost of more than $100 million per aircraft) to replace its older subsonic B-52s. The decision was also highly unpopular with conservatives, who were quick to point out that the B-1 cancellation itself provided few budgetary benefits. In addition, the development of cruise missiles would be expensive, as would the refurbishing of the aging B-52's requested by the Air Force.

In reality, Carter's decision against the B-1 was not accompanied by immediate cuts in overall defense spending. In fact, the defense budget was allowed to increase. Congress, in 1978, approved a record $117.3 billion defense budget, up almost 17 percent from the previous year and accounting for almost one-quarter of the entire budget. The only budget item larger than defense spending was income-security payments — Social Security benefits, unemployment insurance, public assistance, federal civilian pension benefits, and food stamps—which accounted for over 30 percent of the budget. Thus some critics accused Carter of not fulfilling his campaign promises to cut defense spending.[72]

The president's response to his critics quickly became entangled with the growing debate about the future of the U.S. Navy. The problem had its roots back in 1969 when John Lehman, an aide to national security adviser Henry Kissinger, developed a rationale for a 600-ship navy, heavy with large carriers and what Lehman called a "forward strategy" of attacking the Soviet navy in its home waters and ports.

Lehman's proposal became very popular with conservative Republican and Democratic hawks and provided a rationale and a slogan—"the 600-ship" navy—for strong navy-oriented defense advocates, including senators John Tower of Texas and John Warner of Virginia, powerful figures on the Armed Services Committee. Afterwards, as a consultant on naval affairs, Lehman helped Tower and Warner battle the president for more carriers.

On August 17, 1978, Carter surprisingly vetoed the Defense Department fiscal 1979 weapons procurement bill—the first president since James K. Polk in the 1840s to do so—because it authorized construction of a fifth nuclear aircraft carrier which would cost a "budget busting" $2 billion. Carter said the ship was unnecessary and wasteful and that it would divert money from other important weapons programs. In the end, Congress, under intense pressure from the White House, accepted the cut of the nuclear carrier and sustained the president's veto.

The 1978 Congressional Elections and the Democratic Midterm Conference

In the congressional elections of 1978 to select members of the Ninety-sixth Congress, the voters added three Republicans in the Senate and eleven in the House of Representatives. Elected to the Senate were Republicans William S. Cohen in Maine and David Durenberger and Rudy Boschwitz in Minnesota, all of whom replaced Democrats. But the Democrats lost national figures in Clifford P. Case, who was defeated in the New Jersey primary, and James B. Pearson of Kansas, who retired and was replaced by Nancy Landon Kassebaum, the daughter of 1936 GOP presidential candidate Alf Landon.

The Republicans lost Senator Edward W. Brooke, who was defeated in the Massachusetts general election by Paul Tsongas. Although Tsongas was a Democrat, his victory was viewed as an ominous sign by Carter's supporters, many of whom assumed that Tsongas had been backed (in fact, handpicked) by Ted Kennedy to look after Kennedy's interests in Massachusetts should Kennedy decide to run for the presidency in 1980.[73]

Turned out of office were several liberal Democratic senators: William Hathaway of Maine, Thomas McIntyre of New Hampshire, Wendell Anderson of Minnesota, Dick Clark of Iowa, Floyd Haskell of Colorado. Including incumbents and newcomers the GOP elected twenty senators in 1978—more than in any year since 1952—which encouraged the GOP to entertain the notion that it was on the way back in national politics. (The Republicans were defending half the seats at stake.)

The most politically significant changes, however, came in the elections to the House of Representatives of thirty-six new-breed Republican freshmen, the vanguard of a New Right swing toward Reaganite conservatism. One of the more prominent of these representatives was Newt Gingrich, a go-getting, forty-five year old, outspoken former history professor from Georgia who, Hedrick Smith says, has more interest in promoting confrontations and ideas than in passing legislation. As he campaigned, he savaged Jimmy Carter, Speaker O'Neill, and the "liberal welfare state."

Also elected to the House as a Democrat was Phil Gramm, a supremely self-confident ex-professor and Reaganite economist from Texas. Gramm shot to prominence by combining a shrewd sense of timing, brilliant legislative packaging, and a knack for self-promotion and selling his ideas on television.[74]

The outcome of the congressional elections put the Democrats in a downbeat mood when they met in Memphis on December 8–10 of 1978 to hold their second midterm conference. Carter's overlong opening speech drew only polite applause. However, on the next night Senator Ted Kennedy touched off a cheering, stomping ovation with a fiery (though indirect) attack on the president's emphasis on military spending at the expense, Kennedy charged, of programs for the poor. Many observers concluded that Kennedy's attack on Carter in Memphis was an early warning signal that the Massachusetts senator, after nearly two years of saying that he expected the president to be renominated and reelected, might be actively considering a try for the nomination himself in 1980. Speaking in Carter's defense, Vice President Mondale warned the president's critics prophetically—and in vain—that unless they supported the president's austerity measures, inflation would sweep the Democrats from office in 1980.

Before the conference adjourned, a "dissident budget," maintaining the current levels of social expenditures, was proposed by United Auto Workers president Douglas Fraser. Although it lost by 822 to 521, it was clear that the liberals were up in arms about what they regarded as the administration's conservative economic policies.

Jimmy Carter and the Ninety-sixth Congress

President Carter's congressional relations improved somewhat during 1979, and he got much more of what he wanted from Congress. There were, however, several protracted struggles during which Congress rejected or substantially rewrote several of Carter's proposals.

WELFARE REFORM. Carter's experience as governor of Georgia had convinced him that the national welfare system was highly destructive of family values in America. Moreover, it was corrupting people by preventing them from working. He was prepared to push hard for welfare reform because public opinion was favorable, and as a candidate, he promised several times to attempt to persuade Congress to move on the overhaul of the nation's welfare system.[75]

To fulfill his pledge, in August 1977 he sent to Congress a comprehensive income-assistance program. Describing the program as "pro-work" and "pro-family," he stated that it would fundamentally reform current programs to assist the poor by shifting the financial burden from the cities to the states and Washington, and would establish one uniform payment across the nation. Although the president's welfare goals were received well by the media and the public (the *Washington Post* commented editorially, "Work, equity, generosity, economy, efficiency, family stability—a social policy could hardly be based on a more desirable set of values"), the administration's bills floundered in Congress. The high cost ($20 billion) was cited as the reason for failure.

President Carter made a second try at welfare reform in May 1979 when he submitted two bills, the Social Welfare Reform Amendments of 1979 and the Work and Training Opportunities Act of 1979. Neither was as ambitious in scope as the initial proposal.

Under the new proposals existing and expanded employment programs would be used to put able-bodied welfare recipients to work (although emphasis would be placed on employment by the private sector), and states would get federal funds to expand their job-search assistance programs. For people who could not work or find work, the proposal guaranteed an income of no less than 65 percent of the national poverty level, ensuring that a family of four would have at least $4,654 to live on.

The House of Representatives passed this version in November 1979, but it was opposed by Senator Long's Senate Finance Committee, and the Senate took no action on the bill in 1979. In March 1980, as part of the effort to balance the budget, President Carter proposed a one-year deferral of the welfare reform plan. However, since Carter did not subsequently press for the bill, the deferral of the administration's 1979 plan seemed likely to become abandonment.[76]

HOSPITAL COST CONTROLS. Probably President Carter's most disappointing legislative defeat came when the Ninety-sixth Congress rejected the hospital cost control bill that he had called his top-priority anti-inflation measure of 1979.[77]

As a candidate in 1976, Carter promised voters that he would ease their medical care burden by implementing health care cost controls as a part of a broader national health insurance program. In 1977, after his election as president, Carter proposed to Congress a bill to curb soaring hospital costs, which had quintupled in the preceding decade. His program was aimed at holding the future rise of hospital costs to 9.6 percent a year, which the Department of Health, Education and Welfare estimated would save consumers about $27 billion through 1982.

Predictably, the president's program invoked a storm of protest from the American Medical Association and the hospital industry, who instead pressed a program of cooperative voluntary efforts to cut down spending increases by hospitals. On July 18, 1978, the House Commerce Committee defeated the Carter proposal by a single vote, 21–22, and the bill went no further that year.

In March of 1979, the administration resurrected the 1977 bill and revamped it to make it more palatable. This time the bill (The Hospital Cost-Containment Act of 1979) provided that if the hospital industry as a whole maintained cost increases within an 11.6 percent ceiling—up from 1977's 9.6—no mandatory controls would be imposed. If, on the other hand, the industry failed through voluntary efforts to keep spending within the prescribed guidelines of increase, the federal government would regulate hospital revenues. Carter estimated that savings to consumers and to federal, state, and local governments would amount to $53 billion over the ensuing five years—about $10 billion a year.

In November 1979, the bill was considered in the House. In a 321 to 75 vote, the House approved Carter's plan, but without mandatory controls as a backup to the voluntary guidelines. The Senate Finance Committee tabled the bill, and the president, no longer interested in pushing a bill so watered down that he considered it meaningless, let it die.

THE ISSUE OF NATIONAL HEALTH INSURANCE. The president also failed to persuade Congress to move on national health insurance, an issue since the early days of the Nixon administration.

Candidate Carter, recognizing the country's health care problems, promised voters in 1976 a "national, comprehensive, mandatory health insurance program." On "Face the Nation" he said, "I'm committed to that and will work hard as president to get it implemented." However, the Carter administration chose to concentrate its health-care efforts on the containment of rapidly rising hospital costs, and no legislative proposals on the subject were forthcoming from the White House in 1977.

In 1979 President Carter finally came up with a health insurance proposal—his National Health Plan—which linked hospital cost controls with catastrophic health insurance. The major elements in Carter's bill were a unified public program, merging and improving Medicaid and Medicare, and mandatory catastrophic coverage that would protect working Americans against ruinously expensive illnesses with employers and employees sharing the cost. In this case, Carter favored a step-by-step approach, with benefits or coverage of groups phased in as the economy permitted. The nation, the president said, could afford no more than gradual changes. The plan, which would cost $24.1 billion annually with no money being spent until 1983, ended up stalled in Congress, a victim of the budget struggle.

The issue of national health insurance exacerbated the growing rift between the president and Senator Kennedy, who had long been the Senate's principal advocate of national health insurance. Kennedy angrily denounced Carter's unwillingness to push for an immediate broad-based, comprehensive national health insurance plan, which he argued was the only way to eliminate the costly inequities and duplications of the existing "non-system."

In May 1979, Kennedy introduced a new labor-backed health insurance bill—a more comprehensive plan than Carter's—which, he argued, in the long run would be less costly than Carter's piecemeal approach. In Kennedy's view Carter's plan was so deficient that their differences were irreconcilable.[78]

Both of the national health plans languished in Congress. Administration and congressional sources were optimistic that political pressures in the 1980 election year would push "something we can call national health insurance" through the Senate and possibly even the House of Representatives.[79]

CARTER'S SECOND ENERGY PROGRAM. By early 1979 serious gasoline shortages were once again playing havoc with the lives of Americans. A revolution in Iran during January and February of 1979, which forced the Shah to flee his country, brought Iranian oil production nearly to a halt. The resulting shortages of crude oil soon resulted in a substantial drop in the supply of gasoline available in the United States, and in many parts of the country gasoline, once again, became difficult to obtain. Prices soared while motorists were forced to wait in long lines to fill their gas tanks. "Sorry, Out of Gas" signs became increasingly common in March and April.

By early July most Americans were apprehensive, angry, and contemptuous of the administration's efforts to ease their deprivations. Many suspected that the oil companies had deliberately engineered the shortage to raise prices. As gasoline supplies dwindled and tempers of drivers rose, Carter's approval rating slipped—from 50 percent in early January to 28 percent in mid–June, the lowest public approval of his presidency.

The Ninety-sixth Congress gave Carter an especially hard time on energy matters. In February 1979, when Carter asked Congress for standby power to impose national gasoline rationing, the House of Representatives voted it down 246-159—a humiliating defeat for the Carter administration—forcing the individual states to find their own solutions. Then, in April, when Carter announced that he planned to proceed with the gradual phase-out of price controls on domestically produced oil, the House Democratic Caucus voted 153-82 against the move (it was an embarrassing partisan rebuke but had no binding legal effect). Despite this setback, President Carter proceeded with decontrol. As his critics had predicted, decontrol resulted in higher prices of gasoline and heating oil.

At the same time that Carter announced oil price decontrol, he also proposed a modest tax on the huge profits decontrol would assure oil firms. This so-called windfall profits tax would be used for such purposes as subsidizing the poor's heating bills ($24 billion), funding synthetic fuels development ($88 billion), and improving mass transit ($16.5 billion). However, the windfall profits tax was strongly resisted by oil interests. The additional revenue generated by decontrol, they argued, should be given to the oil companies as an incentive for further exploration. The proposal was soon mired in interminable congressional debate.

On July 5, 1979, the frustrated president announced a nationwide address to outline to the nation his plans for dealing with the energy crisis. However, the day before the speech he cancelled it without explanation—a move that caused confusion both in the United States and abroad. The air of mystery intensified when Carter summoned his top aides and more than 130 prominent national figures to a "national retreat" at the presidential lodge at Camp David to discuss a full agenda of topics, including not only the energy crisis but also the mood of the nation, the functioning of the administration, and his own political future.

The "Malaise Speech" and the Cabinet Shakeup

Finally, on Sunday, July 15, 1979, amid much anticipation, a somber President Carter delivered a nationally televised address in which he warned of a "crisis of confidence" in the country that posed a "fundamental threat to American democracy." Americans, he said, were suffering from a national malaise.[80] For the first time in the history of the country, he suggested, "a majority of our people believe that the next five years will be worse then the past five years." The answer, Carter continued, was for

Americans to "snap out of it" and meet the challenge from the nation. The greatest of these challenges, he said, was the energy problem. He closed with a ringing call: "Let us commit ourselves together to a rebirth of the American spirit. Working together with our common faith, we cannot fail."[81]

Carter's speech (or the visible crisis) did change a few opinions. A week later a *New York Times*/CBS News poll showed that public support for his administration had rebounded to 37 percent and that, while before the speech 74 percent of Americans believed the energy shortage was a hoax, after the speech that proportion fell to 65 percent.

President Carter followed his national address with a cabinet reorgnization which he needed, he said, to improve efficiency in the administration. On July 19, two days after he had requested and received offers of resignation from all cabinet members, the pending departures of Joseph Califano (Health, Education and Welfare) and W. Michael Blumenthal (Treasury) were announced. The following day James Schlesinger (Energy) and Brock Adams (Transportation) departed. Hedrick Smith reports that it was an open secret that the White House staff aides wanted to settle scores with all four, especially Califano and Blumenthal, who had repeatedly crossed swords with them.[82]

Califano had not been a team player (a high priority with Carter). He had used his extensive contacts in Congress to try to circumvent decisions affecting HEW that he did not like. He was also unpopular in Southern, tobacco-producing states, such as North Carolina, for his outspoken opposition to smoking and his school desegregation plans. In addition, he had made no secret of his opposition to the Department of Education that Carter had proposed or his lack of enthusiasm for Carter's policy on national health insurance. Carter moved his secretary of housing and urban development, Patricia Harris, into the HEW slot vacated by Califano, and former New Orleans mayor Moon Landrieu took over for Harris at HUD.

Blumenthal had never seemed to fit in. He was ineffective with Congress. Also, Germond and Witcover suggest that some members of the White House staff had never forgiven him for the fact that Bert Lance's downfall in 1977 was caused largely by agencies under Blumenthal's control.[83] G. William Miller, the former head of Textron, who was then serving as chairman of the Federal Reserve Board, replaced Blumenthal. Carter then awarded Miller's old job at the Fed to Paul Volcker, who was then serving as president of the Federal Reserve Bank of New York, a director of the Council on Foreign Relations, and a member of the Trilateral Commission.

Schlesinger had several times indicated a desire to leave the administration before the 1980 primaries because he felt that he had exhausted his usefulness during the long and bitter struggles with Congress over the energy legislation and that his staying would hurt Carter politically. Carter selected Deputy Secretary of Defense Charles W. Duncan, Jr., as Schlesinger's successor at the Department of Energy.

Adams had questioned frequently what he considered inadequate attention to mass transit and energy-efficient automobile research, and he was asked to leave. Portland, Oregon, mayor Neil Goldschmidt replaced Adams. In November, Philip Klutznick, a prominent leader in national Jewish organizations, was appointed secretary of commerce.

After it was all over, the president told reporters that the changes were "all constructive" and that there would be no further firings. At the onset of his administration, Carter had said that he wanted to keep his cabinet intact for four years to promote stability. However, the cabinet reorganization made that impossible. Even so, after two and a half years in office, he had kept his cabinet in place longer than any president in the twentieth century.

Although most of the discharges were not unexpected and would, in fact, have gone unnoticed under different circumstances, the cabinet shakeup produced consternation in Washington and beyond. Democratic congressman Charles Wilson of Texas exploded: "Good grief! They're cutting down the biggest trees and keeping the monkeys!"[84] Many observers concluded that Carter regarded loyalty more highly than independence and competence. Republican reaction was more caustic. As Republican House Minority Whip Robert H. Michel of Illinois put it: "The Carter administration resembles a badly-run elementary school more than it does a government."[85]

THE SELECTION OF HAMILTON JORDAN AS CHIEF OF STAFF. Throughout the transition period between the Ford and Carter administrations, Carter made it clear that he would have no Nixonian-type "palace guard." "I will never permit my White House staff to try to run the major departments of government," he said. The White House staff would be serving in a staff capacity only — not in an administrative capacity. As he had promised, he did not name a chief of staff to oversee the work of other aides. Rather, Carter established a White House staff structure somewhat like the spokes of a wheel, with himself at the center and advisers arrayed around him in a circle. Since there was no chief of staff, the president directed senior presidential assistants to desist from giving directions to cabinet officers.

Very soon, however, divisive staff rivalries and his distaste for hierarchy left Carter at a serious disadvantage when dealing with the members of the cabinet and Congress. Even so, it came as a surprise when, on July 18, in the midst of the cabinet shakeup, the president announced the appointment of his controversial political adviser Hamilton Jordan to be chief of staff. The move, the president said, would expedite decision-making, enable him to "become less involved in minutiae and more in the broad directions," and free him to "get around the country more." In naming Jordan his chief aide, Carter acknowledged that the White House had to be run in a more centralized fashion.

The Democratic leadership in Congress, with whom Jordan would have to work, had little affection for "Hannibal Jerkin" as Tip O'Neill dubbed him (which was tame compared to what Jordan is reputed to have called *him*). In reality, few Democratic members of Congress actually knew Jordan. For the most part he remained aloof from political or social contact with congressional leaders, leading to a widespread belief on their part that Jordan held them all in contempt. O'Neill himself complained that Jordan was so remote that he had never met the president's right-hand man. Jordan's appointment was "a victory of mediocracy," remarked Representative David R. Obey, Democrat of Wisconsin. Others expressed concern that Jordan would become like H. R. Haldeman, President Nixon's hard-nosed chief of staff.[86]

In short order Carter was seriously embarrassed when several people accused Jordan (through the media) of having sniffed cocaine at two Beverly Hills parties and at the Studio 54 disco in New York. Jordan denied the charges, but a stream of Jordan horror stories ranging from the trivial to the very serious made the round of Washington. The bad publicity hurt Carter; this was an administration whose leader had come to power using such phrases as "why not the best?" and emphasizing the necessity for "a government as good as its people."[87]

The Energy Crisis (Continued)

THE STANDBY GASOLINE RATIONING PLAN. Despite the president's efforts, during the remainder of 1979, gasoline supplies dwindled and prices continued their upward spiral (reaching one dollar per gallon). At last, Congress, on October 23, 1979, approved a standby plan to ration gasoline should a huge shortage occur. The bill gave the president the major responsibility for drawing up a standby gasoline rationing plan, and Congress the power to approve it or reject it. However, the Ninety-sixth Congress went home in October 1979 without giving the president authority to force electric utilities to switch from oil and natural gas to coal, which the United States had in abundant quantities.

THE WINDFALL PROFITS TAX. As we have seen, the windfall profits tax proposed by Carter was strongly resisted in the Ninety-fifth Congress by the oil interests. Finally, on March 28, 1980, the Ninety-sixth Congress, under pressure from the oil-state members from both parties, enacted a watered-down windfall profits tax on domestic oil companies.

Although the bill would create considerably less net revenue than Carter had asked for, he nevertheless hailed it as a significant victory for the administration and signed the bill into law on April 2, 1980. The windfall profits tax was expected to bring in over $227 billion over the next decade—the largest tax ever levied on an American industry.

THE SYNFUELS CORPORATION. This victory was followed on June 26 by congressional approval of a massive program designed to nudge private industry into the business of synthetic fuels (such as oil from shale and gas from coal). Carter's position on "synfuels" represented a significant shift from his campaign stand. In 1975, when President Ford had proposed a $100 billion subsidy to the oil industry to develop synthetic fuels, candidate Carter had opposed the proposal, saying, "A decision to subsidize the production of fuels for which there is no genuine market—for example, the synthetic fuels commercialization now before Congress—would divert capital away from the production of useful energy and create even more pressure to raise prices of all energy."

However, as the gasoline lines lengthened (they often stretched for blocks) and citizens' tempers mounted, the president and members of Congress yielded to public pressure. On July 1, 1980, President Carter signed a law which established a federally chartered corporation to disburse loans, loan guarantees, price supports, and purchase agreements. The program, Carter said, would produce by 1980 the equivalent of 2.5 million barrels of oil per day from coal, oil shale, and tar sands.

Congress started the synthetic fuels program with a $20 billion authorization (with more to come later if needed) and said it could eventually go as high as $88 billion. It seemed as if the president would see his entire energy package implemented before the year was out. However, President Carter's now announced Republican challenger, Ronald Reagan, had declared his opposition to the synthetic fuels program and threatened, if elected, to trim the program drastically. Because of the impending election, the Republicans, joined by some Democrats, blocked Senate confirmation of board members for the Synthetic Fuels Corporation to preserve the choices for Reagan.

THE ENERGY MOBILIZATION BOARD. Moreover, Republicans in the House, noting Reagan's opposition to the Energy Mobilization Board, stuck together and succeeded in killing it.

With his decision to decontrol both oil and natural gas and to commit billions of dollars to the synthetic fuels program, Carter had made a major switch in his position on energy policy. Now, increasing the supply of energy—rather than controlling demand—would be his primary strategy for dealing with the energy crisis. Predictably, his critics charged that he had backed away from conservation and social equity.

The Department of Education

On September 27, 1979, after hard lobbying by President Carter, Congress gave final approval to a bill creating a separate Department of Education. The department was a longtime goal of the National Education Association, the nation's largest teachers' organization, which, as we have seen, gave its first endorsement to Carter in 1976 after he promised to push for such a department. The creation of the new department was a major victory for President Carter. It gave him an important victory in Congress when he really needed it. One day after Congress cleared the measure, the board of directors of the NEA endorsed Carter for reelection.

The Education Department bill was supported by about 100 education groups, who felt their interests would receive more sympathetic consideration from an Education Department than they had from the Department of Health, Education and Welfare (HEW). In opposition was an unusual coalition of liberals and conservatives—including the American Federation of Teachers (AFT), an arch rival of the NEA for the allegiance of the nation's teachers, who feared the department would result in federal domination of education (at least by the NEA, which was certain to dominate the department). Also opposed was the Committee Against a Separate Department of Education, a coalition of the presidents of more than fifty colleges and universities, including some of the most prestigious academic institutions in the country—Harvard, Columbia, and Stanford, and the massive state universities of Illinois, California, and Michigan. Also opposing the bill initially was Joseph A. Califano, Jr., the Secretary of HEW, until it became explicit presidential policy. Although Congress imposed specific personnel and spending limitations on the agency, it was still the fifth largest of the thirteen cabinet departments. Its annual budget was the eighth largest.[88]

Carter's Economic Policies

President Carter's most frustrating domestic policy defeats probably came as he attempted to bring order out of an economy which he had inherited and which was in serious disarray, with an unemployment rate over 7 percent, inflation between 5 and 6 percent, and the federal government running a $66 billion annual deficit. He entered office optimistic that he could set them all right in one term: By 1980 he would reduce unemployment, curb inflation, and balance the budget.[89]

During the two decades prior to Carter's decision to seek the presidency, Americans had enjoyed unprecedented prosperity—the

American dream, a good job, a car or two, and college for their children seemed within the grasp of most people. But during the early 1970s increasing unemployment, rising interest rates and inflation, trade deficits, unbalanced budgets, and a growing deficit began to cool down the economy. Carter was convinced that the downturn was the result of the policies of the previous Republican administrations.

The most urgent problem, as he saw it, was to reverse the increase in unemployment: "A government which cannot ensure for its citizens an opportunity to work does not deserve their support." In September 1976, in his first debate with Ford, he said of the unemployment rate: "Seven point nine percent unemployment is a terrible tragedy for this country." "The Republicans say it's too expensive to put our people back to work. I say it is too expensive not to." He acknowledged that inflation was a worrisome problem, but he argued that if the government concentrated on reducing unemployment, inflation would take care of itself. He also pledged that he would "never use unemployment and recession as a tool to fight inflation."

THE ECONOMIC STIMULUS PACKAGE. Carter was also convinced that the economy had to be stimulated in order to bring down the rate of unemployment in the country. In January 1977, in the first policy initiative of his administration, he submitted to Congress an economic stimulus package, amounting to $31 billion spread equally over two years. The centerpiece for the first year was something called the "rebate"—an immediate one-time cash grant of $50 for each taxpayer in the United States, which the president estimated would channel about $11 billion in purchasing power to consumers. As a result of the rebate, he said, spending and consumption would be increased, jobs would be created, and the deficit would be reduced.

Both Al Ullmann, chairman of the House Ways and Means Committee, and Senator Edmund Muskie, chairman of the Senate Budget Committee (these committees are charged with raising revenue for the government) responded negatively to the rebate proposal; they feared that it would increase the budget deficit. However, they both supported the program publicly. Also, neither OMB head Bert Lance nor Secretary of the Treasury Blumenthal liked the rebate idea, but they also agreed to publicly support the program. They did, however, warn the president that it would most likely overstimulate the economy and thus increase the likelihood of inflation, and that inflation was his real problem. If inflation continued to increase by 1980, they warned him, he would not be reelected.

When the economic stimulus package reached Congress, the tax rebate proposal passed the House quite easily (219–194) but was delayed in the Senate, where it had no chance of passing without the support of

Louisiana's Russell Long, the Senate Finance Committee chairman. Long's support was not forthcoming. As we have seen, five of the water projects the president sought to eliminate were located in Long's home state. Long said that he was delaying action on the rebate to give the president time for "thoughtful consideration" of the targeted projects. Senator Byrd, the Senate majority leader, observed that Carter's crusade against the dams was hurting efforts to muster a majority behind the rebate. The message was clear: The president was in a losing confrontation with Congress unless he backed off the water projects. The president refused the offer to trade budget-busting water projects, which he considered were not needed, for a vote on the tax refund he thought *was* needed—no matter how politically expedient such a trade appeared to be. (Inability to "trade" was one of Carter's political defects.) Meanwhile, on a rhetorical level, the liberals charged that the rebates would not create jobs as effectively as direct programs, such as public works projects. They preferred more substantial, visible, long-term programs rather than the one-shot action proposed by the president. The conservatives also said that the business community did not want the rebate, preferring a permanent tax cut as a rein on government spending.

For whatever reason, on April 14, barely three months later, Carter withdrew his support for the rebate program, explaining that the economy was performing better than expected and the payments were no longer needed to stimulate the ecomony. Political considerations were involved, he said, but "I did not back off because I feared a political defeat." Nevertheless, the abruptness of his 180-degree turn raised questions in Congress and the country about his sureness of purpose and sense of direction.

The Democratic congressional leaders who had supported the rebate and had been left out on a limb by the president's action were incensed. Senator Muskie called Carter's action "a breach of his promise to the people," and Ullman, who had led the battle for the rebate in the House, complained that Carter's decision "was a little less than fair to those of us who supported the rebate against our better judgment and worked hard to get it passed."[90] Expressions of discontent with Carter's leadership soon began to surface in the press and T.V. and, what was perhaps more important, on both sides of the aisle in the Congress of the United States.

THE ANTI-INFLATION PACKAGE. Early in 1977, as inflation rose to 6.8 percent, the threat of rising inflation replaced economic stimulation in the center of Carter's economic thinking. He began to consider methods of controlling inflation, including wage and price restraints, budgetary policy, and monetary restraint. He warned the American public: "There are no major solutions in the battle against inflation." The fight could be won, he said, only by "hard day-to-day, unglamorous, and ... politically unpopular efforts." He renewed his promise to balance the budget and pledged meanwhile "to discipline the growth of government spending." Although his warning proved to be all too correct, the obvious inconsistency in his policy from stimulating the economy to an overall battle against inflation was to plague Carter for a long time.

VOLUNTARY WAGE AND PRICE GUIDELINES. On October 24, 1978, Carter issued a call to business and labor voluntarily to accept guidelines under which pay raises were to be limited to an average of 7 percent a year and price hikes to 6 to 6.5 percent (which was the estimated growth in the cost of living).

Corporate executives, surveyed by the *Wall Street Journal*, heartily endorsed the president's "hold the line on inflation" proposal. However, labor spokesmen expressed strong doubts about the effectiveness of voluntary wage and price guidelines. AFL-CIO president George Meany announced that his confederation would not pressure members to adhere to the guidelines and issued a call for mandatory wage-price controls (which Democratic Senator Ted Kennedy had been pressing for). Since President-elect Carter, who was well aware of President Nixon's failure in resorting to wage and price controls, had assured the American people at a press conference on December 3, 1976, that he had "no intention of asking the Congress" for standby wage and price controls, he was, predictably, charged with ambivalence in his record on inflation.

BUDGETARY POLICIES. Carter, unlike many of his Democratic Party colleagues in the Congress, was convinced that the unbalanced federal budgets of the Republicans were the root cause of the present inflation and unemployment. To this end, he committed himself to achieving a balanced federal budget by the end of his first term.

The first "real" budget as far as President Carter was concerned was the budget for fiscal year 1978 (covering the period October 1, 1977, to September 30, 1978), which had been prepared by President Ford and submitted to Congress before he left office in January 1977. Therefore Carter had only a few weeks to make his imprint on this "lame duck" federal budget.

On February 22, 1977, after just one month in office, Carter sent a revised fiscal 1978 budget, amounting to $500.2 billion, to Congress for its approval. The projected deficit of $57.7 billion, which was almost $11 billion higher than the budget proposed by Ford, would be added to the existing national debt of more than $716 billion at the end of 1977.

The changes Carter proposed included the restoration of many cuts in domestic assistance programs proposed by Ford—especially in the areas of employment, health, education, income security, and housing. While those restorations were pleasing to most members of Congress, Carter also proposed several cuts that raised immediate controversy on

Capitol Hill. The only functional area to show a decline in budget authority and outlays was defense, in which Carter proposed to reduce budget
authority by $2.7 billion. Many of his critics quickly pointed out that dur-
ing his campaign Carter had pledged much larger defense reductions.
Budget Director Lance and other administration officials stressed that
while they believed Carter's budget "corrected the major defects" of the
Ford budget, it did not make all the changes they would have liked.[91]

In January 1978, Carter sent his first complete budget (fiscal 1979:
October 1, 1978, to September 30, 1979) to Congress. He proudly asserted
that this budget was "lean and tight" but still "compassionate" enough to
meet the social needs of the nation. He proposed to hold down the growth
of outlays by limiting drastically the introduction of new programs. The
budget kept public service jobs (under the Comprehensive Employment
Training Act—CETA) at the 1978 level (about 750,000) but increased
funding for youth unemployment programs to provide employment and
training for about 167,000 youths. Even so, urban and black leaders were
distressed since they had urged the funding of up to a million jobs.[92] It
amounted to an abandonment of "whole groups of people who are out of
work," they charged, saying that the budget didn't "really begin to meet
the needs of black youths."

The Tax Reform Proposals

THE TAX BILL OF 1978. As a candidate, Carter had committed himself
to reforming the federal tax system, which he had called "a disgrace to the
human race." To that end, his fiscal 1979 budget included a call for a
substantial tax cut to benefit lower income groups, a change he said was
necessary to continue the economic recovery and help reduce unemployment. Later in the month he followed with a tax reform bill calling for a
net $24.5 billion tax cut, including the elimination of many congression-
ally initiated tax breaks favoring primarily middle and upper income
families. The bill aimed more relief at lower income groups while at the
same time closing loopholes that benefited the well-to-do.

THE CALIFORNIA TAXPAYERS' REVOLT. However, Carter's tax cut proposals received a serious setback when, on June 16, 1978, the voters of
California overwhelmingly approved Proposition 13, an amendment to
the state constitution which forced cuts of 5 percent in California's property taxes. The following November, property tax–cutting initiatives appeared on the ballots of twenty-six states. Waves of alarm over this middle
class–spawned "tax revolution" spread through the nation's liberal community. To many members of Congress the rumble of new thunder they
were hearing from the West indicated that shrinking government, or at

least slowing its growth, had become fashionable. The time had come, it would appear, to help the too long put-upon middle class, even if it was at the expense of low income people.

Carter's tax reforms soon became moribund. Congress was not interested in tax reform and converted the reform bill into a reduction of the capital gains tax. On October 15, 1978, Congress sent the president a tax reduction bill aimed primarily at easing the tax burden on middle and upper income groups. Although he felt "doublecrossed," President Carter signed the measure because, he said, it met his fiscal objectives. However, it did not slow the growth of inflation as he hoped it would. By the third quarter of the year the annual inflation rate had risen to 10.8 percent and showed no signs of easing. This crossing of the line to double-digit inflation had considerable symbolic as well as economic significance.[93] Meanwhile, the ever-rising cost of living was leaving the president very vulnerable politically.

Monetary Policy

As President Carter opened his third presidential year, inflation took another giant step, moving from 10.8 percent in 1978 to 13.3 percent in 1979, nearly double the 7.2 percent rate Carter had inherited from Ford. Eventually, it would top 20 percent.

As it turned out, 1979 was a disastrous year for Carter. The economy suffered a number of severe shocks which he could not have anticipated: a sudden dip in productivity; a growth in unemployment; and above all, a jump in inflation that came with the Iranian revolution, the cut-off of Iranian oil to the West, and the OPEC pricing decision that brought a 120 percent increase in oil prices and raised inflation levels by at least three percentage points.[94] Further, as inflation soared in 1979, spending for entitlement programs also soared because they were indexed to inflation.

With the advent of double-digit inflation, another series of unanticipated problems arose: The trade deficit increased, the value of the dollar on foreign money markets declined, and the foreign currency holders began to sell off their American dollars. A giant run on the dollar soon developed and a dollar crisis began to build.

To restore confidence in the dollar, Carter promised in late October 1978 to loosen up the money supply. As a candidate he had repeatedly faulted the tight money policies of the Ford and Nixon administrations, charging that they had established the wrong priorities — tight constraints on the money supply coupled with high interest rates. The result had been excessive inflation and unacceptable unemployment (which had come to be called "Stagflation"). Instead, Carter proposed to expand the money supply to complement an expansionary fiscal policy, which he contended was the only way the nation would regain its economic health.

However, as domestic inflation continued to rise, Carter concurred in an action taken by the Federal Reserve Board in early November 1978 to tighten up (restrict) the money supply by raising the discount rate (the rate at which money is loaned by the Fed to member banks) a full percentage point to a record-high 9.5 percent — the first time since the Depression of the 1930s that the discount rate had been raised a full point. At the same time the Fed also raised reserve requirements for its member banks, further restricting the money supply.

Unfortunately, after a short recovery, the dollar lost much of the ground it had gained. Also, as a result of the board's action, the prime interest rate (the rate banks charge their best customers), which had fluctuated between 8 and 9 percent for most of 1978, soared to above 11 percent. Home mortgage interest rates climbed into the teens, and many people were frozen out of the housing market.

In the early fall of 1979, to calm the apprehensions of the financial world after William Miller was moved to the Treasury Department, Carter appointed Paul A. Volcker, a conservative Republican "monetarist," to be the new chairman of the Federal Reserve Board. On October 6, 1979, Volcker announced several actions to tighten the money supply. The discount rate was raised again, this time to 12 percent, and new reserve requirements were imposed on bank borrowing, even though such actions made the prospect of recession more likely. Once again, the president supported the move as necessary to cut "inflationary expectations" and buoy the dollar overseas.

Unfortunately, the Fed's actions led immediately to soaring interest rates. The prime rate jumped to 15.75 percent, which sent interest-sensitive stocks and bonds plummeting. On October 9, 1979, the Dow Jones industrial average (which had been consistently moving upward) dropped 26.45 points, the largest one-day loss recorded in six years. Heavy selling the following day further worsened the picture. This, in turn, seriously hurt the housing markets and greatly complicated emerging problems in the American auto industry. As it turned out, the tight money strategy had merely helped to bring about recession and aggravated the unemployment problem without bringing down inflation. As the economy worsened, revenues decreased and the budget deficit began to move higher.

THE FISCAL 1980 BUDGET. With inflation reaching 20 percent, Carter was convinced that it was time to abandon his high deficit policy. Accordingly, his fiscal 1980 budget was designed to restrain the growth of government and hold the federal budget deficit under $30 billion in an effort to curb inflation. Presented to the Congress on January 22, 1979, and covering the period October 1, 1979, to September 30, 1980, the budget called for $503 billion in revenues and $532 billion in spending.[95]

As part of this effort the president proposed sharp cuts in the domestic budget, including several major programs such as housing and jobs. He also recommended reductions in Medicare and Social Security. "The policy of restraint," he argued, ". . . is an imperative if we are to overcome the threat of accelerating inflation." Even so, he included a 3 percent increase in military spending (after taking into account the cost of inflation), which could be accomplished only by cuts in domestic programs. It was beginning to appear to his critics that Carter lacked sympathy with the party's traditional support of domestic programs.[96]

Senator Kennedy and other liberal Democrats were certainly not happy. They accused the president of being insensitive to the poor and attempting to draw the Democratic Party away from its long-standing tradition of enacting programs that did things for people despite the necessity for budgetary deficits. After eight years of Republican rule, the liberals had had high hopes for a renewal of the Democratic commitment to social programs. They had been led to believe that this was the year the trend against such programs was to be reversed. And now they were being betrayed by their own president.

Even so, Carter announced on October 28, 1979, his determination to hold the line on the budget deficit. Ironically, his Republican critics charged that the deficit still was too high. On February 22, 1980, after four major New York banks raised their prime interest rate from 15¾ percent to 16¼ percent — triggering a near collapse of the bond market — Carter decided to balance the 1981 budget in an effort to slow the rate of inflation. His hope was that his efforts to eliminate the deficit would also calm the troubled financial markets. Furthermore, he was anxious to fulfill his 1976 promise to balance the budget before he left office.

In mid–March 1980, in a nationally televised address, Carter announced a $14 billion spending cut that would permit the budget to be balanced for the first time since fiscal 1969. The balance in the budget would be brought about not by increasing revenues or taxes, but by significant reductions in expenditures including cuts in state revenue sharing, public service jobs, welfare reform, and anti-recession assistance to local government.

The public and the financial markets responded promptly to news of the balanced budget. Interest rates began to drop about 1 percent per week. Inflation began to creep down. Homebuilding and other industries began a revival. The downward trend in inflation and interest rates, and the indications of recession, worked to lessen public pressure on Congress to hold the line on the budget deficit.[97]

Unfortunately, the squeeze on borrowing (which forced interest rates back up) quickly sent the economy into a state of free fall toward recession and triggered another decline in the already depressed automobile, housing, farming, and small business sectors of the economy. New housing starts plummeted as mortgage rates reached almost 17 percent in mid-1980. Farm income was cut drastically, and small business bankruptcies increased by roughly 50 percent over the level at the end of 1979. When unemployment jumped from 6.2 percent in March to 7.8 percent in May—the number of auto workers laid off by the Big Four passed 300,000, setting a new record—Carter and the Federal Reserve Board came under sharp criticism from many quarters. The country was obviously in a significant recession. By July, it became clear that the recession would cause government spending for such things as unemployment insurance to rise and government tax receipts to fall below expectations.

THE FISCAL 1981 BUDGET. The fiscal 1981 budget, introduced in January 1980, was a "damage control" budget projecting revenues of $600 billion and expenditures of $615 billion for a deficit of only $15 billion (in contrast to the $29 billion originally projected for fiscal 1980). A number of increases were included, including approximately a 10 percent increase in funds for income security, health, education, employment, and urban development programs (about equal to the predicted inflation rate of 9.3 percent). In addition, Carter kept his pledge to increase defense spending 3 percent beyond inflation, with proposals totaling 12 percent. No tax cuts were included in the budget (to stave off the drift into recession), and no new taxes were called for; additional revenue would come as inflation drove up income tax payments. Additional revenue would also come from increased Social Security taxes and the windfall profits tax on oil companies.

However, as the economy continued to slide deeper into recession and the fiscal 1980 budget tilted further out of balance (the deficit was now revised upward to $59 billion—in United States history, it was second only to the $66.4 billion deficit of FY 1976 inherited by Jimmy Carter), it was becoming obvious to the Democrats that there was no way to come close to a balanced budget in 1981. It was also obvious to them that to vote for a deficit just before the November election could be political suicide. The Democratic leadership therefore decided to postpone passing the final budget resolution until after the 1980 election.[98] Meanwhile, the voters, chafing under ever-rising tax rates and deficits, were losing any respect they might have had for Carter's fiscal policies.

CARTER'S FINAL BUDGET. Shortly before leaving office on January 20, 1981, Carter sent Congress a fiscal 1982 budget projecting a deficit of $27.5 billion (with good expectations that it would go higher). In his message of transmittal, he noted that entitlement programs (such as Social Security), interest on the national debt, and other "mandatory contracts" accounted for 75 percent of the total budget. He appealed for restraint on the part of the interest groups that had, he thought, come to dominate Congress: "We can no longer, as individuals or groups, make special pleas for exceptions to budget discipline. Too often we have taken the attitude that there must be alternative sources for reduction in programs that benefit our particular group. That attitude is in part responsible for the rapid budget growth ... [which] we can no longer afford."

The Birth of Reaganomics

A preview of the future course of the economic debate in America came when the Republicans in the House of Representatives sponsored an amendment to the 1978 tax bill based on principles enunciated by economists Arthur Laffer and Robert Mundell, who argued that removal of government-imposed obstacles — especially taxation — was necessary to revive the economy so badly disrupted by Carter's economic policies. High marginal income tax rates, they argued, have irrational disincentive effects at all income levels, and the effects on the wealthy are particularly costly to all levels of society. For people with modest incomes, the rate cuts would enlarge disposable income, thereby expanding their range of comforts and giving a consumption-based push to the economy. For persons of ample means the rate cuts would expand both the means and the ardor for investment. The result would be job creation, rising productivity, and an increase of the supply of goods and services relative to demand. That increase would dampen inflation.[99]

In economic circles, Laffer and Mundell's proposals became known as "supply-side fiscalism." Among politicians, they were simply known as "supply-side economics." (Presumably the opposite of the "demand-side" or "trickle-up" economics so beloved of liberals of the New Deal variety).

THE KEMP-ROTH BILL. Supply-side economics received its political debut when Congressman Jack Kemp of New York unsuccessfully introduced a package of complicated tax benefits for business designed to help his economically blighted constituency in Buffalo. Soon afterwards Kemp met with Senator William Roth, Republican of Delaware, and tried again with a new supply-side tax bill calling for a three-year, across-the-board tax reduction at 10 percent a year. The Kemp-Roth bill was endorsed as party policy by the Republican National Committee late in 1977 (and eventually incorporated in the 1980 Republican platform). It made its appearance on the floor of the House of Representatives when House Republicans sponsored a Kemp-Roth amendment to the 1978 tax bill.

Ronald Reagan promoted Kemp-Roth in the midterm congressional elections of 1978 as the Republican key issue. By 1979 Ronald Reagan had emerged as the political leader of the supply-side movement.[100] More and more often, in his speeches, he quoted Kemp's supply-side rhetoric. Pointing to President Carter's ephemeral balanced budget, Reagan would note that "anybody can balance the budget by raising taxes, and inflation is a tax." Tax rates rising because of inflation constituted "a penalty imposed on working men and women." Tax rate deduction was "another way to balance the budget and another way to end inflation. . . . I do not believe inflation is caused by too many people working."[101]

Carter's Foreign Policy

Jimmy Carter took office with the strong conviction that the time had come to strike out in several new directions in American foreign policy. In his speech accepting the Democratic nomination for president in early July 1976, he said: "Ours was the first nation to dedicate itself clearly to basic moral and philosophical principles . . . a singular act of wisdom and courage . . . a revolutionary development that captured the imagination of the world again."[102]

Unlike his predecessors, Carter was determined not to view the world through the Cold War prism of U.S.–Soviet relations. In a speech at the University of Notre Dame on May 22, 1977, he outlined his vision for United States foreign policy and the world view which underlay it. "Being confident of our own future, we are now free of that inordinate fear of Communism which once led us to embrace any dictator who joined us in our fear." He would approach the Soviet Union not on the basis of confrontation but with a hand of friendship.

American foreign policy, he summarized, should be based on five "cardinal premises": improved relationships with the Soviet Union and the People's Republic of China; a commitment to advance the cause of human rights; close cooperation with the other industrial democracies; an effort to reduce the chasm between the rich and the poor nations; and cooperation with all nations to solve the problems of the threat of nuclear war, racial hatred, the arms race, environmental damage, hunger, and disease.[103] It should have a positive, confident, and moral basis. Before he left office, Carter would accomplish a string of foreign policy successes, from the Panama Canal treaties, to a Middle East summit, to the recognition of the People's Republic of China.

HUMAN RIGHTS IN FOREIGN RELATIONS. An important focus of Carter's foreign policy was his concern over violations of human rights in the Soviet Union, Cuba, Uganda, and other nations. When he announced his candidacy in December 1974 he expressed a dream that the United States would "set a standard within the community of nations of courage, compassion, integrity, and dedication to basic human rights and freedoms."[104] In his campaign he made it clear that he intended to support human rights and "to lessen the injustices in the world." In his inaugural address, as we have seen, he singled out human rights as one of his foreign policy priorities.

Carter was convinced that his crusade for human rights was in line with the 1975 Helsinki Accord, drawn up and signed by thirty-five heads of government (including President Ford and Soviet Communist Party leader Leonid Brezhnev), in which signatory nations agreed to respect human rights and fundamental freedoms, including the freedom of thought, conscience, religion or belief, without distinction as to race, sex, language, or religion. Shortly after his inauguration (February 17, 1977), Carter wrote a letter of support to a Soviet dissident, Andrei Sakharov, in which he assured Sakharov that "the American people and our government will continue our firm commitment to promote respect for human rights not only in our own country but also abroad." He was somewhat surprised to receive a response from Brezhnev in which the Soviet leader warned the president that it was "unthinkable" that Soviet-American relations could develop normally as long as Carter continued his campaign in support of "a renegade who proclaimed himself an enemy of the Soviet State."[105]

Early on, the president realized that if his stand on human rights was to be convincing, it would have to be extended to other countries besides the Soviet Union. At his second press conference on Wednesday, February 23, he stated that there were "deprivations of human rights even more brutal than the ones on which we've commented up till now." The next day the administration announced military aid cutbacks for Argentina, Ethiopia, and Uruguay because they had allegedly violated internationally recognized human rights standards. At the same time, Carter urged continued aid to other countries, including South Korea, despite "great concern" about their human rights policies. When Cyrus Vance explained, "In each case we must balance a political concern for human rights against economic or security goals," he appeared to many observers to undercut Carter's claim that his support of dissenters in the Soviet Union was based on unswerving principle.

Meanwhile, Carter issued a warning that the list of countries designated for cutbacks might be expanded. A week after the warning, Brazil announced that it would not accept *any* United States aid because of statements the Carter people had made about the state of human rights there. On March 17, 1977, Carter made his first address to the United Nations General Assembly and again emphasized the human rights theme of his foreign policy.

Most Americans seemed to welcome Carter's strong stand on human rights. However, there were critics: Conservatives argued that the United States wasn't paying enough attention to the human rights violations of Communist nations such as the Soviet Union, Cuba, Vietnam, and Cambodia, and liberals challenged the administration's near silence on repressive policies toward dissidents in Iran, the Philippines, South Korea, and other nations considered necessary for United States global defense. Also, many critics assailed the president for jeopardizing equally important concerns, such as detente with the Soviets, by his human rights stance. Other observers suggested that the president's efforts in the human rights area were naive, inconsistent, and overly optimistic. The president, in defending his human rights initiatives, replied that supporting the nation's more authoritarian allies and friends while at the same time inducing them to change their repressive policies would provide an environment within those countries in which freedom and democracy could develop, with a resultant improvement in their human rights practices.[106]

The Panama Canal Treaties

President Carter chose the Panama Canal as a powerful symbol to dramatize his new approach to foreign policy. He was convinced that a renegotiation of the Panama Canal treaties would demonstrate to all of Latin America that the United States, not the Soviet Union, had their best interests at heart.

The canal had been American property since it was built in President Theodore Roosevelt's day. Over the intervening years, the Panamanians had increasingly expressed their resentment over control of the canal by Americans. This resentment flared up on January 9, 1964, when a group of students raised the Stars and Stripes on a Canal Zone campus. In the bloody, Yankee-go-home rioting that followed, four American soldiers and twenty Panamanians were killed and dozens more injured. The government of Panama immediately broke diplomatic relations with the United States and informed President Lyndon Johnson that all existing treaties between the two countries must be completely revised to prevent further explosions of violence.

President Johnson agreed with the Panamanians that the Panama Canal treaties should be renegotiated, and by June 1967, agreement had been reached on three treaties. However, despite support for the treaties by Presidents Nixon and Ford, opposition within the United States Congress was so intense that they were never submitted for ratification. A widespread fear persisted that hints being dispensed by General Omar

Torrijos Herrera, Panama's de facto leader, implying that the canal would be sabotaged if the United States didn't hand it over, might become reality. Also, a potent argument of the opponents was that the Panamanian government might go the way of Cuba's Castro and invite in the Soviets.

During the fall of 1975 a Senate resolution sponsored by thirty-eight senators, four more than the one-third needed to prevent ratification of a treaty, had been introduced opposing any new treaty and expressing strong opposition to any termination of United States sovereignty over the Canal Zone. Furthermore, opinion polls showed that the American public strongly opposed relinquishing control of the canal. And, as we have seen, Ronald Reagan gave the "giveaway" of the Panama Canal special prominence during the 1976 presidential primaries: "When it comes to the Canal, we built it, we paid for it, it's ours and we . . . are going to keep it." Reagan's position appealed to many Americans. Ford later believed that he lost several primaries to Reagan over Panama.[107] Negotiations stopped in early 1976.

Soon after President Carter assumed office he reopened negotiations with Panama over the canal. On March 13, 1977, the United States negotiators proposed two treaties. One would set forth new arrangements for the joint operation of the canal for the rest of the century, at the end of which Panama would assume total control. The other would guarantee the permanent neutrality of the canal and the rights of the United States to defend it.[108] The treaty was signed on September 7, 1977, at an elaborate, televised Washington ceremony that was attended by the heads of eighteen different nations of the hemisphere.[109]

THE STRUGGLE FOR RATIFICATION. Once the treaties were signed the Senate committees could begin hearings. In view of the opposition to the treaties, in and out of Congress, ratification seemed unlikely (at least without a vigorous fight by the administration). In the Senate, ratification was fiercely opposed by a coalition of conservative organizations and members of Congress of both parties who charged the treaties were a "giveaway" of the canal. Republican Senators Jesse Helms (North Carolina), Strom Thurmond (South Carolina), Robert Dole (Kansas), and Orrin Hatch (Utah) assumed leadership of the opposition to the treaties in the Senate. The American Conservative Union sent out more than two million pieces of mail trying to defeat the treaties. Ronald Reagan traveled the country and sent his radio and television tapes to hundreds of stations to rally opposition. On September 30, 1977, the Republican National Committee overwhelmingly approved a resolution opposing ratification, contending that the treaties endangered American security.

To gain support for the treaties, the president gave personal White House briefings to key senators, state leaders, editors, college presidents, political party leaders, elected officials, campaign contributors, and other influential people.[110] Meanwhile, cabinet officials and surrogates from the State and Defense departments made hundreds of appearances throughout the nation to explain the treaties directly to the people. They were joined in their efforts by labor unions, business leaders, community service clubs, the Jaycees, garden clubs, religious groups, senior citizens, schoolteachers, Common Cause, and other organizations.[111]

The tide turned in mid–January 1978 when Senator Robert Byrd, the Democratic Senate majority leader, and Senator Howard Baker, the Republican Senate minority leader, both endorsed the treaties. At the end of January the Senate Foreign Relations Committee voted to recommend that the treaties be considered favorably by the Senate.[112] On March 16, 1978, the Senate approved the first of the Panama Canal treaties with only one vote to spare for the two-thirds majority (sixty-eight to thirty-two) and only after the Senate had added a reservation which provided that the United States could intervene with armed forces at any time to insure the security and continued operation of the canal (which severely compromised the sovereignty of the Panamanians). The second treaty, ratified April 18, 1978, with all senators voting as they had on the first treaty, gave Panama "full responsibility" for running the canal as of December 31, 1999. In the end sixteen Republicans supported the president and provided the margin of victory.[113]

It was an important victory for Carter's leadership in foreign affairs. (Unfortunately for Carter, deliberation on the canal delayed consideration on other, more important bills, such as energy.) On June 16, two months after the treaty vote, Carter visited Panama, where he and General Torrijos signed the official transfer documents to conclude the treaty exchange.

Recognition of the People's Republic of China

As we have seen, Jimmy Carter as a candidate and as president was very much interested in normalizing relations between the United States and the People's Republic of China. He saw cooperation with China as a means to promote peace and better understanding between the United States and the nations of the Pacific Rim — Japan, South Korea, and the Philippines — who were anxious for the establishment of political and military stability in the Western Pacific, as well as some of the other nations of the Third World with which it had been difficult for the United States to communicate.[114]

Shortly after taking office Carter instructed Secretary of State Vance to continue the exploratory discussions with Beijing which had been initiated by President Nixon when he visited Mainland China in 1972. At that time Nixon and Premier Chou En-lai had issued a joint communique in Shanghai acknowledging that there was only one China. By doing so, the United States was implicitly saying it could not continue diplomatic relations with Taiwan once full relations with the mainland were established. In 1973 liaison offices were established in Beijing and Washington. (George Bush, a two-term member of the House of Representatives from Texas, was selected by President Ford to serve as United States government liaison.) During the years since, many American officials had visited Beijing, but the officials of the PRC declined to visit the United States "as long as there is a Taiwanese ambassador in Washington."[115]

To maintain an American presence in China, Carter appointed Leonard Woodcock, former president of the United Automobile Workers, to be the chief of the United States liaison office in Beijing. In May 1978, he sent Zbigniew Brzezinski to test the waters for subsequent progress.

Vance and Woodcock's negotiations with the Chinese leaders were so successful that on December 15, 1978, the president was able to announce, dramatically and unexpectedly, that he planned to formally recognize the People's Republic of China and to end United States ties with the nationalist regime on Taiwan.

Carter's announcement caught many members of Congress by surprise, especially conservatives, who charged that in abrogating the Taiwan defense treaty the United States was "abandoning an old ally." Also, they objected that the president had not consulted with them before severing the treaty relationship with Taiwan—an unconstitutional act on the part of Carter since the Constitution required Senate action on treaties. Despite these objections the Congress approved the implementing legislation, and on January 1, 1979, full diplomatic relations were established between the United States and the People's Republic of China. Carter interpreted the generally positive worldwide reaction as a sign that most countries recognized this development as a historic one, which would contribute to peace and would open China further to the outside world.[116]

DENG XIAOPING'S VISIT. Chinese vice premier Deng Xiaoping visited the United States on a goodwill visit from January 28 to February 5, 1979, visiting with congressional leaders and seeing the sights around the nation's capital. He toured automobile plants and airplane factories, ate barbecued spareribs, wore a ten-gallon hat, and attended a reception at the Kennedy Center where several little children sang a Chinese song (whereupon several opponents of normalization simply gave up the fight; there was no way, they said, to vote against little children singing Chinese songs). Deng even made the cover of *Time* magazine as "Man of the Year." At the conclusion of his visit to Washington, Deng and Carter signed agreements concerning consular exchanges, trade, science and technology, and cultural exchanges.

The Soviets severely criticized United States recognition of the People's Republic of China, Russia's old ally. President Carter was well aware that such a move inevitably put considerable strain on U.S.–Soviet relations and changed the nature of the strategic alignments in the world. However, most observers suggested that it would be beneficial to the United States in the long run.

TAIWAN IMPLEMENTING LEGISLATION. Three months after it severed diplomatic relations with Taiwan, Congress cleared and Carter signed legislation establishing unofficial relations with Taiwan. The United States agreed to conduct its relations with the island republic through a private corporation, the American Institute in Taiwan. There was little serious opposition in the country or in Congress to the final agreement. The press treatment was favorable. The worldwide reaction was generally positive.

The Middle East Settlement

Perhaps the most significant foreign policy success for President Carter, and the most satisfying for him, was the negotiation of the settlement of the Middle East crisis.

THE CAMP DAVID ACCORDS. The search for peace and stability in the Middle East was a foreign policy priority for the Carter administration from beginning to end. There were many reasons. One was the strong support of Israel by Democratic and Republican administrations alike. Another was the unremitting pressure by the American Jewish community to keep that support at maximum strength. A third was the growing dependence of the United States upon oil imported from the Persian Gulf states. Finally, there was the ever-present possibility of a direct and perhaps catastrophic confrontation with the Soviet Union in the area.[117]

A promising initiative for peace with Israel was launched by Egypt's president, Anwar Sadat, in November 1977 when he announced to the Egyptian parliament that he would be willing to go to Jerusalem and talk peace with Israeli prime minister Menachem Begin. It was a risky proposal. He would be the first president of an Arab nation to go to Israel in a time when it was not popular to visit the Jewish state. Surprisingly, Israel responded with an invitation to Sadat to speak to the Israeli Knesset (parliament). Carter's efforts were turned immediately to supporting and encouraging Sadat's initiative and seeking ways to involve other leaders in the process.[118]

However, negotiations broke down over Israel's unwillingness to discuss autonomy for the West Bank Palestinians and their refusal to surrender strategic territory captured in the Six Day War of 1967. By August 1978, relations between Egypt and Israel had so far worsened that another blowup in the Middle East seemed imminent. So grave was the danger that Carter courageously decided to risk almost certain failure by inviting President Sadat of Egypt and Prime Minister Begin of Israel to meet at Camp David.

After nearly two weeks of patient and masterful bargaining between the two leaders, with Carter serving as active mediator between them, they finally arrived at a "framework for peace" in the Middle East that held considerable promise of peace, at least between Egypt and Israel. At a prime-time televised ceremony at the White House on September 17, 1978, Begin and Sadat signed the accords and Carter signed as a witness. The next day, with Begin and Sadat seated in the balcony of the House of Representatives, Carter described to a joint session of Congress what was a major achievement in American diplomacy. The agreements were also manifestly a personal triumph for President Carter—his popularity rating shot up seventeen points (to 56 percent approval) in the Gallup Poll within two weeks after the summit.[119]

However, full implementation of the 1978 Camp David agreements proved difficult. Both Begin and Sadat continued to be under heavy pressure. To assuage the feelings of some of his political allies who had now turned against him, Begin announced plans to expand the West Bank settlements and revealed that he was thinking of moving his office to East Jerusalem. When December 17, the deadline for a Middle East settlement, passed without a treaty, President Carter, who was determined to keep the peace effort alive, intervened again. After hectic shuttle diplomacy by Carter between Cairo and Jerusalem, Egypt and Israel signed the historic Egyptian-Israeli peace treaty at a ceremony at the White House on March 26, 1979. The signing of the treaty officially ended the hostilities between the two principal antagonists in the Arab-Israeli conflict. Ironically, despite his unprecedented negotiating breakthroughs, Carter received little credit for his accomplishments. When his public opinion polls plummeted soon after, Jody Powell concluded that the entire Middle East effort, taken as a whole, was decidedly a net minus for Jimmy Carter politically.[120]

The Arab world reacted quickly (and adversely) to the signing of the peace treaty. At a meeting in Baghdad, Iraq, at the end of March, representatives of eighteen Arab League states and the Palestine Liberation Organization voted to sever diplomatic and economic ties with Egypt, and high officials in the Syrian, Libyan, and Iraqi governments called for Sadat's assassination. Unfortunately, the treaty further alienated Sadat from his Arab neighbors, crippling the chances for a comprehensive Middle East peace. Although the Carter administration made several overtures during the late summer and early fall of 1979 to revive the stalled talks, little progress had been made when the two sides met with United States officials for two days of discussions in mid–October. A one-day negotiating session was held in Cairo on November 17.

U.S.–ISRAELI RELATIONS. U.S.–Israeli relations also went through an uneasy period during 1979. American Jews bitterly resented Carter's apparent attempts to pressure Israel into making concessions to the Arabs in the interest of world peace. They were also disturbed that the Carter administration had been openly critical of Israel's announcement that it would allow its citizens to buy land from Arabs in the occupied West Bank for the purpose of establishing new settlements. (The administration stated that the action was "contrary" to the "spirit and the intent of the peace process.") When President Carter expressed his displeasure over "preemptive" raids by Israel in southern Lebanon, the location of several PLO strongholds, Israel expressed concern over what it saw as a tilt in United States relations towards the Palestinians.

Of even greater concern to Jerusalem was the disclosure in early June of 1979 that United States Ambassador to the United Nations Andrew Young had held unauthorized meetings with the PLO's United Nations observer, a meeting that precipitated an uproar in the United States and led to Young's resignation.[121]

The Second Strategic Arms Limitation Treaty (SALT II)

The highest priority on President Carter's foreign policy agenda was the immediate reduction of nuclear arsenals and the ultimate elimination of all nuclear weapons from the earth, as he had pledged in his inaugural address. A few days after the inauguration, in his first interview as president, Carter called for a new treaty, "eliminating the testing of all nuclear devices instantly and completely," and "a fairly rapid ratification" of the strategic arms reduction agreements reached by President Ford with the Soviets at Vladivostok in 1974. Meanwhile, the nuclear arms race continued to cause nightmares, enlivened by the horrible prospect that terrorists would ultimately construct bombs with stolen plutonium and extort ransom from whole cities.

On January 26, 1977, President Carter, in an attempt to open discussion of the issue with the Soviets, sent the first of a series of personal letters to Soviet president Leonid Brezhnev suggesting the need for the two nations to proceed with nuclear arms control. When he received no encouragement from Brezhnev, Carter, in an effort to mobilize world opinion for nuclear disarmament, in February 1977 went public with his proposals to greatly reduce Soviet and American long-range missiles and bombers. Predictably, the Soviets, who preferred to work in secret, rejected such a forthright approach. Brezhnev characterized Carter's proposals as "deliberately unacceptable."[122]

In mid–March 1977 Secretary of State Vance visited the Soviet Union with a whole portfolio of new proposals. Brezhnev, stung by President Carter's outspoken criticism of human rights violations in the Soviet Union, gave him a cool reception. Unless the United States accepted the principle of "noninterference in internal affairs," the Soviet leader said, efforts to improve relations between the two countries would be impossible. He refused to discuss any proposals or make any counteroffers, and Vance left for home empty-handed. In an angry postscript, Soviet foreign minister Andrei Gromyko held an extraordinary press conference, calling the United States approach a "cheap and shady maneuver" and an attempt to renege on the Vladivostok agreement. The two countries did agree to meet again in May to consider much more limited options. President Carter said that he was "not discouraged at all" by the breakdown of the talks. In any case, he said, he was not going to modify his human rights commitment.

By the time of the May meeting, however, pressure was mounting on both the United States and the Soviet Union to reach a new agreement on the limitation of strategic arms. The first Strategic Arms Limitation Treaty (SALT I), signed in 1972, would expire in October of 1977, and although both sides had agreed to abide by the terms of the pact until a new agreement could be reached, both had been moving ahead rapidly with new weapons systems — the United States with the cruise missile and the USSR with the so-called "backfire" bomber. It appeared that the time to talk had arrived.

In May 1977 Secretary of State Vance and Soviet foreign minister Gromyko met in Geneva, Switzerland, and agreed to resume the SALT negotiations. By October the elements of a second SALT agreement had been worked out. The accord would reduce slightly the number of strategic missiles and bombers allowed to each nation and would permit the United States to deploy intermediate-range, airborne cruise missiles. The Soviet Union could exclude its backfire bombers from the overall strategic weapons total and would also be able to equip its heavy missiles with multiple warheads, athough an overall limitation of some 800 to 850 would be imposed on its total land-based multiple-warhead missile force.

During the ensuing negotiations, the Carter administration faced strong opposition to the treaty at home and abroad. Many members of Congress were concerned that, despite the SALT negotiations, thousands of Cuban troops, assisted by Soviet advisers, had appeared in Angola, Ethiopia, and elsewhere in Africa to support "wars of national liberation" mounted by left-wing revolutionary factions. The Soviets also were in the process of penetrating Yemen and were supplying arms to terrorists and client states in the Middle East and Central America. Especially alarming was the Cuban-Soviet penetration in or near the Horn of Africa. Soviet naval bases in this area could be used to cut off shipments of Arab oil to the United States and its allies in the event of a Soviet-American war. The United States, critics charged, was being out-bargained by the Soviet Union in the negotiations for the treaty.

The treaty's critics also argued that the first SALT agreement had limited the ability of the United States to develop new weapons but had not prevented the Soviet Union from continuing its rapid buildup of strategic forces. Their fear was that a new SALT agreement would have the same effect, with the ultimate result being Soviet achievement of strategic superiority. From a political point of view, few Republicans could afford to support a Democratic president in the face of such a fear. It would have been suicidal for those who depended on rich conservatives to finance their campaigns.

Nevertheless, the SALT negotiations continued to make some progress during the summer months of 1978. However, no treaty was ready to be sent to the Senate before the congressional elections of 1978, which prevented SALT from becoming a central issue in the campaign. A SALT II agreement was finally achieved and subsequently signed in Vienna, Austria, on June 18, 1979, by Carter and Brezhnev, who kissed each other on both cheeks to seal the bargain.[123]

THE RATIFICATION BATTLE. Despite what he knew would be formidable opposition, President Carter sent SALT II to the Senate in the summer of 1979. Rather than the almost perfunctory debate which the first SALT treaty received in the Senate, this time the debate was long and often acrimonious. The central issue which emerged was whether the Soviet threat to United States security would be strengthened or weakened by the pact. Backers of SALT argued that the treaty clearly was advantageous to the United States since it limited several ongoing Soviet weapons programs while imposing no significant limits on any planned United States program. However, the opponents argued that the treaty would not enhance United States security and, at worst, might lull the American people into believing that a vigilant defense policy was no longer necessary. In any case, Republican members, in view of the upcoming presidential election in which Carter was almost sure to be a candidate, were unwilling to endorse an agreement that would be politically favorable to a Democratic president seeking reelection.

Senator Jackson, on the eve of the treaty signing, in a sharp attack characterized the treaty as appeasement—one more in a long line of gratuitous concessions made to Moscow by an administration that he felt was too eager to maintain the appearance of U.S.–Soviet accord. Jackson promised a fight to amend the treaty.

THE RUSSIAN TROOPS IN CUBA. During the 1979 Labor Day holiday, just as chances for Senate ratification of the SALT II treaty were improving, it was revealed that the USSR had stationed a combat brigade (2,000 to 3,000 troops) in Cuba. Many senators who had originally said they would support the treaty now said they would do so only if the Soviets removed their troops. When President Carter protested to Moscow, the Soviets asserted that the brigade served a training function only and would not threaten the United States, and they steadfastly refused to remove the troops or make any other face-saving gesture for Carter. Predictably, Carter received considerable scorn for his inability to get Moscow to remove the troops. In a televised speech on October 1, 1979, President Carter promised to increase surveillance of Cuba and to establish a task force in Key West, Florida, to carry out naval observations in the Caribbean. But he asserted that the incident was "certainly no reason to return to the cold war," and appealed to the Senate not to use the issue to block the SALT II treaty.

In November 1979 the Senate Foreign Relations Committee voted to send the treaty to the full Senate, after having defeated a series of amendments that would have significantly altered the pact.

The Iran Crisis

The issue of the Soviet troops in Cuba soon was overshadowed by an even more disquieting event. On a bleak Sunday morning, November 4, 1979 (exactly one year before the 1980 general elections), a howling mob of armed students seized the United States Embassy in Teheran, Iran, and took more than sixty Americans hostage. The students were aroused by a seventy-nine year old Moslem fundamentalist, the Ayatollah Ruhallah Khomeini, who was in Paris organizing opposition to the shah. As mobs chanted hatred for America and burned American flags, the students paraded bound and blindfolded hostages in the embassy compound. The captors then demanded that the American authorities ship back to Iran the exiled shah, who had arrived in the United States two weeks earlier for medical treatment, to face trial for "crimes against the Iranian People" with which he had been charged.

The seizing of the hostages caught President Carter (and most of the rest of the world) by surprise. In retrospect it was obvious that the trouble had been brewing for a long time. From 1950, when the United States put the young shah back on the throne of Iran with the help of the CIA, until 1977 when anti-shah demonstrations took place at the gates of the White

House, American belief in the shah of Iran, a frequent visitor to the White House, was unswerving. President Richard Nixon had referred to the shah as the linchpin of America's entire foreign policy in the Middle East.

After Carter became president, he continued to consider the shah a strong ally, and his support for the shah was unshaken even though the shah was coming under serious pressure from the Iranian student radicals, Moslem religious groups, and supporters of the Ayatollah Khomeini: "We look upon Iran's strength as an extension of our own strength and they look upon our strength as an extension of theirs. We look upon Iran as a very stabilizing force in the world at large. The future looks bright when we have friends like this great country." Those words would return to haunt Jimmy Carter.[124]

President Carter refused the captors' demands and denounced the hostage taking as a flagrant violation of international law. In the next few days he asked the Algerians, Syrians, Turks, Pakistanis, Libyans, PLO, and others to intercede on behalf of the release of the hostages. He also called on the United Nations Security Council to condemn the takeover of the American Embassy and to call for the hostages' release. The Security Council on December 31, 1979, condemned the holding of hostages but delayed action on sanctions under the threat of a Soviet veto. Carter instructed immigration authorities to look into deporting any Iranian students in the United States illegally, ordered the freezing of Iranian government assets in United States banks, made a commitment to greater spending on defense, stationed United States aircraft carriers and destroyers in the Indian Ocean, and stepped up aid to other Middle Eastern nations. In early December, Secretary of State Vance went to Western Europe to enlist the support of the NATO countries for strong economic sanctions against Iran.

The president also imposed an embargo on United States oil imports from Iran. When he was reminded that cutting off Iranian oil would decrease the world supply and drive the cost of gasoline even higher (and would probably bring back angry Americans standing in long lines at gasoline pumps), he refused to budge. It would be, he said, an act of "self-discipline" for the American people to boycott Iran's oil and a clear signal to United States allies in Europe that America meant business and expected their help. Most important, it would signify that American lives were more valuable than oil.[125]

Meanwhile, the anti–American demonstrations continued daily outside the embassy in Teheran, and the ayatollah denounced the United States as "the great Satan" and President Carter as its corrupt and lying leader for having given sanctuary to the "great criminal shah." He threatened to try the hostages as spies if the shah were not returned. In the United States, questions were raised about why Carter had not supported the shah more firmly and why America had not taken tougher action against Iran after the hostages were seized.

Dramatic scenes from Iran depicting the anti–American fervor were shown nightly on American television, accompanied by the networks' relentless count of days that the hostages had been held. Many Americans were left feeling outraged, frustrated, and impotent. In honor of the captives, Americans tied yellow ribbons around trees, flew giant-sized flags, rang church bells each noon, and played songs like "Take Your Oil and Shove It." The crisis actually boosted Carter's slumping popularity. An ABC News–Lou Harris Poll taken in late November showed Carter pulling ahead of Kennedy for the first time, 48 to 46 percent, among Democrats and Independents.[126]

The shah's medical treatment in New York ended in late November, and he prepared to leave for Mexico, where he had been living previously. However, when Mexico announced unexpectedly that he would not be permitted to return to his exile home in Cuernavaca, the shah was flown to a United States military hospital in Texas to continue his convalescense pending a decision on a permanent place of residence. Eventually, Panama provided a new haven after Hamilton Jordan flew there secretly and made arrangements with General Torrijos. But the shah's departure on December 15 for a Panamanian island resort proved of no use in negotiations with the Iranians, who made new demands that the United States use its influence to see that he was sent back to Iran. Again the president refused. The shah, needing surgery and not trusting Panamanian authorities, chose to leave on March 23, 1980, for Egypt, where he died.

CARTER'S ANNOUNCEMENT OF CANDIDACY. On December 4, Carter formally announced his candidacy for renomination and reelection but said that he would engage in no active campaigning or other partisan activity until the hostage crisis was resolved. As the Christmas season approached, the president cancelled his plans to go to Georgia—the first time in twenty-seven years that the Carter family would not spend the holidays together.[127] At the annual lighting of the White House Christmas tree, the president lit only the top light, saying that the rest would be turned on when the hostages were returned. Carter became the rallying point for Americans. The Gallup Poll reported that President Carter's approval rating had doubled from the 32 percent range just before the hostages were taken, to 61 percent by Christmas. This stunning turnabout made Carter, Austin Ranney suggests, the recipient of the most dramatic "rally-round-the-flag" effect ever recorded.[128]

After Carter's ratings in the polls improved so dramatically, his support in the Democratic Party also improved. Several Democratic members of Congress, who had been afraid to be associated with Carter earlier, made it clear that now they were not eager to have Kennedy make appearances with them. Also, more of them showed up at the annual White House Christmas Ball than had in recent years, and those who attended seemed more willing to shake the president's hand.

The Afghanistan Crisis

Then, on Christmas Day, 1979, the Soviet Union without warning invaded Afghanistan to bolster up a shaky pro–Communist regime in that country. On January 7, the United Nations Security Council voted thirteen to two to condemn the Soviet invasion, but the resolution was nullified by a Soviet veto. On January 13, the Soviet Union vetoed another United States–sponsored resolution calling for economic sanctions against Iran until the hostages were released. The Soviet actions (which looked like a resurgence of Soviet expansionism and a renewal of the cold war) finally convinced the president that Moscow's human rights policies had to be his concern after all. He told ABC anchorman Frank Reynolds, "The intervention made a more dramatic change in my opinion of what the Soviet goals are" than anything else during his administration.[129] It was no longer possible "to do business as usual with the Soviet Union."

To express American diapproval, on January 4, 1980, a few days before the Iowa caucuses, Carter ordered an embargo on sales to the Soviet Union of United States grain and high technology items such as computers. When Vice President Mondale objected strenuously to the grain embargo, concerned about possible injury to American grain-belt farmers, Carter assured him that the administration would do everything possible to maintain grain prices. He pleaded for understanding: "How am I going to lead the West and persuade our allies to impose sanctions against the Russians if we aren't willing to make some sacrifices ourselves? What can I say to Margaret Thatcher or Helmut Schmidt if we fail to exercise the single option that hurts the Russians most? ... This is an emergency and I'm going to have to impose the embargo, and we'll just have to make the best of it. Farmers are patriotic people."[130]

Kennedy quickly criticized the move, charging, "A weak foreign policy can't be redeemed by suddenly getting tough on farmers." Predictably, all of the Republican candidates except John Anderson joined in the criticism. Senator Bob Dole said, "Carter took a poke at the Soviet bear and knocked out the American farmer." Ronald Reagan, who had been calling for an administration that would get tough with the USSR, said that "pigs, cows, or chickens" had not invaded Afghanistan and "no one segment of the economy should be asked to bear the brunt of American countermeasures to deal with the Soviet invasion of Afghanistan."[131]

THE OLYMPIC BOYCOTT. Also, Carter announced that unless Soviet troops were withdrawn from Afghanistan by February 20, he would use all his influence either to get the summer Olympics moved from Moscow (which the International Olympic Committee declined to do) or else to get the United States Olympic Committee and the athletes of other nations to boycott the games. Only after much debate and with manifest reluctance did the United States Olympic Committee vote in April 1980 to boycott. The Soviets responded by denouncing the punitive measures as a "flagrant violation" of the United States commitment to detente (whatever detente meant).

The Carter administration found it difficult to muster support abroad or at home for the boycott. It was supported by only sixty-seven countries—many would not have sent teams anyway—and eighty countries participated. The boycott was also generally unpopular with American athletes. The administration failed to achieve the united front it sought.

American athletes, of course, participated in the winter Olympic games held in Lake Placid, New York. Americans seized on evidence of national prowess, like the unexpected come-from-behind victory of an inexperienced United States hockey team over the all-powerful Soviet Union team. When the team went on to win the gold medal by defeating Finland, the crowd sang "God Bless America" and chanted "We're Number One." Unfortunately for Carter, this victory and the gold medal were not omens of better days ahead.[132]

SALT II WITHDRAWAL. Reflecting the political reality in the country, on January 3, 1980, Carter reluctantly asked Senate Majority Leader Robert Byrd to delay Senate floor debate on ratification of the SALT II treaty. He recognized that Soviet action in Afghanistan had created an atmosphere in which Senate leaders did not even dare bring the treaty up. He still believed SALT II was in the national interest, he said, and he left open the possibility that it could be taken up later, saying, "The purpose of this request is not to withdraw the treaty, but to defer the debate so that the Congress and I . . . can assess Soviet actions."

In his memoirs Carter said that "our failure to ratify the SALT II treaty and to secure even more far-reaching agreements on nuclear arms control was the most profound disappointment of my Presidency."[133]

3. The Loss of Leadership

As the fall of 1979 and the presidential nomination season approached, President Carter found himself increasingly combating charges that he had permitted the nation to drift because of his ineffectiveness and incompetence. To make matters worse, he also suffered a serious embarrassment in the summer of 1979 when Andrew Young, the United States representative to the United Nations, was forced to resign under fire.

Ambassador Young seemed determined to voice his own opinion on foreign policy matters — often to the discomfort of both Secretary of State Vance and President Carter himself.[1] In July 1978, just when President Carter was officially protesting the trials of Soviet dissidents, Young told a French newspaper that there were "hundreds, perhaps thousands, of political prisoners in the United States." Although Carter gently rebuked Young in private, he continued to publicly declare his full faith in the ambassador.

However, a major storm broke out in June 1979 when it became known that Young had held a secret meeting with a representative of the Palestine Liberation Organization, violating the official United States policy against negotiation with the PLO. The ambassador, when queried about the meeting, explained that it was just a chance social encounter, and that he had left "after social amenities." Subsequently, Young changed his story, saying that he had planned the encounter to talk about delaying a United Nations Security Council discussion of Palestinian rights. "I didn't lie, I didn't tell the whole truth," he explained.

Young's off-the-cuff remarks caused a serious dilemma for the president. The ambassador was clearly a valuable asset at the United Nations, where he was credited with greatly improving United States relations with the Third World. And, as a black with visible influence in the Oval Office, Young had helped the administration's stature among blacks and other minorities.

To spare the president further embarrassment, Young offered his

115

resignation on July 15, 1979. Carter accepted it "with deep regret." Nevertheless, both Israeli officials and American Jews, always influential in Democratic Party politics, remained suspicious that United States policy was tilting toward the Palestinians. Also, some black leaders in the United States, without whose support Carter would not have won election in 1976, charged that the most independent and most visible black member of the Carter political team had been unfairly made a scapegoat for administration problems. Young's supporters reminded Carter that the United States ambassador to Austria had held a serious discussion with a PLO official earlier in the year, and had received nothing worse than a "reminder" of United States policy from the State Department and a warning not to repeat the incident. It was clearly a no-win situation for the president.

Meanwhile, Carter's popularity as revealed by the polls was plummeting. By the summer of 1979 an Associated Press/NBC Poll showed that only 19 percent of those interviewed gave Carter's performance a favorable rating—the lowest job rating given a president since Harry Truman in the midst of the Korean War and Richard Nixon at the depths of the Watergate scandal. It was suggested that Carter, like Lewis Carroll's Cheshire Cat, was fading away, leaving only a smile behind.

The Democratic Candidates

EDMUND G. "JERRY" BROWN. President Carter's political weakness stimulated challenges for the 1980 nomination within his own party.[2] The first Democratic challenge came from Governor Jerry Brown of California.[3] Brown had been unofficially campaigning since his string of impressive primary victories over Carter in 1976. As we have seen, in that first bid for the presidency, after a late start he had defeated Carter in five of the six primaries he entered, creating considerable attention—dubbed the "Brown phenomenon" by reporters. After an overwhelming reelection victory (by 1.3 million votes) as California's governor in 1978, Brown began preparing for a full-scale effort to win the presidential nomination.

The governor was difficult to categorize as either liberal or conservative. As Theodore H. White put it, "He belongs somewhere in the future of the eighties or nineties ... [he is] a man arrived before his time."[4] Brown's main pitch, as best anyone could figure out, was an amalgam of environmentalism, fiscal and budgetary prudence, opposition to nuclear power, and support of high-tech expansionism. It was all summed up in his campaign slogan: "Protect the earth, serve the people, and explore the universe."[5] At least that is what his supporters stenciled on their tee-shirts. In 1979 the governor traveled the country on behalf of a federal constitutional amendment mandating a balanced budget, garnering extensive publicity (mostly bad) in the process. Balanced budgets and conservation of resources were part of one whole, he said. "If you look at the budget, what do you find?" Brown asked his college audiences. "Welfare, warfare, and interest on the debt. That's the big picture of the USA and I think it is a very sorry one. I say, let's balance the budget and pay our bills as they come due."

On November 8, standing behind a poster that said "Wow! Brown Now!," he announced his candidacy at the National Press Club in Washington, D.C. When a television reporter asked what he thought his chances were, he replied that the odds were one in three: "There's Kennedy and there's Carter and there's me."[6]

SENATOR EDWARD M. "TED" KENNEDY. Potentially the most serious Democratic challenge to Carter came from Massachusetts Senator Ted Kennedy.[7] The signals that he was now ready to be president came early. As we have seen, in December 1978 he made a speech at the party's midterm conference in Memphis attacking the president's plan to increase military spending (by 3 percentage points above inflation) and to hold down increases for social spending. Some observers concluded this speech was intended to demonstrate his obvious popularity with the delegates.[8]

By the spring of 1979, "Kennedy in 1980" groups had mushroomed across the country. By midsummer 1979, polls were showing Kennedy to be more than a two-to-one favorite over President Carter among Democrats for their party's nomination. But for months Kennedy, when asked if he would run, gave his standard answer: "I expect the president to be renominated, and I expect the president to be reelected, and I intend to support him. If Carter withdraws, of course, I'll give it [candidacy] serious consideration."

In reality, Kennedy had already been giving candidacy serious consideration. The last three years had been for him a period of disenchantment with a presidency that from the start had been alien to his own political ideology, objectives, and style. Out of loyalty to the party he had backed Carter on Capitol Hill on most issues for most of the time, but his heart was never in it. All through 1979 the pressure had built to challenge Carter, and he had doggedly resisted it, but his rationale for staying on the sidelines was now rapidly eroding.[9] Kennedy had also been upset by Carter's "Malaise Speech." He thought it violated the spirit of America — the things Kennedy believed the American people wanted to do and feel about themselves. It was also an indictment of a lot of things that Kennedy believed in. *New York Times* correspondent Adam Clymer suggests that the "Malaise Speech" was most likely the turning point in the senator's decision to run.[10]

After Labor Day 1979, when Kennedy returned to Washington for the opening of the Ninety-sixth Congress, he had given his supporters a major boost by backing away a bit from his blanket statement of noncandidacy and by generally sounding more and more like a potential candidate. He was, he said, "concerned about Carter's failure of leadership." As if on cue, a "dump Carter" campaign, launched earlier in California, quickly grew into a national "draft Kennedy" movement.

Finally, on November 7, Kennedy formally announced his candidacy for the presidency. Unfortunately for Kennedy, because of the Iran crisis, his announcement was the ninth story on all three networks following eight stories on Iran. Even so, the polls were still showing Kennedy to be strongly favored over President Carter among Democrats, and the press generally declared Kennedy the victor with his entrance into the race. Carter, however, professed to be unperturbed by Kennedy's entry. "I'll whip his ass," he told a group of congressmen when informed of Kennedy's challenge. The Carter White House made sure that the world knew he had said it.[11]

Ironically, Kennedy's popularity declined rapidly once it became clear that he actually was a candidate. He was no longer one of the Kennedy brothers; now he was Ted Kennedy, a serious candidate for the presidency, who could expect to be open to careful scrutiny and who could also expect to inherit the considerable amount of animosity which had developed toward the Kennedy family over the years. People started attacking him or began to consider problems they had brushed aside. Also, Kennedy's earlier-than-planned entry left him unprepared. He had no organization in place and little money raised, in sharp contrast to Carter at that point in time.[12]

THE CHARACTER ISSUE. One factor in Kennedy's decline in popularity was the so-called character issue. Many who would otherwise have supported him had nagging doubts about his personal integrity, his sexual morality, and his stability in a crisis, doubts raised largely by the now famous 1969 incident at Chappaquiddick Island, Massachusetts. Kennedy attempted to defuse the issue early in the campaign by admitting his remorse and the irrationality of his actions, but it was not enough to sway those who perceived him as someone who did not have his life together.

THE KENNEDY-MUDD INTERVIEW. Another important reason for Kennedy's decline in popularity was his disastrous interview with CBS correspondent Roger Mudd (ironically, a family friend), broadcast on Sunday, November 5, 1979, on CBS television.[13] The event had been heavily promoted by the network, and the text had been leaked to certain reporters and columnists. Mudd's questions had touched all of the major controversial elements of Kennedy's political career, from Chappaquiddick to rumors about his alleged womanizing. In responding Kennedy had hemmed and hawed and talked in vague generalities over questions that should have been easy enough for a veteran politician—like: "Why do you want to be president?"[14]

Questions were also raised about Kennedy's political views. Long an active "New Deal style" liberal, he was seen by many as out of step with an era in which inflation and relatively slow economic growth seemed to call for fiscal conservatism.

THE IRAN CRISIS. Unfortunately for Kennedy, his interview with Mudd was broadcast the same day that the American Embassy in Teheran was stormed by a mob and sixty-six American citizens were taken hostage. Almost at once, the entire political landscape changed. When, shortly after the seizure of the hostages, Kennedy commented in a television interview that the shah of Iran was "one of history's worst tyrants" who should not be given permanent residence in the United States, he was widely criticized for not maintaining a united front against the Iranian militants. (Ronald Reagan had just said that the shah should be given permanent residence.) Kennedy later insisted that he had been misquoted, but the damage was done.[15]

However, fortunately for Kennedy, the political columnists soon turned their attention to Teheran, and his shah gaffe and the Kennedy-Mudd interview largely disappeared from sight.

The Republican Candidates

As the 1980 presidential election approached, the Republicans made no secret of their eagerness to take on Jimmy Carter or whomever else the Democrats would nominate. Into this political arena stepped an impressive lineup of declared or potential GOP candidates, ranging across the political spectrum from former California governor Ronald Reagan on the ideological right to Representative John B. Anderson of Illinois in the progressive center.[16]

PRESIDENT FORD. By logic and tradition, the GOP candidate should be former president Gerald Ford, who was living the good life in semi-retirement, golfing in Palm Springs, California, skiing at Vail, Colorado, writing his memoirs, and enjoying the respectful treatment rightfully accorded to an ex-president.

Ford had a half-developed idea that he wanted to be president again. But as the last Republican president, he did not feel that he should have to slug it out with Ronald Reagan in the primaries, repeating the unpleasant campaign of 1976. However, he had a low opinion of Reagan and did not want Reagan to secure the nomination by default. At the same time, the fact that Ford had lost the White House as an incumbent president minimized the demand within the GOP for him to seek the nomination for himself. His advisers urged him to wait a few months into the next year to see what would happen, and then to decide what to do.

In the meantime, Ford sent out conflicting signals. He had responded to a newspaper reporter's question: "If something happens, it happens. I'm a fatalist." And he added, "I never say 'never' in politics." Then, a few days later, at a press conference, he announced that he had made a firm decision not to become an active candidate. But, he said, he would "be a candidate if my political party wanted it" and would respond in the "very remote" chance the Republican Convention became deadlocked.[17]

RONALD WILSON REAGAN. The smart money was on the sixty-nine year old Ronald Reagan, who had lost the party's nomination to Ford in 1976 by a mere 117 votes. Almost from the moment of Gerald Ford's defeat at the hands of Jimmy Carter in 1976, the even-featured and heavily tanned Reagan had been accepted throughout the party as its leading candidate for the 1980 nomination. In a party turning ever more to the right, Reagan, the party's most resolute conservative ideologue, seemed ideally positioned to lead.

Reagan had announced his candidacy in a nationally televised address on November 3, 1978, from the ballroom of the Hilton Hotel in traditionally liberal New York City. He had decried government as "distributor of gifts and privileges." In his address he had borrowed three times from FDR's phrase "rendezvous with destiny" to describe the country's future.

Ronald Reagan's latest bid for the presidency had really begun almost a year earlier when Reagan had created a political action committee — Citizens for the Republic, with himself as chairman — to support conservative candidates, and to "try to help broaden the conservative Republican base," and to organize conservatives in the nation. Throughout 1977, CFTR newsletters stoked conservative fires with attacks on the treaties that "gave away the Panama Canal," the USSR, Cuba, government "destruction" of the work ethic, and the supposed duplicity of the Carter administration.[18]

From 1977 until late 1979 Reagan had taped radio editorials and written a widely read newspaper column. He had given dozens of speeches around the country in which he had focused upon the inconsistencies in the Carter energy policy, the condition of the economy, and the president's purported lack of leadership. Reagan's extensive tours and contacts with party and interest groups around the nation made him the first choice of Republican voters by the fall of 1978.[19]

John Sears III, a politically astute Washington, D.C., lawyer who had managed Reagan's nomination bid in 1976, was brought back to be the working chairman of the Reagan for President Committee (its nominal chairman was Senator Paul Laxalt). However, Sears's authority was considerably murkier than in 1976 because of the opposition of several of the old Reagan retainers, including Lyn Nofziger, Michael Deaver, and Edwin Meese, who thought that Sears had cost Reagan the 1976 nomination with his Schweiker ploy, the futile fight over Rule 16-C at the convention, and other actions. But, for now, Ron and Nancy Reagan were willing to follow Sears's advice.

Reagan was confident of winning the nomination and regarded the prenomination period as a time for drawing the Republican coalition together (and adding to it if possible), healing the wounds left over from 1976, and building an issue agenda. Thus his strategy, at least initially, was to ignore the other Republican hopefuls. It would be divisive, he said, to openly criticize his fellow candidates, and he again referred to his personal Eleventh Commandment: "Thou shalt not speak ill of any fellow Republican."

Reagan's entry into the race for the nomination created problems for all the other potential Republican candidates. Because of his widespread popularity in the Republican Party (which it was estimated would assure him of at least 35 to 40 percent of the primary vote), every candidate who entered had to develop a strategy with regard to Reagan—he was for Reagan, *but*; he was against Reagan, *but*; he was an alternative to Reagan; he was a young Reagan. The idea was to avoid antagonizing Reagan or the Reagan supporters on whom the candidate would have to call for help if he got the nomination.

Sears was not seriously troubled by Reagan's age, which almost everyone else considered his greatest liability. Once Reagan displayed his remarkable physical vitality on the campaign trail, Sears felt, such misgivings would fade away. Rather, Sears worried about the same thing he had in 1976: whether Reagan's identification in the public mind as Mr. Conservative would destroy him against Carter. The problem was how to convince the ordinary citizen that Reagan was no extremist, but the friend of the forgotten American he had talked about in the famous 1964 speech; not the creature of corporate boardrooms, but the populist of the right.

JOHN CONNALLY. Running close behind Reagan in the polls was "Big John" Connally, the silver-haired, three-term former Democratic governor of Texas.

The flamboyant Texan projected an image of a man who could get impossible things done for business. This image brought him strong support from multi-nationalists, who wanted free trade and an open global economy; somewhat illogically, it also won him fans among protectionists, who sought shelter from international competition—and who suspected that Reagan lacked the proper business orientation and experience.

Connally's biggest drawbacks appeared to be that he was a political turncoat (he had switched parties in 1973 along with millions of other white Southerners) at a time of disaster for the Republicans, and that he had stood trial in 1974 for taking $10,000 in bribes from the Associated Milk Producers in exchange for persuading President Nixon to support a hike in milk price support. Although he was acquitted of the charges, in the public mind he was perceived as having some connection with Watergate.

Connally's primary election strategy was to take away the southern base from Reagan by defeating him decisively in a key southern state where the conservative Reagan would be presumed to be at his best. Then he would go on to contest Reagan in the Midwest and the late primaries. However, Connally was convinced that he could not defeat Reagan if he could not outspend him. Therefore, because his initial fundraising was so successful (by mid-December 1979 he had already raised $8 million— more than any other Republican), he decided to forego public financing and matching funds, which would enable him to spend whatever he could raise wherever he chose to spend it.[20] Connally's refusal to accept matching funds quickly caught the eyes of the reporters, who dubbed him the "millionaire candidate" and the "Fortune 500 candidate."

Unfortunately for Connally, after the hostages were taken in Iran in early November the national television networks (where he had planned to spend most of his campaign budget) were jammed with news from Iran, and Connally was unable to purchase television network prime time. When he lost the TV news coverage and could not buy TV spots, he could not sustain a national campaign, and Connally dropped out of sight (as did everyone else).

GEORGE BUSH. George Herbert Walker Bush was born on June 12, 1924, in Milton, Massachusetts, the second son of Prescott Bush, a Wall Street financier and Republican United States senator from Connecticut for ten years. An authentic hero in World War II, George Bush enlisted at eighteen, became a naval pilot, and flew fifty-eight missions, earning the Distinguished Flying Cross and three Air Medals for service in the Pacific. After his discharge from the navy, he attended Yale University, where he captained the baseball team and graduated Phi Beta Kappa.

After the war, Bush, with his family, moved to West Texas, where he made himself a millionaire through holdings in oil and oil-drilling equipment. When he had acquired the minimum fortune for a Texas businessman, he ran for the Senate (with the support of Richard Nixon), running a Goldwater race—opposition to the Civil Rights Act—in Barry Goldwater's year, 1964. But Bush had gone too far to the right and was defeated. In 1966 he was elected from a Houston district to the United States House of Representatives, where he compiled a generally conservative voting record during two terms in office. After losing another

Senate race in 1970 to Lloyd Bentsen, he was appointed by Nixon to be chief United States delegate to the United Nations.

In 1972 Bush left his United Nations assignment, a post he liked, to become chairman of the Republican National Committee (with the promise from Nixon of a cabinet post after the 1974 elections). Subsequently, it was his thankless task to defend Richard Nixon and the Republican Party through the darkest days of Watergate. In 1974, as a reward for his service under fire, President Ford named Bush head of the United States Liaison Office in China (although Bush had hoped for the vice presidency given to Nelson Rockefeller). Bush later (1976-1977) served as head of the Central Intelligence Agency during a time of turmoil. Thus over the years Bush had filled a longer list of important jobs than most people who run for the presidency—"experience *and* leadership" would be his theme.[21] Unfortunately for Bush, it was primarily an appointive resume—a little thin on electoral successes for one who sought the highest elective post in the nation.

George Bush, who was believed to be an essentially "moderate"— some described him as "somewhere to the center of center"—Republican, was very popular with the Jerry Ford–type Republicans and with Independents, many of whom remained wary of Reagan. He was well known among the party people, though he had little public recognition. Although he had lost twice in seeking a Senate seat in Texas, Bush was convinced that he could mount a successful campaign for the presidency.

Bush thought Ronald Reagan was a "lightweight," but he recognized that the Californian's political support was widespread and that he would disadvantage himself if he alienated Reagan's support. He therefore refused to become an anti-Reagan or a Stop Reagan candidate.

The well-mannered Bush would suffer from "softness"—something akin to "wimpishness." Because he spoke in the diction of good breeding, strangers tended to regard him as soft when he was merely cordial, and petulant when he was genuinely angry.

SENATOR HOWARD BAKER. Senator Howard Baker's credentials were impeccable. After fourteen years in the Senate the fifty-five year old Tennessee Republican could count any number of major accomplishments. As minority leader he had proved to be an effective director of Republican opposition to a Democratic majority in the Senate. He was a proven votegetter as well as a much-appreciated rarity—a repeatedly reelected Republican senator from a traditionally Democratic state. He also had another advantage in that he came from the border South. He enjoyed consistent strength among a broad range of Republicans, although his political philosophy placed him smack in the center of the Republican political spectrum. He followed close behind Ford and Reagan in the early polls.

Baker hoped to capitalize on the popularity he had gained by his evenhanded role in the Watergate Select Committee hearing with his now-famous question: "What did the president know and when did he know it?" He had also hoped to star in the Senate debate on SALT (which he opposed) and then announce his candidacy. However, when the SALT agreement was delayed in getting to the Senate, Baker had been seriously delayed in getting a campaign organization together.[22] On November 1, when he finally declared his candidacy in the Senate Caucus Room (before a sign which read, "Tough, Honest, Right for the 80's"), he stressed his experience, noting that he knew Washington "well enough to change Washington." He would run as an "insider"—a *Washington* politician. He concluded: "Watch me. Judge me. Then come with me. Let's reach for the future and make it ours!"[23]

Baker's announcement stirred few sparks. Although the Tennessean looked good on paper, there was a nagging question about whether he had sufficient fire in the belly to do the things necessary to win the presidency.[24] Also, Baker would have problems with the southern conservatives in the party, in large measure because he had voted for the Panama Canal accords. Somewhat ironically, both President Carter and Vice President Mondale considered Baker the most formidable of their potential adversaries—a view shared by several knowledgeable political reporters and observers.[25] Even Reagan thought that, aside from Ford, Baker was potentially his strongest competitor.[26]

PHILIP CRANE. Actually the first declared candidate for the 1980 Republican nomination was Philip Crane, a five-term member of the House of Representatives from Illinois. He announced his intentions on August 2, 1978, two years before the 1980 general election—the earliest anyone had ever announced, and well before Ronald Reagan had made public his intention to run. As a former chairman of the American Conservative Union, Crane's ability to articulate conservative theory had built a small but dedicated following for him, especially among members of the New Right who were concerned about Reagan's age and looking for a "young Reagan."[27]

Although Crane had been a strong supporter of Ronald Reagan in both 1968 and 1976, he felt that, considering Reagan's age, it would be well for the conservatives to have a backup candidate if Reagan should decide not to run. However, after Reagan announced his candidacy and Crane did not withdraw from the race, many observers concluded that Crane was really more concerned with putting himself forward as heir to the Reagan mantle than with actually capturing the nomination.

ROBERT DOLE. Senator Robert Dole, the acerbic senior senator from Kansas ("the fastest lip in politics"), who had been the Republican vice-presidential nominee in 1976, announced his candidacy on May 14, 1979.

Dole, a dark, handsome man, had established a good record in the Senate. He had also revealed himself as a tough campaigner. The Kansan saw himself not only as an alternative to Reagan but as the choice beyond Reagan. He also, like Crane, saw himself as a young Ronald Reagan. He could personally identify with farmers, veterans, and handicapped persons with whom he had worked on a one-to-one basis over the years.[28]

JOHN B. ANDERSON. John B. Anderson, elected to Congress from Illinois in 1960 as a conservative, had become recognized as a moderate by the late 1960s. Nevertheless, he had become a member of the House Republican leadership — chairman of the Republican Conference, the third-ranking Republican in the House of Representatives. Like Bush and Dole, Anderson was an authentic war hero.

Silver-haired and distinguished, the fifty-eight year old Anderson had early established a reputation as an intellectually honest, strongly issue-oriented congressman who was always willing to speak his mind. His independent style had not endeared him to the rest of the House GOP leadership, and by being one of the first Republican representatives to say publicly that President Nixon was culpable on Watergate, he had further estranged himself from his party colleagues. However, Anderson's "politics of differentness" had caught on with a substantial number of voters — mostly the well educated and affluent, as well as some students.

On March 4, 1979, a Gallup Poll of Republican voters on prospective presidential candidates revealed Reagan with 31 percent, Ford with 26 percent, Connally with 12 percent, and Baker with 8 percent.

The Republican Primaries

IOWA. The first major confrontation among the Republican candidates came in the Iowa precinct caucuses on Monday, January 21, 1980.[29] In the past, Republicans had generally ignored Iowa; New Hampshire had traditionally been the official kickoff of the Republican nominating season. Since Carter's victory in 1976, however, the Iowa caucuses had been transformed into what Howard Baker characterized as "the functional equivalent of a primary." Moreover, in 1980, the significance of Iowa increased when the *Des Moines Register and Tribune,* one of the nation's few truly statewide papers with a quarter of a million subscribers, decided to sponsor the season's first nationally televised debates between the presidential candidates — the Republicans on Saturday, January 5, and the Democrats two days later.

Six of the invited Republican candidates — Connally, Baker, Bush, Anderson, Crane, and Dole — accepted the debate invitation. Reagan, who was easily the best speaker of the group, rejected it, arguing that the debate would be "divisive" and would adversely affect party harmony. In truth, his campaign advisers didn't think it was necessary—only 22,000 Republicans had participated in the Iowa caucuses of 1976, and in 1980 they would be selecting only 37 of the 1,994 delegates to the Republican National Convention. It was more important for him, they concluded, to conserve his energy and resources, to husband his lead in the polls, and to avoid getting involved in the normal give-and-take of campaigning. Rather than being disruptive of party harmony, as Reagan had predicted, the New York Times editorialized that the debate "conveyed an overriding sense of earnest, ordered democracy."[30]

There was no general agreement on who won the debates in Iowa, although Ronald Reagan was uniformly cited as the loser for not showing up.[31] The popular favorite with the reporters and commentators appeared to be John Anderson. In reporting the debate, CBS even used clips from "Saturday Night Live"—a phony missing persons report on candidate John Anderson—to conclude that Anderson "has been found."[32]

Bush prepared for the Iowa caucuses very carefully, basing his bid on Jimmy Carter's early-bird strategy four years before. He hit the Iowa roads early in 1979, eleven months before the caucuses, and visited the state twenty-two times, building a strong organization in the state.[33] He campaigned vigorously and used the media to increase name recall. He went to every coffee klatch, every service club meeting where six or more Republicans were likely to show up (especially if they were going to have a straw poll). As Bush liked to say, he had seen the entire planting cycle in the state of Iowa.[34]

Campaigning in Iowa, Bush painted himself as a solid conservative who was, in truth, a younger version of Reagan. He zeroed in on the one serious disagreement he had with Reagan: taxation. Supply-side economics, he said, was "voodoo economics" (a memorable phrase which would one day rise up to haunt him).

In contrast, Reagan made only a few brief visits to the state and did not participate in any joint appearances with other Republican candidates. Also, he bought a mere half-hour of television time—which the Republicans of Iowa resented, since it appeared that he was downgrading the importance of the Iowa Republican's voice in the nominating process. He preferred to spend his time wooing political leaders in New Hampshire, Vermont, Connecticut, and New York—four states which had given Ford 204 delegates and Reagan only 23 at the 1976 convention.[35] In addition, because of recent developments in Iran and Afghanistan, Reagan was convinced that the attention of the media had turned toward foreign affairs, which would rob his lesser-known opponents of potential coverage and thus enhance his chances of victory as the best known of the Republican candidates.

Bush's efforts paid off. He won the Iowa caucuses with 33,530 votes (31.5 percent)—one-third of the total—in contrast to Reagan's 31,348 (29.4 percent). Howard Baker had come in third with 15.2 percent; Connally had 9.3 percent; Crane, 6.7 percent; Anderson, 4.3 percent; and Bob Dole, 1.5 percent. Surprisingly, more than five times more Republicans had participated in the 1980 caucuses than in the 1976 event.[36]

Iowa was an important win for Bush, who was working hard to be taken seriously as a valid contender for moderate Republican support. Realistically, if Bush had not won this initial victory (or another important one—most likely New Hampshire), it is unlikely that his campaign would have gotten off the ground. In any case, it elevated Bush to the status of a serious contender—so serious that he could not lower expectations for future engagements.[37]

What Reagan, and the other candidates, had not reckoned with was the interest of the press in the Iowa outcome. Mindful of the importance of Iowa to Jimmy Carter's 1976 presidential bid, nearly every newspaper and broadcasting outlet had a reporter on the scene weeks before caucus time. Not suprisingly, Bush's unexpected win over the front-running Reagan received extensive media coverage. In the ensuing days the media built up the Bush victory to a point where many newspaper readers and television viewers must have thought that Bush had the nomination in the bag. *Newsweek* magazine even put him on its cover. Suddenly, the number of reporters vying for places in the Bush campaign entourage swelled to forty. (The bad news for Bush was that winning in Iowa meant that in the future he would be treated to the same intense media scrutiny accorded candidates like Reagan and Senator Edward Kennedy.[38]) Bush's media-based "big victory" gave the moderate wing of the Republican Party their first glimmer of hope in sixteen years.[39]

The Iowa loss was, of course, a rude awakening for Reagan. The daily media "medical status reports" on his ailing campaign made him realize that no one was going to hand him the nomination. He was going to have to work for it. More importantly, such a loss in the very state where he had spent part of his youth led the Reagan supporters to an uncomfortable conclusion: Perhaps the Iowa Republicans had decided that a man nearing his sixty-ninth birthday and carrying so much right-wing ideological baggage was not the Republican who could beat Jimmy Carter. Or perhaps they felt that Bush really was a younger, more vigorous, more interesting version of Reagan. (If the Republicans of Iowa had reached that conclusion, so also could the Republicans of New Hampshire, etc.) In any case, the loss raised serious questions about the wisdom of Sears's cautious, "above the fray," non-ideological campaign strategy designed to make the governor look more presidential.[40]

NEW HAMPSHIRE. Reagan reversed his previous aloof stance and campaigned in New Hampshire as if his life depended upon it—as indeed it did, since losing that state would almost certainly write the end of Reagan's political life.[41] He was, he said, less concerned about unity in the party and more concerned about self-survival. During one stretch, he bounced around the back roads of the Granite State on campaign buses for twenty-one consecutive below-freezing days. He responded warmly to the crowds, answering questions easily and openly. He offered to debate other Republicans, and he ran anti-Bush television commercials.

Reagan devoted most of his attention in New Hampshire to George Bush, charging the Texan with favoring a liberalized abortion law, the Equal Rights Amendment, and a guaranteed-income welfare plan.[42] He also hit hard on Jimmy Carter—the budget deficits, the Soviet Union, gun control, the Panama Canal treaties, SALT II, and permissive abortion laws were all popular issues in the largely conservative state.

Bush, for his part, raced from shopping mall to department store and back to shopping mall, admonishing those potential voters who were reluctant to come see. "No fair hiding. You can't escape. I'm George Bush. I would love to have your vote." He was on one of the toughest schedules ever developed for a presidential candidate, but in public he appeared to thrive on it. Meanwhile, William Loeb, the publisher and editor of the powerful Manchester, New Hampshire, *Union Leader* and a Reagan supporter, attacked Bush on a daily basis, bombarding his readers with everything negative he could possibly find about the former Texas congressman.

Anderson and Baker competed for the moderate vote with Bayh. Phil Crane had been working the state since the summer of 1978, hoping to use the primary to establish himself as a realistic possibility for the nomination after his disastrous (6.7 percent) finish in Iowa.

Ironically, by absenting himself from Iowa, Reagan had raised the most serious issue of the New Hampshire primary—that of "age and vitality." However, his appearance (he was careful about his weight, didn't smoke, chopped wood, rode horseback—and was often pictured doing so—and swam) projected an image of robust good health for men much younger than he. Then, on his sixty-ninth birthday, the "Oldest and Wisest Candidate," as the reporters dubbed him, suspended campaigning in New Hampshire long enough to lead the press on twenty-eight campaign appearances in seven states stretching from California to South Carolina. Before he had finished, several of the younger reporters withdrew, pleading exhaustion. After New Hampshire Reagan's age never really became an issue.[43]

Also, Reagan effectively dealt with the age issue by using various self-deprecating jokes. After watching himself play the role of George Gipp in a rerun of *Knute Rockne—All American*, he said, "It's like seeing a younger son I never knew I had." He often quoted Thomas Jefferson's comment that a person's chronological age should be no barrier to his service to his country. Then, pausing for effect, he would add, "Ever since he told me that. . ."[44]

On February 20, Reagan joined with the six Republican candidates he had eluded in Iowa for a joint appearance in Manchester sponsored by the League of Women Voters. The event was generally uneventful to the point of being boring as the candidates — with the exception of John Anderson, who stubbornly insisted on proposing liberal remedies and expounding ideas that could only cost him votes among the majority of New Hampshire Republicans — revealed little of themselves or their positions on the issues.

In the open question period at the end of the debate, Reagan defused a potentially damaging situation when he was asked by a member of the audience about his use of ethnic jokes.[45] He deflected the inquiry with an audience-pleasing, self-deprecatingly humorous remark. Reagan had skillfully managed to put the lid on an incident which might have caused him further embarrassment, and he had demonstrated his considerable agility before a national television audience. The incident did give rise to some observers concluding that "the Great Deflector" was wearing his "teflon suit."

A second debate held three days later at the high school in Nashua, Hew Hampshire, provided a great deal more interest and excitement. The night of the debate all the candidates except John Connally, who was campaigning in South Carolina, showed up prepared to do verbal battle. Bush objected to their presence on the platform, arguing (correctly) that the debate's sponsor, the *Nashua Telegraph*, had agreed that the debate would be between him and Reagan. However, Reagan, maintaining his position as one above personal battles, genially invited them all in. When the nominal host, Jon Breen, executive editor of the *Telegraph*, decided to stick to the original two-person format and refused to permit the other four to participate, Reagan, his voice a mixture of anger and righteousness, grabbed the microphone and the headlines (and the audience) by pointing out in barely controlled, determined tones that he had paid the $3,500 required to rent the hall (Bush had declined to share the cost). The crowd greeted Reagan's announcement with cheers.[46]

In the end, the four excluded guests (two senior United States senators and two congressmen) stalked off to another room, where they roundly denounced Bush as a bad sport for refusing to let them participate. Although the debate itself was televised only locally, newscasts across the country featured the pre-debate controversy. By Monday morning, all New Hampshire voters and most other Americans had heard of or seen the incident. Considerable damage was done to Bush's image as the candidate eager to have all points of view presented; instead, the voters were left with the impression that he was an uptight eastern elitist who hadn't much of importance to say.

On the other hand, Reagan's image as one who could make prompt, firm decisions, and would back his decisions with action, was enhanced. His campaign was back on track. The Bush boom, so enthusiastically promoted by the media since the Iowa caucuses, was considerably deflated.

On primary day Reagan wiped out Bush and the five other candidates by receiving half the votes cast.[47] Bush finished second, but he was seen as severely damaged. Anderson, who finished behind Bush, still continued to receive more favorable media coverage than the Texan.[48]

Reagan's top-heavy win in New Hampshire saved his candidacy. The latest polls showed Reagan, once a ten-point underdog, was now even with Bush. It did not, however, save Sears's job (even though Sears had done brilliant work in New Hampshire). In a surprise move Reagan fired the chief of his campaign and replaced him with William Casey, a sixty-seven year old Manhattan lawyer with limited political experience and, several of the Reagan aides charged, few political instincts.

In reality, long before the New Hampshire primary, Sears's leadership of the campaign had been under challenge from Lyn Nofziger and Michael Deaver. In the summer of 1979 Nofziger, who was pretty tough and wily himself, lost in the power struggle to Sears and was shunted off to fundraising duties but soon left the campaign. After Nofziger's resignation the campaign staff was stacked with Sears loyalists. The word was soon out that no one was safe, and in November 1979 Deaver resigned rather than have the team broken up on the eve of the primary campaigns. Ed Meese was the sole remaining obstacle in Sears's path to total control. After Iowa, Sears went after Meese—a fatal mistake. Reagan could not bring himself to throw his old friend Meese overboard, and he sacked Sears.

Needless to say, Reagan's campaign was in turmoil. Morale was very low. The campaign was almost broke. Sears and his crew had been spending money hand over fist without any recognition that the new election law restrictions on campaign contributions would soon leave the Reagan campaign with no funds.[49] Casey imposed strict spending limits and was able to save and raise enough money to get the campaign all the way to the convention in July.

MASSACHUSETTS AND VERMONT. On March 4, in a close three-way race, heavily favored George Bush, with a great deal of support from independents, edged out Anderson and Reagan in the Massachusetts open primary.[50] Unfortunately for Bush, even though he won the contest, the media attention was on Anderson, the surprise second-place finisher.[51] On the same day, Reagan won the Vermont primary, narrowly edging

Anderson 31 percent to 30 percent.[52] Bush had drawn a disappointing 23 percent of the ballots. Anderson, of course, was ecstatic over the outcome in Vermont. Pointing to the heavy crossover vote that had enabled him to do so well, he insisted that he, unlike Bush and Reagan, could draw the votes of Independents and Democrats as well as Republicans, which would be absolutely essential to capturing the White House in November. Overnight the Illinois congressman's campaign contributions and volunteer support increased dramatically.

Baker and Dole found that the Reagan victories in New Hampshire and Vermont injected a sense of urgency into the question of whether to remain in the contest. On March 5 Baker, after finishing fourth in both Massachusetts and Vermont, decided to call it quits: "It was not in the cards." He had already spent $4 million by then on an effort he admitted wasn't "going anywhere." Ten days later, Dole also withdrew, explaining that he lacked the "five M's"—money, management, manpower, media, and momentum.

For Gerald Ford the problem was somewhat different. With Baker out of the race the old Ford constituency was left without a candidate unless the ex-president could be persuaded to run. However, if Ford was to enter the race he had to do so soon or there was a strong possibility that the party would rush toward Reagan's bandwagon. Practically speaking, the last possible minute Ford could enter the fray and have any chance at victory would be March 21, 1980—the deadline for entering both the California and Michigan primaries.[53] Although Ford was being strongly urged to run by a "Draft Ford" committee, on March 15 he announced that he had reached a firm decision—the toughest of his life. He would not be a candidate. "Our country is in very deep trouble," he said. "America needs a new president." But he did not want to divide his party, and so he would not become a candidate. He would, however, support the party nominee with all the energy he had.

SOUTH CAROLINA. In South Carolina on Saturday, March 8, Reagan and Connally went head-to-head for the first time. Although Connally was supported by the popular (and politically powerful) South Carolina senator Strom Thurmond, Reagan was expected to win.[54] The big Texan had skipped the earlier New England primaries to concentrate all his efforts on the Palmetto State, hoping that if he could stop Reagan there he might go on and sweep the South. He frankly admitted that for him the future of the race would depend upon a first-place finish or a close second to Reagan. In the voting, Connally finished a distant second with less than 30 percent to Reagan's nearly 55 percent.[55] Connally's plans for a Southern ambush had been shattered. The following day Connally quit the race, saying Reagan was "still the champ." He had spent nearly $12 million and had won only one delegate: Mrs. Ada Mills of Clarksville,

Arkansas, probably the most expensive delegate in American political history.[56]

ILLINOIS. Ten days after his win in South Carolina, Reagan faced John Anderson in the Illinois open primary. Anderson held a home-state advantage, and with Ford out, Bush fading, and potentially large numbers of Democrats and Independents voting in the Republican primary, some political observers suggested that Anderson had a real chance of winning and becoming Reagan's leading opponent.[57] Anderson was also being endorsed by two powerful Chicago newspapers, the *Sun Times* and the *Tribune*. Anderson himself was confident about his chances: "I'm going to be the Republican nominee," he was quoted as saying.[58]

Anderson had conducted a campaign which emphasized the differences between himself and the other Republicans. At the Iowa debates, he was the only candidate to support Carter's embargo of grain shipments to the USSR because of the invasion of Afghanistan—a politically naive thing to do in a grain-growing state. Also, Anderson enraged a meeting of the Gun Owners of New Hampshire in Concord when he asked them, "What is so wrong about telling the law-abiding public of the country we will license gun owners?" He also took liberal positions diametrically opposed to those of Reagan, such as support of abortion and opposition to enlarged military spending.[59]

Because Anderson's strong second-place finishes in Massachusetts (to Bush) and Vermont (to Reagan) had established the congressman as a serious, moderate-to-liberal alternative to Reagan, the Illinois contest was a crucial confrontation for Bush, who had seemed on the verge of successfully assuming that role himself. Bush was well aware that he was in "the squeeze"—caught in the middle between Reagan on his right and Anderson on his left. Although Anderson had won no primaries, Bush did not do well when Anderson was competing.

Reagan went on to win the Illinois primary in a walkaway, beating Anderson by more than eleven percentage points. Defeating Anderson in the congressman's home state was a very impressive demonstration of Reagan's drawing power among Independents and crossover Democrats (fully one-third cast their ballots for him),[60] and the news media began to concede the nomination to the Californian. Despite the twenty-two remaining primaries, the *New York Times* said Reagan "appears to be virtually impossible to beat, barring some major error."[61]

Anthony Lewis of the *New York Times* warned the Democrats who had been pooh-poohing Reagan's chances of beating Carter that, after Illinois, they "had better think again about how easy it would be to defeat Reagan in November."[62]

John Anderson's considerable loss in the Illinois primary pushed him a giant step toward decision time about an Independent candidacy.[63] On

April 24, after running poorly in the Pennsylvania primary, he conceded the Republican nomination to Reagan, withdrew from that contest, and announced that he would seek an Independent presidential bid to offer "a choice . . . for the nation."

By May the GOP contest was reduced to Bush's frantic efforts to catch Reagan. On May 5, in a hard-fought contest, Bush lost to Reagan in Texas, his adopted state. After Texas, Bush was so far behind that he would have needed to win 98 percent of the remaining delegates to take the nomination—a prospect which he called "a tough scenario." Waiting for an upbeat moment to make his exit, Bush quit the race shortly after defeating Reagan in Michigan on May 20. That evening both ABC and CBS reported that Reagan had acquired more than enough delegates to ensure his nomination by the Republican National Convention. On May 26, Bush conceded, noting: "I am an optimist. But I also know how to count to 998" (the number of delegates needed to nominate).[64] He asked his delegates to support Reagan.

The Californian was now out in front—all alone. The final round of primaries was anticlimactic. By July Reagan had the nomination secured. He had moved steadily through the largest number of Republican primaries in history, winning twenty-nine, losing just six (all to Bush). The convention would be more like a coronation.

Between May 26 and the Republican Convention on July 13, Reagan made good political use of his time by healing party wounds. He agreed to help the losers pay off nearly $3 million in campaign debts at a series of Republican unity dinners.

The Democratic Primaries

President Carter was well aware that his changed status and situation in 1980 required a new strategy.[65] He was now an incumbent president, and under normal circumstances, he could expect to be renominated (although incumbents had not fared too well recently). However, as we have seen, he was to be challenged for that nomination by Ted Kennedy and Jerry Brown, both formidable opponents. As in 1976, he assumed that the nomination would be decided in the early caucuses and primaries.[66] It would thus be necessary to emphasize the early contests, to run simultaneously in a variety of states, and to make a broad-based appeal to a significant portion of the Democratic coalition. Also, given his low standing in the polls, it would be necessary for Carter to adopt a strategy that would maximize the political clout of his office and, at the same time, minimize public expectations of his performance as president.[67]

Carter would use the authority of his office to control events so as to bolster his political support. Grants and appointments would be timed to enhance endorsements of Carter by leading state and local officials. In addition, White House personnel with campaign experience would be given exended leaves of absence to work in the primaries and caucuses, and cabinet members would campaign around the country as surrogates for the president. Also, the formidable resources of the Democratic Party—the majority party—would be used to the extent they could be marshalled.[68]

Vice President Mondale would be assigned what has become the traditional role of the vice-presidential candidate—the attack dog. With Kennedy in the race it would be a difficult role for Mondale. Since both he and Kennedy were "old-fashioned liberals" and generally represented the same constituency in the Democratic Party, they were fairly close on the issues and were frequently allied in the Senate.

In anticipation of Kennedy's entering the race, beginning in 1979, the Carter organization attempted to rearrange the dates of several southern primaries and caucuses so that those in which Carter expected to do well would be at the beginning of the primary season, and those in which he was likely to do poorly would be scheduled on the same day as states that he was likely to win.[69] They were only partially successful. They were able to advance the dates of several southern primaries and to delay the date of at least one Northern one, Connecticut, for about a month. However, they failed in their attempt to move the Massachusetts primary (which Carter was sure to lose to Kennedy) from March 4, a week after the New Hampshire primary, to March 11, where it would be one among a number in southern states.

FLORIDA. The importance of the Iowa primary in Carter's successful 1976 bid forced the opening of his second primary campaign season back into 1979. The Florida Democrats, determined to capitalize on the media attention they could receive by holding a "first-in-the-nation" straw vote of their members, moved their caucuses to October 13, 1979.

Kennedy and Carter, seeing the opportunity of attention and an early victory, both campaigned in Florida. Each hoped to win delegates to the November state party convention, where a non-binding presidential straw poll would be conducted. To help out, Carter invited 200 Florida citizens to the White House for an "issues briefing." The media, billing the contest as the first confrontation between the president and Kennedy, turned what had always been a "non-event" into a "must enter" in the quest for the nomination.

Carter came out narrowly ahead in the Florida caucuses—a victory not totally unexpected, since he was a Southerner running in his own back yard. He then went on to win the straw vote in November, an indication that Kennedy would not have an easy time. Even so, Kennedy shrugged off the loss with a taunt: "Wait till Iowa — that is the first *real* contest." As it turned out, placing emphasis on the Iowa caucuses was a mistake for Kennedy because it heightened expectations of his performance there. Probably a more serious blow for Kennedy was that Carter's victory in Florida had forced him into the race before he and his organization were ready.[70]

IOWA. The Iowa precinct caucuses, the first of the four steps in choosing the state's fifty delegates (of 3,331) to the Democratic National Convention, were scheduled for January 1980; the final step would not come until mid-June. The opening shots would be fired at the *Des Moines Register and Tribune*-sponsored Democratic Party debates on Monday, January 7. Kennedy and Brown had already indicated their intention to participate, and it was expected that President Carter would join with them because he was trailing Kennedy in the polls.

However, when his ratings improved after the seizure of the hostages in Iran and the Soviet invasion of Afghanistan on December 27, Carter decided not to leave the White House until he had succeeded in freeing the hostages. On December 28 he withdrew from the debate on the grounds that the crisis required that he stay in Washington. "In times of crisis for our country," he said, "I believe it is very important for the President not to assume, in a public way, the role of a partisan campaigner in a political contest." Iran, he suggested, might deliberately "precipitate a crisis or an incident during any absence."[71]

Under the circumstances it was a shrewd strategy. As long as Americans remained captive in Iran, the president's challengers were severely limited in criticizing his handling of the affair, since their remarks might somehow jeopardize the hostages' safety. The President, meanwhile, could generate much favorable media attention by merely acting "presidential" while his opponents were being "political." He could sign and veto legislation; he could receive visiting dignitaries, hold press conferences, and make announcements, which the television networks were bound to report at no cost to his campaign. His opponents, on the other hand, had to buy time to get themselves and their views before the public. In the meantime, Carter's day-by-day campaigning was carried on by his wife Rosalynn, Vice President and Mrs. Mondale, Secretary of Agriculture Robert Bergland, and even Muriel Humphrey.

Carter, in reality, had been cultivating Iowans since his election in 1976. He had returned to the state several times and had in fact spent a vacation there. In 1978, he had sponsored an Iowa Day at the White House commemorating the second anniversary of his "victory." Also, a large number of Iowans were invited to briefings and dinners at the White House.[72]

Carter's withdrawal from the debates was a great disappointment to

Kennedy. He had hoped to confront Carter head-to-head in Iowa, where he expected to trounce the president. As he campaigned across the state, Kennedy bore down hard on the president's refusal to debate, saying he should appear and defend his decision on the grain embargo issue, which had hit Iowa hard and was widely unpopular. He reminded his hearers that Carter had promised in 1976 that he would not place an embargo on grain. The embargo, he said, was the wrong kind of response to the invasion of Afghanistan. "We can show the Soviets we're strong by beefing up our military presence in Southwest Asia, and stopping the sale of sophisticated technology to the Soviet Union; we can provide military assistance to countries in that part of the world"—steps that the Carter administration was taking—"but I don't think food ought to be the weapon."[73] The grain embargo, Kennedy charged, was just another example of a disjointed foreign policy that hurt the wrong people.

Kennedy was also highly critical of Carter's domestic policy. He identified the central concern as inflation (now 13 percent, up from 5 percent when Carter took office) and high interest rates. The current interest rate of 15 percent, he said, made it difficult for people to buy homes, for young families to get started, for people to send their children to college, and for the elderly to pay rising home-heating bills and to purchase prescription drugs. "These are not problems—energy problems, health-care problems—that we cannot deal with. After all, this is America, and we have faced up to such problems effectively. . . . There is no reason we cannot face up to those problems and restore respect and dignity for the United States."[74] The real question, Kennedy said, was "whether we are going to continue a policy of drift here at home and a policy of lurching from crisis to crisis overseas."[75]

The "Rose Garden strategy" of remaining at the White House seemed to pay off for the president. His ratings in the polls, which had fallen disastrously, now climbed dramatically. In October 1979, before the taking of the hostages, Carter's popularity rating among all Americans was 30 percent. By February 1980, as the primaries began, he had scored a 26 percent increase, the largest short-term rise in presidential popularity since Gallup began asking the question in 1938.[76] His approval rating among Democrats went from 37 percent in November to an overwhelming 62 percent in February.

When the Democrats of Iowa cast their caucus ballots the president defeated both challengers handily—Kennedy by a two-to-one vote margin out of an incredibly high voter turnout of 100,000 (20 percent).[77] Kennedy's loss in Iowa was the big story on the evening news. It was also a real blow to Brown, who had not made a serious effort in Iowa; he had pinned all his hopes on a three-way debate with Carter and Kennedy in which he could present his ideas to a mass audience. (As it turned out, the question most often asked Brown in his press conferences was "Where's Linda?"—referring to Brown's friend pop singer Linda Ronstadt.) After Brown's failure to win a delegate in Iowa, the press generally lost interest in him, and his name disappeared from the news.[78]

The Iowa loss was a staggering blow to Kennedy and led to a change in his strategy. He "came home" to his liberal roots. In a speech at Georgetown University in late January, he told the student audience that it was time to return to traditional liberalism. He talked of the need for programs to meet human problems—placing controls on prices, profits, dividends, interest rates, wages and rents; national health insurance; and the closing of tax loopholes which Carter was refusing to support. His proposals might not be perfect, Kennedy said, but they were preferable to putting people out of work and slashing the budget for health, education, and housing. After the speech there was bound to be increasing polarization in the Democratic Party.[79]

MAINE. After Iowa, Kennedy focused a major effort on the Maine caucuses, which Carter had won in 1976 and was likely to win again in 1980 because of his close ties with Maine senator Edmund Muskie. Carter won, but narrowly—45.2 percent to 39.4 percent—and the press focus was on how close Kennedy had come. "We won the election but lost the interpretation," a Carter campaign strategist moaned.[80]

NEW HAMPSHIRE. Two weeks after the Maine caucuses the voters of New Hampshire would meet for the first primary election in the 1980 nominating season. By the first week in January 1980, the president's conduct of the Iran crisis and Kennedy's statement about the shah had reversed Carter's downward slide, and his polls revealed him running ahead of Kennedy, 35 to 31 percent. The figures made it clear that Kennedy, to remain a serious rival of Jimmy Carter, had to beat or finish close behind the president in New Hampshire's open primary on February 26, and win in Massachusetts the following Tuesday. A defeat (or even a near-defeat) for Kennedy in either primary would surely trigger demands that he withdraw from the campaign.

Kennedy received a significant boost on February 22, the Friday before the New Hampshire contest, when the Consumer Price Index soared to a record high annual rate of 18.2 percent—almost four and a half points above the figure for the previous month—a rate which, if it persisted, would alter American life forever.[81] Kennedy hit hard at the inflation figures ("the greatest economic crisis since the depression"). To scotch the character issue, he polished his image as a good family man by campaigning with his children, his sister, nieces and nephews, his mother, and his wife, Joan.[82]

On the eve of the New Hampshire primary, the president defused much of the bad economic news by welcoming to the White House the

American Olympic hockey team, which had scored an upset victory over the defending champions from the Soviet Union and had then gone on to defeat Finland for the gold medal. Hockey-crazed New Hampshire loved it and gave Carter a 49 to 38 percent victory over Kennedy. However, the dangerous rise in the Consumer Price Index had pretty well set inflation at the top of the political agenda for the rest of the year.

New Hampshire was a great embarrassment to Kennedy. After he lost in a New England state, in his own back yard, his capacity to win at all was seriously questioned. And what he had feared now happened: He began to receive strong suggestions that he withdraw from the race.

Although Theodore H. White suggests that Kennedy had been thinking about a way to withdraw[83] (and although the Kennedy family appeared ready to support him in his decision), it really was unlikely that the senator would seriously consider dropping out of the contest. For one thing, doing so would be tantamount to saying that he was beaten — a hard thing for a Kennedy to say. Also, in making his challenge in 1980, Kennedy was laying on the line a legend and a legacy for which he felt responsible.[84]

ILLINOIS. Both Carter and Kennedy hoped that Illinois would be the breakaway state. It was clearly a crucial state for Carter. Since 1920, in seventeen presidential elections, it had voted with the winner sixteen times. Its only miss was in 1976 when it preferred Ford over Carter.[85] It was also vital to Carter that he beat Kennedy in the first big battle in a big state. However, he wasn't given much hope.[86] Illinois, heavily ethnic and Catholic in population, an urban Midwestern industrial and agricultural state with considerable unemployment, was just the kind of state where Kennedy was expected to do well. Also the Massachusetts senator had the endorsement of Chicago mayor Jane M. Byrne (who had promised to endorse Carter but changed her mind) in time to beat out the Cook County Central Committee which had also planned to endorse him. Carter, who had been warned that Mrs. Byrne was highly unpredictable and that it was very likely that if she endorsed someone it would be Kennedy, shrugged it off: "Anybody who does business that way must have a hell of a lot of enemies. If we can get everyone in Chicago who doesn't like Jane Byrne to vote for me, we can win."[87]

Carter humiliated Kennedy by a thumping 780,787 to 359,875 popular votes and captured the Illinois delegation by the almost unbelievable margin of 165 to 14 (thus embarrassing Mayor Byrne in her own city). The following day the New York Times stated that "Kennedy's chances are all but eliminated" and the Washington Post judged that Carter had "clinched the nomination." With his victory in Illinois, Carter had accumulated almost a quarter of the votes needed for nomination. He had what appeared to be a lead that Kennedy under no conceivable set of circumstances would overtake before the convention.[88]

After the Illinois primary, Kennedy's campaign, now in severe financial difficulty, turned rough. The president's budget, the senator charged, was "harsh" and "insensitive" toward the poor, the sick, the cities, and above all, the unemployed. However, when Kennedy's campaign polls indicated that the public did not react well to personal attacks on President Carter, who people generally believed was a decent man who was trying hard, Kennedy was forced to moderate his attacks.

NEW YORK. Carter targeted New York as the place to knock Kennedy out of the race. For Kennedy, in turn, New York was a "must win" situation. If he lost there, he would have little rationale left to continue his challenge to Carter.[89] But Kennedy ended up taking 59 percent of the popular vote to Carter's 41 percent—a major setback for an incumbent president on a winning streak. (Ironically, as a result of the Democratic Party's proportional allocation of delegates, Carter won nearly half of New York's national convention delegates.) The *New York Times* was inspired to proclaim the challenger was "back in the race."

In New York the Kennedy cause was greatly helped by the bad economic news. In the ten days before the primary election the stock market had fallen from 811 to 765 on the Dow Jones Average, largely because of the Federal Reserve Board's new credit rules which were clamping off credit-card buying. With Easter coming and sales down, the financial and business community was raising more and more questions about the Carter administration's ability to ward off a recession.

Kennedy was also helped by the overwhelming support of Jewish voters in New York City who were upset by a vote of the United States in the United Nations on March 1. In that vote, the United Nations Security Council unanimously condemned Israel and ordered the dismantling of civilian Israeli settlements in occupied Arab territories including Jerusalem. Even though the United States had reversed its vote on the resolution, with President Carter explaining that the United States vote in the Security Council was an error—the result of "a failure to communicate" between the president and Secretary of State Vance—the flap hadn't cooled off, and the mood in New York's large Jewish community was very hostile. Many people concluded that Vance had been selected to take the fall for the president, which only worsened the embarrassment for Carter. After the New York primary the consensus among the observers was that the contest was not won by Kennedy, it was lost by Carter—a protest vote to send the president a message. "We're back to the 'incompetence problem,'" said a White House aide.[90]

The polls also revealed that the president was losing his Iranian advantage. The *New York Times*/CBS News Poll reported that approval of his handling of the hostage crisis had declined from a high of 77 percent in December 1979 to 49 percent by the time of the New York balloting.

WISCONSIN. After he lost the New York and Connecticut contests, Carter faced a showdown with Kennedy in the April 1 Wisconsin primary. On the day before the primary the president set a deadline for the transfer of the hostages being held in Iran. The next day at 7:00 A.M., just as voting was starting, Carter dramatically invited reporters and television cameras into the Oval Office, where he announced that there had been "a positive development" in the negotiations for the release of the hostages.

Carter won the Wisconsin primary, no doubt partly as a result of the "Tuesday happening."[91] The voting on primary day brought in Carter with 56 percent of the vote, Kennedy with 30 percent, and Brown with 12 percent. Carter's 7,000-vote "come-from-behind" victory was proclaimed a miracle and was the day's top news story.

The progress Carter promised in resolving the hostage crisis never materialized. The announcement did, however, add to the growing public cynicism regarding Carter's credibility. Now he appeared to be manipulating the hostage crisis for personal political gain (he had never before held an early morning press conference). Shortly afterward polls for the first time registered greater disapproval than approval of Carter's handling of the hostage problem.[92]

The anti–Carter cynicism virtually eliminated the "character issue" which had been so available for use by Carter against Kennedy (Carter's people had consistently insinuated that Kennedy was not a "moral man" by describing Carter as a faithful husband and father, home loving, etc.).[93] In future, it meant that the president's performance in office, not his personality, would be the issue. Fortunately for Kennedy, his character as an issue continued to recede throughout the rest of the campaign. Unfortunately for him, it came too late to change the outcome of the primaries. Almost without notice, however, Kennedy's candidacy changed; instead of a viable campaigner for the nomination, he became the leader of a protest movement against the president.

JERRY BROWN'S CAMPAIGN. The day after the Wisconsin primary, Jerry Brown said goodbye to his 1980 White House ambitions: "It is obvious that the voters have spoken and have given their verdict on my 1980 campaign. . . ." Brown's campaign had never gotten off the ground. After netting 14 percent of the vote in the February 10 Maine caucuses—his best showing—Brown (whom the press, who were really more concerned with style than substance, had dubbed variously "Governor Moonbeam," "Governor Beige," "Governor Mork") won less than 10 percent of the votes in the New Hampshire (February 26) and Massachusetts (March 4) primaries. By failing to obtain at least 10 percent of the vote in two consecutive primaries he became disqualified for federal matching funds, and when he ran a poor third in Wisconsin he left the race and just disappeared (literally, into the wilds of Africa with Linda Ronstadt). Before he withdrew, Brown had spent $3 million, much of it raised through rock concerts featuring Ronstadt. However, he managed to garner only a single delegate. After Brown's withdrawal, the 1980 Democratic primary contest was quickly trimmed down to two candidates, Carter and Kennedy.

The Iran Crisis (Continued)

By April 1980 the mood in Washington over the holding of the hostages had changed from patience to active hostility. On April 7 Carter announced that he was banning all exports to Iran except for food and medicine and that he was severing diplomatic relations with Iran. Economic sanctions were imposed, and travel by Americans to Iran was forbidden. United States allies were urged to take the same measures (after much debate, most imposed less stringent sanctions than Washington had sought), and the Iranians were warned through the press that if the hostages were not freed by the middle of May, a naval blockade was likely. When Carter began openly to suggest that military steps might be taken to free the hostages if nothing else worked, both Democrats and Republicans on the Senate Foreign Relations Committee sent him a letter, dated April 24, pointing out that the Senate War Powers Resolution of 1973 required any president to consult with Congress before taking military action.

OPERATION BLUE LIGHT. Nevertheless, on the night of April 24, 1980, just after he had narrowly lost the Pennsylvania primary, the president gave the go-ahead for a military rescue mission (code-named Operation Blue Light). A successful rescue mission, the president concluded, would prove to the columnists and his political opponents that he was not an indecisive chief executive who was afraid to act. Also, it would bolster a world community that was increasingly skeptical about American power and would right the great wrong done to the United States and its citizens.[94] After multiple equipment failures, however, the mission was aborted in the Iranian desert — an unmitigated disaster. Eight commandos were killed when a C-130 transport plane and a helicopter collided while preparing for takeoff for the return trip. In response to the incident, Iran scattered the hostages to different locations, making further rescue attempts impossible. The failure of the rescue mission enveloped the president in a storm of criticism over United States military preparedness and over his unilateral decision to proceed with the operation.[95]

Within days of the failed effort to rescue the hostages by military means, President Carter abandoned his Rose Garden strategy and returned to the campaign trail. The situation was "manageable," he announced, and he was coming out of the White House. Although he had appeared to be obsessed with the hostages before the rescue mission failed, in the remaining primaries he de-emphasized the crisis. Surprisingly, no tough questions were raised by the media about Blue Light and whether Carter had given up on the hostages. There wasn't much that Kennedy could say about it without appearing ghoulish. Meanwhile, the death of the shah of Iran in a hospital outside Cairo on July 27 eliminated the possibility of his being returned to Iran and, everyone hoped, removed one major obstacle to a settlement.

In a matter of days Carter suffered a serious loss to his official family when Cyrus Vance resigned as secretary of state as a result of the rescue operation (he had opposed it from the beginning). Vance was replaced the following day by Edmund Muskie of Maine.[96]

SUPER TUESDAY. By June, Carter was far ahead in the delegate count, but more than a third of the number of delegates needed for the nomination remained to be chosen. The Kennedy people knew that it was impossible to catch up mathematically (they would have to win more than 60 percent of the delegates remaining to be chosen), but they—and some others—argued that there was a difference between the "arithmetic" and the "psychology." If Kennedy started beating Carter regularly, a mood could develop in the Democratic Party to take the nomination away from Carter.

At this point, Kennedy promised to concede the nomination if Carter agreed to debate him before the final primary day—so-called "Super Tuesday," June 3—and if the president won the majority of votes in the eight primaries to be held that day. It was, in reality, a no-lose proposition for Kennedy, and both he and Carter knew it. Carter also knew that whatever happened on June 3, the Democratic Party's system of proportional representation would provide him with enough pledged delegates to assure his nomination. Carter, as was to be expected, did not accept (which was probably a mistake).

In the end, Kennedy, in a blazing windup, captured five of the eight primaries, with a 200,000-vote edge in the overall popular vote, ominously underscoring Carter's weakness in such crucial states as California and New Jersey. Elated, Kennedy announced that he would pursue the nomination right into the convention. "Today Democrats from coast to coast were unwilling to concede the nomination to Jimmy Carter. We are determined to move on to victory at the convention and in the election next November."[97]

It was not good news for a president who was already deeply concerned about the growing cost of Kennedy's campaign, not only to himself, but also to the Democratic Party in terms of lost opportunities to raise money and to prepare for the general election.

The Republican Convention

The Republican Party's thirty-second national convention opened on July 14, 1980, in Detroit, Michigan—possibly, on that date, the most un-Republican city in the United States. Heavily black, largely blue-collar, Detroit had an unemployment rate of 18.4 percent—one of the nation's highest. As the delegates met inside the Joe Louis Arena, picketers marched outside, carrying placards pleading for jobs and protection from Japanese automobile imports. Automobiles rolled through the streets bearing bumper stickers: "Unemployment—Made in Japan." Inside the convention hall the Reagan convention leaders were conspicuous in red and yellow golf caps (which the Ford forces had worn four years before). The most prominent name missing from the proceedings was that of Richard M. Nixon.

Former president Ford delivered a rousing speech on the opening night of the convention in which he denounced the Democrats in general and Jimmy Carter, and his "trust me" administration, in particular. Many of the delegates concluded that Ford was sending a message that he would be open to a draft for nomination as president or possibly vice president. "Elder statesmen are supposed to sit quietly and smile wisely from the sidelines," Ford said. "I've never been much for sitting. I've never spent much time on the sidelines. Betty tells me that this country means too much to me to comfortably park on the bench. So, when this convention fields the team for Governor Reagan, count me in."[98]

The convention erupted with joy at this signal that the simmering Ford-Reagan feud might at last be at an end. The delegates were well aware that Ford did not think much of Reagan. In his autobiography Ford said that he found Reagan "thin"—prone to offering simplistic solutions to hideously complex problems. Also, Ford still resented the fact that Reagan had not exerted himself on Ford's behalf in the 1976 election. Ford also knew that Reagan needed him to give legitimacy among moderates. However, Ford's far greater distaste for Jimmy Carter had led him to support the former California governor.

Reagan, at least, took Ford's remarks as a sign that the door was open to the idea of Ford taking second place on the ticket. Clearly, on its face, a Reagan-Ford pairing would be a potent ticket. Together they could dominate the right and center of the political spectrum, plus carry the two key states of California and Michigan. However, when the two men met privately the next afternoon and Reagan urged Ford to reconsider his earlier rejection of the vice-presidential nomination, Ford said he didn't think he could do it. He could be of more help to Reagan, he said, off the ticket. Even so, Reagan came away from the meeting thinking he might be able to persuade Ford to change his mind.

THE REPUBLICAN PLATFORM. The Republicans' 1980 platform, embodying the "New Beginning" pledged by Ronald Reagan, was a blueprint for victory in November rather than a definitive statement of party views.[99] Four years before, platform deliberations had been marked by discord between the Ford backers and the Reagan faction. This time around, the party's moderate and conservative wings agreed to submerge their differences in order to appear united, to broaden the party's appeal, and to smooth the way to the White House for their nominee. There were calls for the enactment of the Kemp-Roth tax bill that would reduce personal income taxes by 30 percent over a three-year period—the first time supply-side economics had been included in a Republican platform. Also included were promises of less government regulation, better enforcement of civil rights laws, help for American workers whose jobs were threatened by imports, and aid for the cities. Finally, the platform's foreign policy provisions marked a departure from policies supported by Nixon and Ford by rejecting detente and calling for a much harder line in United States relations with the Soviet Union. In advocating a policy of "peace through strength" it urged increased defense expenditures, opposition to Soviet expansionism, and new guidelines for providing foreign aid.

Since Reagan opposed ratification of the Equal Rights Amendment, the Republican platform, for the first time in forty years, did not endorse it. On the abortion issue, the Republicans took a much stronger position than in prior platforms, supporting a constitutional amendment that would outlaw abortion.[100]

THE NOMINATION OF REAGAN. As expected, the nomination of Reagan was strictly routine. His name was placed in nomination by a close friend, Senator Paul Laxalt of Nevada. Then followed a tumultuous demonstration—it was a time of celebration for Reagan's supporters, many of whom had waited more than a dozen years for this moment—and when Montana's twenty votes put Reagan over the magic 998 he required, the place went crazy. The delegates on the floor and the spectators in the galleries jumped on their chairs, blew horns, shouted themselves hoarse drowning out the brass band, and waved banners reading, "Shell That Peanut," "Ron Turns Us On," "Elephants Eat Peanuts," "Life, Liberty, And The Pursuit Of Reagan." Meanwhile, as the band played "It's a Grand Old Flag," "Anchors Aweigh," "California Here I Come," the Marine Hymn, and "God Bless America," thousands of red, white, and blue balloons showered down from the roof of the arena.

THE SELECTION OF GEORGE BUSH AS VICE PRESIDENT. As it turned out, the choosing of the vice-presidential nominee provided the only suspense at the convention. In the pre-convention jockeying the delegates seemed to be moving toward the selection of either George Bush or Howard Baker to be Reagan's running mate.[101] Then Baker closed the door on his selection. He had started out by running for president but had gotten nowhere, and he did not want to go through that again. The Reagan insiders then turned their attention to George Bush as the running mate most likely to bring unity to the party. However, neither Reagan nor his wife, Nancy, was much impressed with Bush. Their dislike for the Texan seemed to date back to the debates at Nashua, New Hampshire. Reagan could not understand Bush just sitting there in his chair and not speaking to Reagan or the other candidates who filed onto the stage. Reagan apparently concluded that the incident confirmed that Bush was some kind of a "wimp."

Meanwhile, groups described as "friends of Ronald Reagan"[102] and "friends of Gerald Ford"[103] met to discuss the possibility of forging a Reagan-Ford ticket.

On July 15, Reagan and Ford met in person to discuss Ford's joining the ticket. Although no formal offer was made, Reagan encouraged Ford to think it over. The pair met again the following morning, but nothing was resolved. Then, on the evening of July 16, while being interviewed on nationwide television by CBS News anchorman Walter Cronkite, Ford was asked how he would respond to a draft from the convention floor. He responded, "I would not go to Washington and be a figurehead Vice President. If I go to Washington I have to be there in the belief that I would play a meaningful role."[104] After the interview, rumors spread like wildfire throughout the convention hall and nationwide that Ford had changed his mind again, and was now willing to be the vice-presidential nominee. The delegates were ecstatic over the possibility of what appeared to be a dream ticket.

However, the dream never materialized. Reportedly, negotiations broke down after Ford demanded assurances that the power of the vice president (an office John Nance Garner, FDR's Vice President, said was not worth a "bucket of warm spit"[105]) be raised almost to the level of co-president—including responsibility for agencies such as the Office of Management and Budget, the National Security Council, the domestic policy staff, and the Council of Economic Advisers.

Unwilling to go so far,[106] Reagan turned away from Ford and settled on Bush, despite his talk of "voodoo economics." Although Bush was opposed by the party's most conservative faction (including Senator Jesse Helms, who threatened to place his own name in nomination to forestall Bush's selection) he had considerable support from those in the party who thought that Bush's background would balance the ticket geographically and that his extensive government service would overcome criticism that Reagan did not have any Washington experience. Also, Bush's presence on the ticket would help Reagan to reach outside the right wing of the Republican Party and would broaden his appeal in November.[107]

To announce his selection, and to quell the rumors, a hoarse and tired Reagan made an unprecedented post-midnight appearance before the convention. He and Ford, he said, had come to the conclusion that Ford could "be of more value as the former president campaigning his heart out, which he has pledged to do, and not as a member of the ticket." He then said he was recommending that the convention nominate George Bush as his running mate. Bush was happy to accept; he told Reagan he would enthusiastically support him and the platform (although Bush had earlier opposed several of the more controversial planks) and pledged to "work, work, work" for a Republican victory. On an anticlimactic roll call Bush was nominated by 1,832 votes. His nomination was not unanimous, however. One hundred and nineteen die-hard conservatives refused to go along with their presidential candidate and gave Senator Helms of North Carolina fifty-four delegate votes, Congressman Jack Kemp of New York forty-two votes, and Congressman Philip Crane of Illinois twenty-three votes, even though none of these men had been nominated for vice president.

George Bush delivered a short acceptance speech following his nomination. The band, attempting to touch all of Bush's far-flung bases, then struck up "The Eyes of Texas" and "Boola Boola" (which many delegates did not recognize as the drinking song of Yale, Bush's alma mater).[108] When it was all over David Broder concluded that the vice president incident was a "fiasco" and that Reagan "did enough damage himself to make Mr. Carter seem smart to have left Mr. Reagan onstage alone."[109]

REAGAN'S ACCEPTANCE SPEECH. On Thursday, the last night of the convention, Reagan delivered an acceptance speech designed to echo the themes of the platform. His speech had been preceded by a film which emphasized his roots in the heartland of America, his union membership and his administrative ability. "He believes in the boundless opportunities of the American Idea," the announcer assured the hearers.

"My first thrill tonight," Reagan admitted as he began his acceptance address, "was to find myself, for the first time in a long time, in a movie in prime time." He went on to promise to "bring our government back under control and make it acceptable to the people." The old virtues of "family, work, neighborhood, peace and freedom," he said, would be coupled with the new theme of economy in government, to be the basis of a "new consensus" in which traditional Democrats would join with Independents and Republicans to replace "the mediocre leadership" of Jimmy Carter with a president who would simultaneously balance the budget and reduce taxes, and who would build up United States military capability while pursuing an objective of "lasting world peace." He called for "a new beginning," and promised "to restore to the federal government the capacity to do the people's work without dominating their lives. .... The time is *now*, my fellow Americans, to recapture our destiny, to take it into our own hands." Observers said that the speech touched the right political bases.[110]

When Reagan finished the prepared text of his acceptance speech, he added a dramatic touch: "I have thought of something that is not part of my speech and I am worried over whether I should do it." Then, with voice quavering, he asked the delegates to join his "crusade" to "recapture our destiny" with a moment of silent prayer. He bowed his head. Then, after fifteen spellbinding seconds, he lifted it and said emotionally, "God bless America." *Washington Post* reporter Tom Shales commented, "He never made a movie with a better ending than that."[111]

Ford and Reagan made a clear gesture of mutual respect and good-will, and the Republican Party emerged from the convention more unified than it had been in years. As the Republicans happily left Detroit, they could smell the sweet scent of victory on the breeze.[112]

The Democratic Convention

When the Democratic National Convention opened on August 11, 1980, in New York City's Madison Square Garden,[113] President Carter could count 1,981.1 delegates pledged to him—315 more than he needed for the nomination. Senator Kennedy had 1,225.8 delegates. There were 122.1 uncommitted delegates and two for other candidates. Despite (or because of) the party reforms, it was perhaps the most unrepresentative convention in modern Democratic Party history.[114]

Special interests were heavily over-represented. The National Education Association, which in 1976 had given its support to Carter in exchange for a pledge to work hard for the establishment of a Department of Education, claimed 302 delegates—more than any state except California. As we have seen, Carter made good on his promise to the teachers to create a Department of Education. Now, the NEA delegates were present to insure that the party did not nominate someone who would dismantle the new department. Also, because of the new Democratic Party reform rules which virtually eliminated public or party officials as delegates, only eight senators and thirty-seven representatives ended up as delegates. Half of the delegates, as stipulated by the new rules, were women. Blacks, the largest minority group at the convention, claimed between 470 and 480 delegates.[115] Back in Washington after the convention, the president sounded the warning: "Our party can't survive the way it's going if we don't figure out some way to nominate a convention that also represents the mainstream of life in this country."[116]

THE FIGHT FOR RULE F(3)C. Kennedy had only a remote chance to secure the nomination. To do so he would have to persuade the convention to overturn a dreary clause called party rule F(3)c, rammed through a committee packed by Carter forces in 1978, that required all delegates to vote on the first ballot for the candidate for whom they were publicly pledged at the time they were chosen to attend the convention. Then he would have to convince more than 400 additional delegates to come over to his side. Regardless of the odds against him, Kennedy refused to give up. He and his supporters were determined to open up the convention so that delegates "could vote their conscience" even though it almost certainly would disrupt party unity. The Kennedy forces were convinced that Kennedy was the only Democrat who could beat Ronald Reagan (as the convention opened, Reagan was leading Carter in the polls by eleven percentage points), and they were willing to go to great lengths to get their candidate nominated. Publicly, Kennedy justified his call for an open convention on the grounds that circumstances had changed substantially in the months since the primaries had been held. (Many delegates had been selected more than a year before.)

Although many of those calling for an open convention were Kennedy supporters or tied closely to other Kennedy constituencies — big city mayors, for example — they also claimed powerful support from quarters that had no special ties to Kennedy.[117] Many Democratic members of Congress were afraid that Carter was unelectable and that if he were renominated their own chances for reelection would be jeopardized.[118] However, many also feared that Kennedy was unacceptable to too great a portion of the party and were pushing Vice President Mondale, Secretary of State Edmund Muskie, or Senator Henry Jackson of Washington State.[119]

Edward Bennet Williams — a Washington attorney, an uncommitted delegate, and a moving force in the effort to unseat the president — described the binding delegate rule as a change in party tradition: "For the first time in 150 years, delegates . . . are being asked to deliver their final freedom of choice, and to vote themselves into bondage to a candidate." He pointed out that "nineteen million Democrats never voted for Rule F(3)c. They voted instead for men and women of conscience and character."[120] Making a direct appeal to Carter supporters, Williams urged: "If your man is President Carter, vote for him in freedom. Vote for him because you want to, but not because you have to."[121]

The case for the binding rule was presented by Connecticut senator Abraham Ribicoff. The issue, he said, "is one of fairness. . . . Nineteen million Americans voted in fifty-five Democratic primaries and caucuses. They went to the polls expecting their votes to mean something. . . . It isn't fair to change the rules now." Dianne Feinstein, the mayor of San

Francisco, seconded the fairness theme: "We don't change the rules after the game has been played." Only when it was apparent that Carter was winning, claimed Atlanta mayor Maynard Jackson, did the Kennedy camp want to change the rules to allow a "fifth ball, a fourth out, or a tenth inning."[122]

As expected, the delegates supported the loyalty rule, although the margin of victory was higher than expected — 1937 to 1390. The open convention forces picked up only about fifty Carter votes. Passage of the rule assured Carter's renomination. An hour later Kennedy, his disappointment clearly showing, formally withdrew from the contest — which had been hopeless from the beginning — by announcing on television that his name would not be placed in nomination. "I'm a realist," he said, "and I know what this result means." But he added that the efforts for Democratic principles must and would continue.

THE PLATFORM BATTLE. The Carter people had hoped they had effectively ended the contest with Kennedy with the solid victory in the rules fight and with Kennedy's withdrawal from the race. They wanted to get on with putting the Democratic Party back together again. But it was not to be. When the platform debate began the next day, the senator's forces persisted in their efforts to mold the party platform by introducing a large number of "minority reports" which reflected the distinct differences between Carter and Kennedy (and which, taken together, represented a repudiation of the president's economic policy: a plank that called for wage and price controls, which the president had always opposed; a $12 billion "stimulus" package, which the president considered excessive; and another plank that gave fighting unemployment priority over the other components of the president's economic game plan).[123]

KENNEDY'S SPEECH. On Tuesday night, August 12, Kennedy electrified the delegates with a rousing New Deal, New Frontier–style speech in which he eloquently articulated his case against Carter. "I have come here tonight not to argue as a candidate but to affirm a cause. . . . I speak out of the deep sense of urgency about the anguish and anxiety I have seen across America. . . ." He warned the delegates, "We cannot let the great purposes of the Democratic Party become the bygone passages of history." The Democratic Party, he charged, "must sail against the wind" of social and economic conservatism. In a dramatic finale he reminded his followers: "For me, a few hours ago, this campaign came to an end. But for all those whose cares have been our concern, the work goes on, the cause endures, the hope still lives, and the dream shall never die."

The audience roared its approval as the teary-eyed Kennedy delegates turned Madison Square Garden into a cheering, stomping madhouse. Kennedy blue banners were hoisted everywhere as delegates jammed the aisles and shrieked, "Go, Teddy, go. Go! Go! Go!" Hamilton

Jordan recorded that it was one of the best speeches of Kennedy's life, and it triggered open the floodgates of memories (Camelot, magic rhetoric, and the shock of assassinations.)[124] Practically speaking, however, the most notable thing about the speech was that Kennedy did not use it to endorse Carter—quite the contrary.

At this point, rather than further dividing the convention, Carter yielded to the Kennedy forces in several areas of the platform, most notably on their proposal for $12 billion to create 800,000 new federal jobs for those who were most in need, as well as on railroad renewal, an expanded housing program, and several other Kennedy-backed proposals which were accepted by voice vote. However, Carter refused to yield on Kennedy's demands for wage and price controls, which Carter recognized as a capitulation rather than a compromise.

After seventeen hours of debate and roll calls that stretched over two days, the bitterly contested, 40,000-word platform was finally accepted on August 13. It was the result of so many concessions to the Kennedy forces that it won only a halfhearted endorsement from the president. It was, in reality, a moderate-to-liberal platform that provided considerable continuity with traditional Democratic positions.[125]

THE NOMINATION OF CARTER. Carter's name was placed in nomination by Florida governor Robert Graham and seconded by Coretta Scott King (widow of slain civil rights leader Martin Luther King, Jr.) and Sol Chaikin, president of the International Ladies Garment Workers Union. The demonstrations did not last very long—about ten minutes (one-third as long as the demonstration after Kennedy's platform speech).

On the first roll call, even though convention chairman Tip O'Neill read a note from Kennedy freeing his delegates to "vote their conscience," Kennedy received the votes of all but seventy-eight of the delegates originally pledged to him (even though he had not been nominated). Victory for President Carter came shortly after midnight when Texas put him over the top (as the band played "The Eyes of Texas Are Upon You"). After the Texas vote, O'Neill read a second Kennedy statement that promised support (grudgingly, it appeared to many) of Carter's candidacy. "I congratulate President Carter on his renomination," the Kennedy statement read. "I endorse the platform of the Democratic Party. I will support and work for the reelection of President Carter. It is imperative that we defeat Ronald Reagan in 1980. I urge all Democrats to join in that effort." And so, concluded Speaker O'Neill, "united we stand." Not quite.

Earlier in the evening, Vice President Walter Mondale, as expected, had been nominated to be Carter's running mate. The Minnesotan's highly partisan acceptance speech was well received. He touched on the symbols of the Democratic Party including Kennedy and Muskie. He then went after the Republicans and their nominee with great relish and talked about the "stark difference" between Reagan and Carter. He closed with his own version of what Hubert Humphrey, his mentor and patron, did to Barry Goldwater at the 1964 Democratic National Convention. He recited a litany of things that "most Americans believe" and added after each, "But not Ronald Reagan." The delegates were soon echoing his responses.

CARTER'S ACCEPTANCE SPEECH. Carter was presented to the convention delegates by a film which showed him in the Oval Office dealing with the enormous complexities of his job and generally looking presidential. "Trust experience," the message said.

In accepting the nomination, Carter led off with praise for Kennedy's tough campaign, thanked him for his concessions during the convention, and appealed (virtually pleaded) for future help: "Ted, your party needs — and I need — you, and your idealism and dedication working for us." Carter then spoke proudly of his accomplishments in office. He had made mistakes, he told the delegates, but "I am wiser tonight than I was four years ago." He had made difficult, sometimes unpopular decisions, but they had been sound for the country. He was grateful, he said, that his four years in office had been marked by peace. Carter's speech was repeatedly interrupted with applause. But the echoes of "We want Ted" followed the president as he spoke — a stark reminder that he still faced the difficult task of rallying a divided party behind the ticket he shared with Vice President Mondale. "Above all," Carter concluded, "I want us to be what the founders of our nation meant us to become — the land of freedom, the land of peace, the land of hope."

Although the president had reservations about several provisions of the platform (the party's abortion stand and the reduction of unemployment through a $12 billion jobs program) he glossed over his differences and emphasized instead his agreement with the basic principles and goals of the party.[126]

At the conclusion of Carter's acceptance speech, the delegates hoisted banners reading, "Reagan — Eat My Grits," and waved their green and white Carter-Mondale placards. Southerners stood and waved the Stars and Bars. Pro-life and pro-choice women waved their banners. The band played "Happy Days Are Here Again" over and over to keep the demonstration for Carter going long enough to give Kennedy time to get to the podium (if he planned to go there). For fifteen long, agonizing minutes, Bob Strauss, the Democratic national chairman, called Democratic celebrities (including a lot of really minor celebrities and politicians whom no one knew) onto the podium. Finally, Kennedy made a stiff and brief appearance on the platform with Carter, Mondale, and a host of Democratic officeholders. He eventually shook hands with Carter, but he did not join in the traditional victor-vanquished, locking-arms, holding-hands-aloft ceremony with the president.

Kennedy's obvious personal coolness left no doubt that he barely forgave Carter (and would find it hard to forget). What it did leave in doubt was the commitment of Kennedy and his supporters to work strenuously for Carter's reelection. To the last, most Kennedy delegates continued to chant, "We want Ted." Any semblance of Democratic Party unity appeared to be a sham. The Democrats would leave New York City with none of their 1976 euphoria.

The Reverend Martin Luther King, Sr., gave the closing prayer. The band struck up in triumphant rhythm the hymn "We Shall Overcome," the hymn of black liberation which had stirred the country for two momentous decades. The convention was finally over. On the whole it had been a disaster for Carter. In front of millions of television viewers, he had invoked the never-to-be-forgotten name of Hubert Horatio "Hornblower." His approach to Kennedy had been rebuffed. And, if that weren't ominous enough, the victory balloons failed to fall from the ceiling.[127]

The Carter Campaign

President Carter opened his fall campaign in the South, as he had in 1976, on Labor Day at an outdoor picnic in Tuscumbia, Alabama, a town in an industrial and agricultural area in the Tennessee Valley. Most of the important Southern labor and political leaders, including George Wallace, were there. After popular singer Charlie Daniels had warmed up the audience (estimated at 40,000),[128] Carter delivered a typical Labor Day speech.[129] He de-emphasized the economy, but with unemployment at more than 7 percent and with double digit inflation and interest rates, he had to say something about it. He then went on to denounce the Ku Klux Klan, about twenty of whose members were demonstrating at the rally. "These people in white sheets do not understand our region and what it's been through," he said. "They do not understand that the South and all America must move forward."[130]

CARTER'S CAMPAIGN STRATEGY. Carter entered the 1980 presidential campaign with several serious handicaps.[131] The often bitter nomination fight with Kennedy left him politically weakened and his party divided. The public, which had rallied to his cause after the seizure of the American hostages in Iran, was growing impatient as the crisis reached its tenth month without resolution.

Carter knew that, as the incumbent president, he would have to defend his record in office; he was also well aware that it would not be an easy record to defend. His challenger, on the other hand, had no such obligation (although Carter could, and did, attack Reagan's record as governor of California). Inflation was still in the double digits and in

January 1980 had reached 20 percent (a record high). Unemployment had risen to almost 8 percent nationwide and reached 20 percent in some areas. Interest rates were at their highest level since the Civil War. In the summer of 1980 Carter had received the lowest approval rating (21 percent) ever recorded for an incumbent president. He was in the league with Herbert Hoover as a highly vulnerable incumbent.[132]

Carter's campaign advisers agreed that the issue had to be Ronald Reagan. They then settled on a campaign strategy designed to accentuate personal and ideological concerns about Reagan: his lack of knowledge and energy, his insensitivity to the average person, his tendency to shoot from the hip, his very conservative ideological and issue positions. Past statements which Reagan had made against Medicare and Medicaid, unemployment benefits, the minimum wage, national health insurance and aid to New York City and Chrysler would be used to present him as a threat to the social welfare benefits of the aged, poor, and minorities. Moreover, Carter would charge Reagan with being inexperienced in national affairs. He hadn't even been a good governor, he would say.[133] Carter was to keep the attention of the voters focused on the importance and extreme sensitivity of the office of president and to emphasize the question of which individual might better be trusted with the responsibility. Above all, the election must not become a referendum on the Carter administration. Carter was to be portrayed as a president who was in the mainstream of American political beliefs, in contrast to Ronald Reagan. As president he had learned and would be a better president in a second term.

Carter's electoral college strategy was focused on the South and the northern industrial states — especially Ohio, Pennsylvania, Illinois, Michigan, New Jersey, and Wisconsin — plus Texas and Missouri. Those two regions had elected Carter in 1976 and should be able to do so again in 1980. Also, if possible, New York or California should be added.[134] Despite the sour economy, the president's advisers thought they could win Michigan, New Jersey, and Illinois, although Ohio would be tough. Because of some expected defections in the South — Texas and Florida — they also needed to win a handful of states that Ford had carried four years earlier in New England (Maine and Connecticut) and the Northwest (Oregon and Washington). Considered "safe" states for Carter were Massachusetts, Georgia, Minnesota, Maryland, West Virginia, Arkansas, Hawaii, and Rhode Island, along with the District of Columbia.[135]

In view of this, the Carter advisers decided that it was time for the president to hit the road and to campaign actively. During the primaries he had not gotten enough attention when he was doing "presidential" deeds at the White House, and he had exhausted the possibilities of the Rose Garden as a backdrop.[136]

THE "BILLYGATE" AFFAIR. Even before the campaign was well under way, embarrassing questions began to surface about the relationship of the president's brother Billy with the government of Libya and its dictator, Mohamar Khaddaffi. It had been revealed on July 14, 1980, as the Republicans were meeting in convention, that the White House and the Justice Department had been unsuccessfully urging Billy Carter to register with the Justice Department as an agent of the Libyan government. On August 3, the *New York Times* referred to the "Billy Carter Problem" as the "Political Sensation of the Election Year."

The following day, President Carter, in a report to the Senate panel investigating his brother's ties to Libya, stated that Billy had not influenced United States foreign policy and that no member of his administration had "violated any law or committed any impropriety." The same day the president went before the press and candidly answered questions concerning what was now being referred to as the "Billygate Affair." At the same time, he conveyed the essence of his relationship with Billy. "I love Billy," the president said gently, "but I cannot control him."[137] Unfortunately for Carter, the charges against his brother made it impossible for him to maintain a low profile until the convention. Inevitably the image of the president mired down again in controversy would encourage those trying to steal the nomination away from him.

As Carter feared, "Billygate" refused to go away. On October 2, 1980, it was revealed that Billy had accepted $220,000 from the Libyan government for lobbying efforts in the United States. A special Senate subcommittee investigating the report concluded that while there were no violations of law, the president was "ill-advised" to try to involve his brother in efforts to influence Iran through the Libyans, and brother Billy merited "severe criticism." When interviewed on the evening news, Billy said, "I'm not apologizing for a damn thing."[138]

Although the episode, in the long run, did the president no perceptible damage, he had been forced to use badly needed time to defuse the issue. The president emerged from the affair appearing to be a man who could not control his brother, much less the country.

The Reagan Campaign

Reagan opened his official campaign on Labor Day in Liberty Park on the New Jersey waterfront, with the Statue of Liberty providing a television backdrop. The event, which was billed as an "ethnic picnic," had attracted people from a variety of eastern European backgrounds. In a media coup, Reagan was joined on the platform by Stanislaw Walesa, the father of Lech Walesa, leader of the Polish workers' movement.

Before he spoke, Reagan turned and looked out at the harbor; then he began, "The lady standing out there in the harbor has never betrayed us once, but this administration has betrayed the working men and women of this country." He then went on to mix attacks on the Carter administration's record in office with patriotic appeals.

REAGAN'S CAMPAIGN STRATEGY. Reagan's campaign strategy was designed to reinforce an image of himself as the embodiment of the "presidential" values a majority of Americans think are important: leadership, competence, strength, and decisiveness. At the same time Carter's major weaknesses would be stressed—his mean spirit, his vacillation in foreign policy, his failed presidency, and his lack of leadership. A sharp contrast would be drawn between Carter's political promises and his performances.[139]

Reagan's electoral college strategy was to build a base that included almost all of the western states plus such Republican strongholds as Indiana and New Hampshire. Prime targets would be the southern states (especially Texas, Florida, Virginia,[140] Mississippi, and Louisiana) and the industrial heartland, specifically Michigan, Illinois, and Ohio. Other states would be added during the campaign if the polls showed them to be within the range of victory. To offset Carter's larger party base (54 percent of the electorate were Democrats or Independents leaning Democratic) and the incumbency advantage, the base of Reagan's support would be expanded to include more Independents, Anderson voters, Southern white Protestants, urban ethnics, blue collar workers in the industrial states, disaffected Democrats—union members, Catholics—and Hispanics, which would require a move to the ideological center by the Reagan campaign.[141]

REAGAN ON CARTER'S DEFENSE POLICY. As he campaigned, Reagan charged that the Carter administration had allowed United States military capabilities to become dangerously weak—so much so that American military weakness could well encourage Soviet aggression. He pointed to the Russian invasion of Afghanistan and the Iranian hostage situation to criticize the foreign policy of the Carter administration and to urge greater expenditures for defense. Reagan also called for a tougher posture against the Soviet Union, which he pictured as an unrelenting adversary and a threat to world peace.

Reagan returned repeatedly to the "unpreparedness" theme. During "Defense Week" in mid-August, Reagan, addressing the Veterans of Foreign Wars, asserted that Carter was following "policies of weakness, inconsistency, vacillation and bluff" on national defense issues while remaining "totally oblivious" to the Soviet Union's drive toward world domination. He told the veterans that the nation had neglected the Vietnam veterans, saying, "We have been shabby in our treatment of those who returned." Then he added, "It is time we recognized that ours, in truth, was a noble cause." His "noble cause" characterization of the Vietnam War provoked angry calls to talk shows and letters to editors from those who has opposed the war. Many Vietnam veterans also bitterly opposed what he had said (although many of them supported him).[142]

Two days later, in a Boston address to the American Legion, he described the United States as "second to one," and said the American people are sick and tired of leadership that tells us "why we can't contain the Russians."

REAGAN ON CARTER'S ECONOMIC POLICY. Reagan also hit hard in great detail on Carter's record on the economy. Carter and the Democratic Congress had mismanaged the United States economy, he charged, to a degree unmatched in modern history. "Thanks to the economic policies of the Democratic Party, millions of people found themselves out of work." During 1980 the inflation rate averaged about 13 percent (nearly three times that of the Ford administration). The Carter inflation, Reagan said, had turned the American dream of a good job, a home, a car or two, and a college education for their children into a nightmare.

The economy was an especially sensitive issue for Carter because in 1976 he had strongly assailed Gerald Ford for a "misery index" (combined inflation and unemployment rates) of 12 percent. Carter now faced a "misery index" of more than 20 percent, and Reagan, or more likely Ford if he campaigned for Reagan, would not hesitate to point out the irony.

INFLATION. Reagan pledged to deal with inflation by a three-year, 30 percent tax cut for individuals as well as a reduction in business taxes. A tax cut, Reagan argued, would stimulate the economy by making available to business people vast sums of money that would otherwise have been taken by the govenment. This money would then be invested in business and industry, leading to an expansion of the economy. The expanded economy would, in turn, provide new jobs and produce an increase in the amount of taxes the government collected. Thus the money lost to the government by virtue of the tax cut would be more than replaced by the new taxes produced by the expanding economy.

Although Reagan called for a drastic reduction in government spending, the one area he believed should not be cut was the military. The Soviet Union, he said, had achieved a dangerous military superiority over the United States. He called, therefore, for a huge increase in defense spending.[143]

Reagan also called for a balanced budget by 1983: "There's enough fat in the government in Washington that if it was rendered and made into soap, it would wash the world." Big government, he said, was a principal cause of the nation's economic problems. Big government spent too much, which led to fraud and mismanagement. American business, he proclaimed in a multitude of campaign speeches, would restore prosperity if only government would "get off its back." What the country needed was "the clarity of vision to see the difference between what is essential and what is merely desirable. and then the courage to bring our government back under control."

Predictably Carter diagreed. In a speech to the National Press Club on October 4, 1980, the president charged that Reagan's plan to drastically cut taxes and sharply increase the defense budget would result in a $140 billion budget deficit by 1983, leaving only a bloated defense budget and a few uncuttable programs like Social Security. In an interview with Barbara Walters the next day, Reagan responded, saying that every economist who had studied his program believed the federal government would have a budget surplus by 1983 that would provide for additional tax cuts. As for Carter's charge that a Reagan presidency would be bad for the country, Reagan flashed a smile, shook his head sadly, and said: "Well, he's kind of an authority on people who are not good Presidents."[144]

REAGAN'S GAFFES. Reagan ran into difficulties from the beginning with off-the-cuff remarks which often provoked negative reactions from the press. For example, in mid–August Reagan stirred anger in Mainland China and concern among the electorate at home. On August 16 he sent running mate George Bush on a fence-mending mission to the People's Republic of China to show he sought peace with all the world. However, just after Bush left for China, Reagan proclaimed himself in favor of reestablishing "official" diplomatic relations with Taiwan (as we have seen, the breaking of official ties with Taiwan had been a precondition for the establishment of diplomatic relations between Washington and Beijing in the treaty negotiated by Carter and would be prohibited by the Taiwan Relations Act of 1979).

After Reagan's announcement, Bush's mission received an especially frosty Chinese reception. The Chinese complained that Reagan was recreating the "two-China" policy, which was unacceptable to the Chinese government. Although he was not very happy about it, Reagan spent much of the next week explaining and apologizing and coming across as inept and inexperienced.

Reagan was still reeling from the blows dealt him on the China issue when he traveled on August 22 to the Reunion Arena in Dallas, Texas, to address a rally of 14,000 fundamentalist Christian business and religious leaders sponsored by the Religious Roundtable. Reagan's political advisers urged him to bypass the meeting. However, Reagan was well aware that the conservative preachers and parishioners of the Moral Majority were upset about his selection of George Bush as his running mate, and he wanted to reassure them and make himself certain of their support.

His remarks were well received as he deplored all the right things:

schools "that educate without ethics"; public policies that have produced "mounting evidence in crime rates, drug abuse, child abuse and human suffering"; "morally neutral government" which gave its resources to "value-free" institutions but denied them to citizens "professing religious beliefs"; and Internal Revenue Service enforcement of affirmative action orders against private (mainly religious) schools. In closing he swore to the group that he would base his policies "on the primacy of parental rights and responsibility," thereby opposing government-financed abortion. Finally, he pledged to "keep big government out of the school and the neighborhood and, above all, the home" and return to that "older American vision."[145]

In the question period which followed, a reporter for a religious publication asked Reagan his views about the theory of evolution. He acknowledged that he had a "great many questions" about the theory.[146] It might be a good idea, he added, if the schools taught the Creationist theory as well. Reagan's answer produced gasps of despair from Republican politicians. The media representatives, however, loved it. For a few days the issue of "Creationism" made Reagan look like an idiot (that issue, the press pointed out repeatedly, had been settled in American politics fifty-five years ago at the Scopes "Monkey" trial in Dayton, Tennessee).[147]

In the end Reagan got away with it. The media passed on to other things—Creationism was not a controversy Reagan would have to deal with as president. In the meantime, by his Creationist statement, he had nailed down the support of the Moral Majority members for the duration of the campaign.

Perhaps Reagan's most politically damaging remark was made on the opening day of his own campaign. Speaking to a crowd at the Michigan State Fair, Reagan noticed a woman with a Carter mask. It reminded him, he said, that the president was opening his campaign the same day in Tuscumbia, Alabama. "Now I am happy to be here while he is opening his campaign down there in that city that gave birth to and is the parent body of the Ku Klux Klan," Reagan said.

The next day Carter seized on this remark. "Anybody who resorts to slurs and innuendos against a whole region of the country based on a false statement and a false premise isn't doing the South or our nation a good service."[148] When seven angry southern Democratic governors pointed out to Reagan that Tuscumbia was not the birthplace of the Klan, he concluded that it was time to apologize to the state of Alabama and the community of Tuscumbia. After it was polished by the media for several days, the incident added considerable luster to Reagan's growing shoot-from-the-lip image.[149]

Then on October 9, 1980, Reagan made another startling announcement to the effect that air pollution was under control and that Mount St. Helen's volcanic eruptions and the country's forests were responsible for a significant amount of air pollution, a claim which was quickly disputed by the Environmental Protection Agency.

Two days later, Reagan was scheduled to address a triumphant homecoming rally in Burbank. The smog was so heavy that his plane, which was supposed to land at the Burbank airport, had to be diverted to Los Angeles International Airport. The next day at Claremont College he was greeted by demonstrators chanting, "Smog, smog," and someone had affixed a poster to a nearby tree: "Chop me down before I kill again." A Reagan aide later remarked that the only bright spot about all the blunders was that the press had to make some choices about which ones to report.

However, Reagan did turn one slip to his advantage. Early in the 1980 campaign he had publicly declared that the country was not in a depression, as President Carter had said, but in a recession. When the press took issue with his definition he replied: "If the President wants a definition, I'll give him one. A recession is when your neighbor loses his job. A depression is when you lose yours. And a recovery will be when Jimmy Carter loses his."[150]

Reagan committed his share of goofs, no doubt about it. But the criticism that followed a Reagan blunder never seemed to put a dent in his popularity. Through all the gaffes, the public maintained a positive attitude about him, due in part, no doubt, to his personality — his optimism and decisiveness, his good cheer and obvious enjoyment of campaigning.

THE STEALTH DISCLOSURE. On September 4, in Jacksonville, Florida, to get the focus off the mistakes he had made, Reagan accused the Defense Department of "a serious breach of national security," charging that it had deliberately leaked secret details of a radar-resistant warplane, the Stealth, in order to benefit President Carter politically.[151] He also charged that the administration's decision to release further data on the new plane was yet another attempt to appear "tough" on defense issues (at the cost of providing important intelligence information to the Soviet Union) and said it was designed to offset Carter's 1977 cancellation of the B-1 bomber. The action, he said, was a "cynical abuse of power and a clear abuse of the public trust."

Carter replied on September 9 that the public admission was made only after news of the project's existence had become widely known. Although he assured his hearers that no technological details were publicized, many Democrats agreed with Reagan, which helped restore Reagan's confidence.

THE BALTIMORE DEBATE. On September 21, in Baltimore, the first presidential debate was scheduled to occur.[152] When the sponsoring

League of Women Voters decided to invite John Anderson because the national polls at the time showed the Illinois Independent with support of 15 percent or more,[153] the Reagan camp accepted, and so, of course, did Anderson. However, Carter declined to participate. It would be unfair for him, he said, to debate two Republicans. Most likely, Carter feared that Anderson was already hurting him and that appearing on the same stage with the president would help the Independent to cut deeper into Carter's support. Also, there was a strong probability that Reagan and Anderson would gang up on him for an hour. In any case, Carter had weathered well his refusal to debate Kennedy in the primaries, and there would undoubtedly be other opportunities later to debate Reagan head-to-head.

Reagan made no objection to Anderson's presence. Although he and Anderson disagreed sharply on a whole range of issues—energy policy, the MX missile, taxes, and abortion among them—Reagan had no stake in trying to cut down Anderson. On the contrary, it was to his advantage to bolster the Independent as a viable force in the campaign. Anderson's first priority was establishing his own credentials as a candidate now that he had finally achieved a national forum.[154] In the end they united to attack Carter.

In different ways, both Reagan and Anderson could claim to be the "winner" later. The ABC/Harris Poll reported that 36 percent of the viewers thought Anderson had performed better, 30 percent favored Reagan, and 17 percent thought they were equally effective.[155] But a subsequent ABC News/Harris Survey indicated that a majority of the respondents thought that the only loser was Carter.[156]

THE WAR-PEACE ISSUE. Early in the campaign, Carter raised the war-peace issue. Carter's own campaign advertising focused on his image as a man of peace by picturing him with Begin and Sadat at the Camp David summit. Carter had warned that Reagan's election would mean "the risk of an uncontrollable, unaffordable, and unwinnable nuclear arms race" and an "alarming, even perilous destiny."[157] The Oval Office, the president cautioned, was not a place for shooting from the hip. He warned that Reagan would set off a "massive nuclear arms race" that could lead to war with the Soviet Union. The presidential choice, Carter said, provided the "sharpest difference" between the major party contenders of any choice in his lifetime.

THE RACISM ISSUE. In mid–September, while speaking to an all-black audience at Martin Luther King, Sr.'s, Ebenezer Baptist Church in Atlanta, Carter appeared to be accusing his challenger of racism. "You've seen in this campaign the stirrings of hate and the rebirth of code words like states' rights . . . relating to the South," he said. "This is a message that creates a cloud on the political horizon."[158]

In the days to follow, the Republicans jumped all over the Atlanta statement. Gerald Ford criticized it as "intemperate and totally misleading" and demeaning to the presidency. George Bush announced that he was appalled at the "ugly, mean, little remark Jimmy Carter made."

When confronted with the charge by Reagan, Carter denied that he was calling Reagan a racist, but a few days later an ad appeared in 100 newspapers aimed at blacks: "Jimmy Carter named thirty-seven black judges. He cracked down on job bias, and created one million jobs. That's why the Republicans are out to beat him." The Republicans charged that this ad was a "smear" by the Democrats.[159]

Then, at a Democratic fundraising event in Chicago on October 6, Carter warned that Reagan's election would split the nation, "black from white, Jew from Christian, North from South, rural from urban."

Reagan's response to these attacks was largely restrained. He was "saddened," he said, by the president's remarks but not "angry." "I think it is inconceivable that anyone, and particularly the President of the United States, would imply . . . that anyone, any person, in this country would want war. And that's what he has been charging and I think it is unforgivable."[160] The accusation that he had injected race hatred into the campaign was "shameful." The reaction of the press and media, however, was much harsher and uniformly critical of the president's conduct.

In time, Carter's personal attacks on Reagan undermined one of his strongest assets — his reputation for compassion and fair play — and made him look mean, nasty, and petty. Critical editorials and cartoons began to appear in the media. Curtis Wilkie, writing in the liberal *Boston Globe*, called the Carter campaign "the symbol of gracelessness under pressure."[161] Herblock, in the equally un–Republican *Washington Post*, drew a Jimmy Carter wallowing in slime with a paint brush poised to smear again.[162] Unfortunately for Carter, people began to look at him more and more as "just another politician." Some of the esteem he had won for his honesty and morality faded.

Carter defended his statements as an excess of campaign rhetoric triggered by massive frustration resulting from his low level of popularity, the intractability of the problems he was being called upon to resolve (particularly the economy and the hostage problem in Iran), and his poor standing in the polls. When the polls indicated that his personal attacks on Reagan were hurting his own standing with voters rather than his opponent's, the president relented somewhat; during an October 8 interview with ABC's Barbara Walters, he acknowledged that he had been excessively harsh on occasions, but he claimed that his rhetorical excesses were hardly more extravagant than what was emerging from the Reagan campaign. He did, however, half-promise that he would refrain from any further personal attacks on Reagan and concentrate his criticisms on his opponent's policies. "Well," said Reagan when he heard what Carter had said, "I think that would be nice if he did. . . . If he decided to straighten up and fly right, that'll be fine."[163]

John Anderson and the Politics of Differentness

John Anderson started out as the least known candidate for the Republican nomination. During the course of the campaign, however, his amalgam of conservative economics and liberal social ideals stirred more interest than many had expected. Many were attracted to him because of his obvious personal integrity and his willingness to take unpopular stands in his campaigning (which garnered him a great deal of media attention). As we have seen, he advocated gun control in New Hampshire and supported the grain embargo against the Soviet Union before an audience of Iowa farmers. Within a few weeks he had persuaded enough voters of the "Anderson difference" to finish a close second in both Vermont and New Hampshire, and some observers were giving him a chance to dethrone the front-running Ronald Reagan.

In late April, when that chance had faded, the "National Unity Campaign" was officially launched in the ballroom of the National Press Club. He would travel the adventurous road of an Independent candidate, Anderson said. "The obstacles pale when one considers that too many people in our nation are disillusioned with the prospective choices our party structures are offering."[164]

Anderson made a strong appeal to college students; educated, affluent suburbanites (who became known as the "brie-and-chablis set"); Republican liberals; and the undecided vote. He no doubt benefited from the fact that (according to the polls) neither Carter nor Reagan was a highly popular choice. On the other hand, he suffered from a widespread belief that he had no chance of winning despite the weakness of the Republican and Democratic candidates. A Gallup Poll in mid–June gave Anderson 23 percent support among voters, but he was down to 15 percent in August and sliding. The polls indicated that Anderson had considerable strength in about half a dozen states in New England (Massachusetts and Connecticut), the upper Great Lakes (Wisconsin and Michigan), and the Pacific Northwest (Oregon and Washington).[165]

In launching his Independent campaign, Anderson said that his purpose was to offer the voters an alternative to Carter and Reagan. He denied being a "spoiler," asking what could be spoiled when the other two major candidates were so wanting. He insisted that he intended to win, but he also said that if it appeared that his candidacy would lead to the election of Reagan, for whom he had contempt, he would drop out.[166]

In late August, Anderson persuaded Patrick J. Lucey, Democratic governor of Wisconsin from 1971 to 1977, to be his running mate in a "National Unity Coalition" (after feelers extended to several more prominent Democrats had failed to produce a candidate). Sixty-two year old Lucey was a veteran of more than twenty years of liberal politics. Most recently, he had served under Carter as ambassador to Mexico. However, after a bitter falling out with the president, he had resigned and joined Ted Kennedy's campaign. Anderson expected Lucey, an Irish Catholic, to contribute ethnic balance (which he did) and also to draw support from Kennedy Democrats (which he didn't—at least not as much as had been hoped).

THE NATIONAL UNITY PARTY PLATFORM. Anderson then announced his campaign platform, a series of proposals that emphasized what he called his "wallet on the right, heart on the left" political philosophy. The platform stressed revitalization of the economy, self-sacrifice, no massive new federal spending but maintenance of a range of liberal social programs.[167] Called for were tax incentives to labor and management for wage and price restraint (an idea that Carter once proposed and then gave up on); a reindustrialization program that would provide tax incentives and bonuses to rehabilitate troubled industries and increase productivity; an urban reinvestment trust fund (the funds to come from federal excise taxes on alcohol and tobacco) to encourage the rebuilding of cities; a community transportation trust fund (also from federal excise taxes) for mass transit; and, of course, the fifty-cent-a-gallon tax on gasoline which Anderson had been espousing. The platform also stressed energy conservation, defended foreign aid, and offered specific proposals for dealing with the pending deficits in Social Security finances.[168]

When Anderson won the New York Liberal Party endorsement in early September—the first time the Liberals had shunned a Democratic presidential contender—Anderson supporters began to think that New York was winnable. Anderson also thought that California was a possibility. As the campaign entered the final four weeks, the Anderson camp was encouraged by the poll findings, which showed that the Carter-Reagan race remained uncertain.

Money was a problem for Anderson and Lucey. Unlike the two major party contenders, Anderson would not get any federal funds before the election but was still limited by the $1000 contribution ceiling. Since Anderson was not assured of federal funds, he had difficulty borrowing money. Unable to secure large bank loans, he had to depend on private contributions and loans. Even so, the campaign raised almost $12 million, largely through direct mail contributions. (Anderson actually received money from more individuals than did the national Democratic Party.)

Anderson got a break on September 4 when the Federal Election

Commission ruled that his candidacy should be treated as a third-party effort: If he received at least 5 percent of the vote on election day, he would qualify for postelection federal funds. This would be anywhere from $3 million to the full $29.4 million, depending on Anderson's share of the vote. The FEC ruling meant that the campaign could borrow money using the expected postelection funds as collateral. It also meant that Anderson would have to stay in the race to pay off his debts (not a happy thought for Jimmy Carter). The Anderson-Lucey ticket secured a place on the ballot of all fifty states, despite formidable legal and political hurdles.[169]

The Carter-Reagan Debate

The long-awaited, much ballyhooed, head-to-head debate between President Carter and Ronald Reagan almost did not take place because of objections of one kind or another by both sides; finally, though, it was held on October 28 (exactly one week before election day) in Cleveland.[170] Sponsored by the League of Women Voters, the nationally televised debate was being discussed in the papers as a "sudden death" event. Because of the closeness of the race — the polls released on October 27 indicated a virtual dead heat — campaign strategists on both sides agreed that the debate could swing the vote either way.

Both candidates, determined to avoid any costly mistakes, carefully prepared for the event. (Reagan practiced by having several of his associates impersonate members of the panel who could be asking the questions, while David Stockman, a young congressman from Michigan, played the role of Carter.) Carter expected to have an edge in the debate because of his detailed knowledge of the issues and his grasp of the presidency. Carter's task, as he saw it, was to use that superior knowledge of the office of president to prevent Reagan from reaching (or passing) the "plausibility threshold" where people would seriously consider him, despite his inexperience, as an acceptable candidate for president. Reagan expected to score well because of his debating presence and his experience as an actor, which would help him to ward off Carter's attacks.

As the debate opened Carter looked tired and tense — as Hamilton Jordan put it, "like a coiled spring, ready to pounce, an overtrained boxer, too ready for the bout."[171] Reagan, on the other hand — tall, erect, and tanned — appeared to be in robust health and relaxed. Reagan obviously rattled the president when he strode across the stage just before the debate (and right afterwards, too) to shake hands. Once the debate started, both men gave standard campaign responses to wide-ranging questions from a panel of four journalists.

Responding to question number one, regarding the differences between the two candidates on how they would use military power, Reagan attacked the incumbent's fumbling performance in foreign policy and asserted that his "first priority must be world peace, and that use of force is always, and only, a last resort when everything else has failed." Carter had been out-negotiated on SALT, Reagan insisted. He proposed that the treaty be renegotiated to mandate actual arms cuts. Reagan charged Carter with increasing the danger of war by weakening the nation's defenses when he cancelled the B-1 bomber; delayed the MX missile, Trident submarine, and Cruise missile; and shut down the Minuteman production line.

As he had all through the campaign, Carter attempted to paint Reagan as "dangerous" to world peace. Reagan's desire to scrap SALT II, Carter charged, would lead to a threatening arms race.

Carter also repeatedly questioned Reagan's experience. To offset such questions, Reagan often referred to his tenure as governor of California (1967–1975), a state he claimed "would be the seventh ranking economic power in the world" if it were a nation. Carter also took the offensive on economic issues, quoting Reagan's own running mate in describing Reagan's three-year, 30 percent tax cut as "voodoo economics." Reagan denied the scheme would stimulate inflation, as Carter contended. "Why is it inflationary to let the people keep more of their money and spend it the way they like?" he asked. Reagan pointed out that the inflation rate had soared under Carter. The issue of inflation permitted Reagan to get off one of his famous one-liners: "We don't have inflation because the people are living too well; we have inflation because the government is living too well."[172]

There was one particularly memorable moment when Reagan, as part of his theme that Carter was desperately distorting his positions on nuclear arms control, Social Security, and other issues, smiled, shook his head in mock disappointment, turned to Carter and said, "There you go again." It was a superb piece of scene stealing, showing that he was in command of the situation, and the viewing audience loved it. That phrase, along with a view of the former California governor chuckling at one of the president's responses, seemed to set the tone for viewer reaction.

Neither candidate made a fatal mistake — the kind that would end not only the debate but also the campaign — but both drew some criticism. Reagan was attacked for saying that when he was a boy no one knew there was a racial problem in the United States. Carter was ridiculed for asserting that his thirteen year old daughter, Amy, had told him that the most important issue in the campaign was nuclear arms control.[173]

Reagan had the last word, and he used it to sum up what the campaign was all about. "Are you better off than you were four years ago? Is it easier for you to go and buy things in the stores than it was four years ago? Is there more or less unemployment in the country than there was four years ago? Is America as respected throughout the world as it was? Do you feel that our security is as safe, that we're as strong as we were four years ago? And if you answer all those questions 'yes,' why I think your choice is very obvious as to who you'll vote for. If you don't think that this course that we've been on for the last four years is what you would like to see us follow for the next four years, then I suggest another choice that you have. . . ." He concluded by saying that he would like to "have a crusade . . . to take the government off the backs of the great people of this country."[174]

Most press observers called the debate a draw. A CBS News Poll the day after the debate indicated that 44 percent of those surveyed thought Reagan had won, while 36 percent gave the debate to Carter. Twenty percent said it was a tie or had no opinion. Six percent said they had changed their vote choice because of the debates; these viewers went for Reagan two to one.[175] However, when the ABC News/Harris Poll showed Reagan the clear winner, Reagan's backers were overjoyed. One of Carter's aides summed it all up by saying: "I just wish we hadn't debated."[176]

Most observers also agreed that Reagan had successfully used his humor and his professional acting skills to defuse Carter's attempts to depict him as the warmonger or racist the Democrats had implied he was in the campaign. He had come across as a calm and self-assured person with a good sense of humor (in contrast to Carter, who appeared tense and colorless).

Reagan emerged from Cleveland with new confidence, which was reflected in the polls. He received endorsements from such unlikely sources as the Teamsters' Union, black mayor Charles D. Evers of Fayette, Mississippi, and the Reverend Ralph David Abernathy, former head of the Southern Christian Leadership Conference, who explained: "We don't need this doctor anymore, because we as the patients are getting sicker. We need to change doctors." Eugene McCarthy, the independent, anti-war candidate in 1968, added his support because, he said, Reagan had "run a more dignified campaign."

Carter returned to the campaign trail with an almost desperate plea to Democrats to "come home" to the party of Franklin Roosevelt, Harry Truman, and Jack Kennedy. But it was too late. Most Democrats knew that for four years Carter had disdained the Democratic Party and its organizations. He appealed directly to Anderson supporters (without much success) by citing issues on which he and Anderson agreed. Union members, one of Carter's strongest allies, had become increasingly cool to the president as layoffs had mounted in basic industries and inflation had reached an annual rate of almost 13 percent in September. Kennedy did campaign some for Carter, although he never appeared to be comfortable doing it. (Reagan made good use of tapes of Kennedy campaigning against Carter in the primaries.) Nevertheless, going into the final week of the campaign, the election was widely viewed as a toss-up. Most of the polls indicated the Americans generally were unenthusiastic about both candidates.

FINAL WEEK OF THE CAMPAIGN. In the final week Reagan, encouraged by the results of the debate, took the offensive with an attack on Carter's inability to manage the presidency and the economy, citing high taxes and prices, unemployment, inadequate defense spending, foreign policy failures, excessive government regulation, and general national demoralization. "Jimmy Carter's doing his best," Reagan mock-seriously conceded. "That's our problem," he inevitably added. As he traveled the nation, Reagan won cheers everywhere with his promises of not just one, not just two, not just three years of tax reductions, but three years plus counterinflationary tax indexing after that.[177] Gerald Ford also hit hard at Carter. He didn't care much for Reagan (whom he had once dismissed as "simplistic"), but now he told people that he and Reagan had become very compatible.

Carter did his best to cement the cracks in the crumbling Democratic coalition, which he needed to win. With liberals and women in mind, he cited his support for the Equal Rights Amendment, which Reagan opposed. For minority viewers, he stressed his record level of appointment of blacks to judgeships and executive branch posts. And he pointed to his regional ties: "I'm a Southerner."

Several events in the closing days of the campaign created problems for Carter. A Justice Department report leaked to the press on Thursday, October 30, charged that the president had not cooperated fully in the inquiry into the Libyan ties of his brother and that Billy Carter had lied under oath. Also, interest rates went up and the stock market went down. Trying to recover, the president raced across the nation, hitting twenty-six cities in fifteen states and flying more than 15,000 miles in the final week, pleading, in a raspy voice, "I need you. Help us!"

THE HOSTAGE PROBLEM. Shortly before the debate in Cleveland, signs out of Iran indicated that the release of the American hostages might be imminent. The Carter officials tried to dampen hopes that the hostages would be released before the election, in case they weren't. The Reagan people tried to diminish the credit that would accrue to Carter if they were released. Reagan responded to the news of the possible release by commenting that he "did not understand why the hostages had been held so long." When Reagan was asked by reporters to explain his comment, he replied: "I believe that this administration's foreign policy helped create the entire situation that made their kidnap possible. And I think the fact that they've been there that long is a humiliation and a disgrace to this country."[178] Asked if he had any ideas of his own for releasing the hostages, Reagan replied, "I think I've had some ideas, but they're—you don't talk about them." Carter landed on this, saying if Reagan did have any ideas he ought to offer them. Carter (somewhat illogically) accused Reagan of turning the hostage issue into "a political football."

On Sunday, November 2, two days before the election, the Iranian Parliament voted to release the hostages if the United States met four conditions: that the United States pledge not to interfere in Iran's internal affairs; that Iran's assets be unfrozen; that the shah's wealth be returned; and that all court claims against Iran be dismissed. With hope revived for a hostage release by Election Day, Carter cut short his campaign and returned to the White House to deal with the issue. However, some of the terms were so legally complicated that they required further negotiations, and the hostages were not freed. Carter attempted to keep the negotiations out of the campaign, but it was impossible. The publicity given to them worked against the president by serving to remind the voters of Carter's haplessness in the crisis.

On election eve Reagan delivered a deliberately emotional television speech. "What kind of country, what kind of legacy, will we leave to the young men and women who will live out America's third century?" he asked. He spoke of "government that has grown too large, too bureaucratic, too wasteful, too unresponsive, too uncaring about people and their problems," and he said, "I believe that we can embark on a new age of reform in this country and an era of national renewal." He found no national malaise, Reagan said. And then he asked a version of the devastating question he had asked at the close of the debate: "Are you happier today than when Mr. Carter became president?"

On that same night, the president learned he was going to lose. En route from a campaign stop in Washington State to Plains, Georgia, aboard Air Force One, press secretary Jody Powell told him that late samplings by pollster Patrick Caddell showed he had fallen irretrievably behind Ronald Reagan. The following morning the president voted in Plains. Then, with breaking voice, he addressed the crowd over the radio. "I've tried to honor my commitment"—long silence—"to you."[179]

THE 1980 OUTCOME. On November 4, by a landslide that astonished even his most optimistic aides, Ronald Reagan buried incumbent Jimmy Carter with a plurality of nearly nine million popular votes to become the nation's president-elect.[180] By carrying forty-four states, Reagan won 489 electoral votes to just forty-nine for Carter, who carried only Georgia, Hawaii, Maryland, Minnesota, Rhode Island, West Virginia, and the District of Columbia.[181] Carter failed to carry a single large industrial state. Significantly, it was the second straight election—but only the fourth in the twentieth century—in which an incumbent president was defeated for reelection.[182]

Reagan made inroads into Carter's victorious coalition of 1976 by scoring well with nearly every voting group except blacks and Hispanics. Blacks held for Carter in 1980 (80 percent) although apparently voting in reduced numbers. Carter ran only narrowly ahead of Reagan among several traditionally Democratic constituencies. Among labor union families, for instance, Carter led by only eight percentage points. Among Jewish voters, he led by only seven percentage points. Several polls also indicated that many blue-collar voters defected to Reagan. The election of 1980 was, in the words of House Speaker Tip O'Neill, a "disaster for the Democrats."

Independent candidate John Anderson won 5.7 million votes (most at Carter's expense—6.6 percent of the total vote) but did not win any states. Falling well behind were the other third-party candidates. Ed Clark (Libertarian Party) drew 921,188 votes (1.1 percent); the remaining half-million votes (0.5) were divided among seventeen other candidates.[183]

THE 1980 CONGRESSIONAL ELECTIONS. More surprising than Carter's defeat at the hands of Reagan was the outcome of the congressional elections. The Republicans won control of the Senate for the first time since 1954—something that not even the GOP had dreamed possible—with a net gain of twelve for an overall majority of fifty-three to forty-six seats; one other seat was held by Independent Senator Harry Byrd of Virginia. Such well-known Democratic liberals as George McGovern, Frank Church, Birch Bayh, John Culver, Gaylord Nelson, and Warren "Maggie" Magnuson, the senior member of the Senate, were turned out of office. Moreover, the Republicans who would gain positions of power in the Senate—the committee and subcommittee chairmanships—were for thre most part very conservative Republicans.

The Reagan landslide failed to overturn the Democratic majority in the House of Representatives, but it was reduced from 276 to 243 out of 435 seats. By and large, as in the Senate, the Democrats who lost were replaced by conservative Republicans. Although the Democrats still claimed a majority in the House of Representatives, it was clearly a conservative majority. The conservatives had been given a striking opportunity to turn the country in a new direction and make progress in solving problems that had been frustrating Democrats in recent years.

CAMPAIGN FINANCING. The 1980 presidential election was the most expensive in the nation's history, when the rise in the Consumer Price Index is figured in. It cost the people $275 million to elect a new president, more than $115 million above 1976 spending. The United States government supplied some $100.6 million—roughly one-third—of that amount.[184]

One of the great surprises of the 1980 election was the amount of money spent on the candidates by Political Action Groups (PACs) and independent committees—estimated to be at least $60 million and possibly as much as $75 million either to support or to oppose. The year 1980 saw a phenomenal growth in their numbers (up to 2,551)[185] and influence (giving three times as much money to support or oppose candidates as the parties). For the first time PAC contributions by the business community exceeded those by labor unions. In 1980, however, these independent committees benefited Reagan and other Republican candidates rather than Carter and Democrats.

The biggest among all PACs were the National Conservative Political Action Committee (NCPAC), Jesse Helms's National Congressional Club, and the Committee for the Survival of a Free Congress, a conservative multi-issue committee formed in 1974. These PACs alone spent $17 million between January 1979 and November 1980, attacking Carter and defending Reagan. The largest share of this money—$1.2 million—was spent by NCPAC to defeat six liberals whom it characterized as the "most distasteful" members of the Senate—Birch Bayh, Frank Church, Alan Cranston, John Culver, George McGovern, and, eventually, Thomas Eagleton.[186] The Moral Majority spent an additional $3 million against liberal senators, backing, among others, Dan Quayle, a thirty-three year old congressman from Indiana, who, in a surprise upset, unseated Senator Birch Bayh. As we have seen, only Cranston (who was reelected by a margin of 1.6 million votes) and Eagleston survived.

CARTER'S CONCESSION SPEECH. By 9:00 Eastern Standard Time on election night the early returns coming in and the private polls had already made clear that President Carter not only was losing his bid for reelection but was losing it badly. Forty-five minutes later, while voters in almost half the states were still going to the polls, Jimmy Carter formally conceded defeat. To a group of his supporters assembled at the Sheraton Washington Hotel, he confided: "I promised you four years ago that I would never lie to you, so I can't stand here tonight and say it doesn't hurt. . . . I have not achieved all I set out to do . . . but we have faced the tough issues. . . . The great principles that have guided this nation since its very founding will continue to guide America through the challenge of the future. . . . We must now come together as a united and a unified people to solve the problems that are still before us, to meet the challenges of a new decade."[187]

Many Democrats were horrified by Carter's early concession. West Coast Democrats reported that after the president conceded, thousands of voters left the voting lines; countless others never showed up. Several Democratic candidates in the region suffered defeat (or thought they did) because of Carter's early concession.[188] Carter later explained that he "thought it would look ungracious" if he waited until eleven; he didn't want people to think he was sulking in the White House, bitter in defeat.

His statement was taken by many as merely another indication of his lack of concern for the Democratic Party. "From beginning to end Carter was very much a loner," says Austin Ranney of the American Enterprise Institute. "Carter showed little interest in the affairs of the party, and with his early concession speech he showed little interest in the welfare of other Democratic candidates."[189]

REAGAN'S VICTORY STATEMENT. At 11:55 P.M., an overjoyed Reagan came onstage at the Century Plaza Hotel in Los Angeles with his wife, Nancy, beside him. "There's never been a more humbling moment in my life," he said. "I am not frightened by what lies ahead. . . . We're going to put America back to work again." Then he quoted what Abraham Lincoln told newsmen when they knew he had won in 1860: "Well boys, your troubles are over now; mine have just begun."[190]

THE AFTERMATH. Carter's humiliating loss to Ronald Reagan was a shock to the Democrats. He had suffered one of the worst electoral defeats ever sustained by an incumbent president. As the first loss of a Democratic incumbent since 1888, when Grover Cleveland was beaten by Republican Benjamin Harrison, Carter's defeat underscored the Democrats' difficulty in winning presidential elections since World War II. Of eleven postwar elections, Republican candidates have won seven. Only twice—in 1964 and 1976—has the Democratic candidate drawn a majority of the popular vote.[191]

The Republicans were, of course, overjoyed. With the victory of Ronald Reagan and the election of a Republican majority in the Senate, it was widely assumed that at long last the nation was witnessing the demise of the party system dominated by the New Deal coalition. It seemed that a party realignment was about to occur and that a Republican Party majority was about to emerge. "For the first time in a generation," David Broder wrote in the *Washington Post*, "it is sensible to ask whether we might be entering a new political era—an era of Republican dominance."[192]

The Democrats began the search for understanding. Certainly one of the problems for Carter was low voter turnout. Only a little more than half of the Americans old enough to vote went to the polls, marking the fifth consecutive election that the presidential turnout had declined. The 1980 figure of 53.9 percent was below the 1976 turnout (54.4 percent) and was the lowest since 1948.[193] And, of course, there was a sizable third-party vote, constituting 4.4 percent of the age-eligible population, or 5.7 million votes. The lack of voter enthusiasm for both Carter and Reagan led one observer to comment that 1980 was "a to-hell-with-them-both election." Carter's defeat was, many thought, the result of the "fed up" vote.[194] After the election, when queried, two of every five Reagan votes explained their choice as a dislike of Carter.[195]

When the election was over, most of the national pollsters were dumbfounded because they had so badly underestimated the magnitude of Reagan's victory.[196] The Gallup Poll had shown a margin of only three percentage points three days before the election, and the CBS/New York Times and Newsweek polls had indicated an even closer race. Only Louis Harris among the public pollsters had pointed to the decisiveness of the victory, and he had Reagan leading by only 5 percent.[197] Whatever the polls said, it was pretty clear that both Carter and Reagan were perceived negatively by a majority of the electorate.[198] The election was not an endorsement of new conservative principles. Reagan, it would appear, simply had more "damn right" issues than Carter.

Carter's defeat was regarded by many as a direct repudiation of his personality and performance as president.[199] To others, including Carter himself, it was more a reflection of the frustration of the voters over developments that no president could control to their satisfaction. Actually, Hamilton Jordan was probably closest to the truth when he said, "The President's chances for reelection probably died in the desert of Iran with the eight brave soldiers who gave their lives trying to free the American hostages."[200]

To the end Jimmy Carter had hoped that the hostages would be freed while he was still president in order to justify the decisions he had made during the preceding months. In anticipation of their release, he had made arrangements to fly to Wiesbaden, West Germany, so that he could greet them in person as their president. But it was not to be. Then, on January 19, when it once again appeared that their freedom might be imminent, he arranged again to fly to Wiesbaden to greet them as his last major official act. At the last minute, however, Iran delayed the signing of the formal agreement until the morning of January 20 — Inauguration Day — because (many thought) the Iranian leaders were determined to further punish Carter. The disappointed Georgian instead joined Ronald Reagan for the traditional ride to the inauguration in the presidential limousine.[201]

Ronald Wilson Reagan was sworn in as the fortieth president of the United States at high noon on a bright, warm, sunny January 20. During the ceremonies, the obviously very tired outgoing president sat tight-lipped and distracted, his face conveying a measure of his final presidential agony. After the ceremony, at the traditional luncheon for congressional leaders in the Capitol, the new president made the first official announcement of the release of the United States hostages. "Some ten minutes ago," he told the legislators, "the planes bearing our prisoners left Iranian airspace, and they're now free of Iran."[202]

The news that the hostages had been released and were on their way from Teheran to Algiers and then to the Wiesbaden United States Air

Force base was telephoned to the emotionally drained ex-president as he flew back to his home in Plains, Georgia. The next day, no longer as president, but at Reagan's invitation, he flew to Wiesbaden to greet the returning hostages. Then, once again, back to Georgia, where he planned to write a history of his presidency (which he did)[203] and to take a break from politics (which he also did—for about five months).

Somewhere between Wiesbaden and Plains, on the long trip home, Carter confided to Hamilton Jordan: "1980 was pure hell—the Kennedy challenge, Afghanistan, having to put the SALT treaty on the shelf, the recession, Ronald Reagan, and the hostages ... always the hostages! It was one crisis after another."[204]

There were many observers who would have agreed that Jimmy Carter's summation of 1980, with a little adjustment, was a rather appropriate epitaph for his presidency.

Epilogue

Leaving the office of president of the United States was very difficult for Jimmy Carter. The first of several severe shocks came when he found that the family business, which he had placed in a blind trust, was heavily in debt and that he and Rosalynn would have to sell all the family businesses to clear up their debts. Then, he suffered the loss of his brother Billy and his two sisters, all cut down in early life by the same terminal disease. On top of these painful events, he had just been brutally rejected by the American public. The future appeared bleak. Yet in the 1990s, polls show him more appreciated than Ronald Reagan, who had defeated him so decisively, or any other recent ex-president. It was a remarkable comeback, in fact unprecedented in American political history.

The creation of the Carter Presidential Center in Atlanta was crucial to Carter's self-rehabilitation. The president's vision of a clearinghouse of ideas and programs intended to address international problems and crises — problems so bad nobody ever addresses them — became reality when the center was established in Atlanta as a part of Emory University in 1982, and even more so when its permanent headquarters opened in 1986. Carter himself holds the title of distinguished professor, lecturing and leading workshops and seminars in human and natural ecology at Emory University, with a special concern for rural problems in the Third World such as agriculture, water purification, modernizing health care — problems that Carter knows well but which to his frustration, he often saw put on Washington's back burner.

Fortunately, selling the family businesses and establishing the Carter Presidential Center gave Jimmy and Rosalynn the resources and time to do many of the things they wanted to do, things no other former "First Family" has done. Now, regularly, without fanfare, the former president supervises Carter Center projects in sub–Saharan Africa to eradicate the Guinea worm (a ghastly human parasite), to introduce new crop hybrids to African subsistence farmers, to immunize Third World children against disease, and to persuade farmers to enlist in the "Green Revolution." He is driven, he says, by "a sense of pleasant obligation." He is, of course, also aided by the fact that he is an ex-president of the United States – the first former president ever to set foot in that part of Africa south of the Sahara. Frequently, on "vacations" from the Carter Center, he and Rosalynn don blue jeans and pound nails for Habitat for Humanity, a nonprofit group that builds homes for the homeless.

Another of his goals is that of promoting human rights through free elections. In Panama, in 1989, after serving as an election monitor, he courageously denounced Manuel Noriega for "taking the elections by fraud." In Nicaragua, he played a prominent role in certifying that that country's presidential election was fair. He was invited to help monitor elections in Hungary, Romania, and the Dominican Republic.

Carter's extensive skills in personal diplomacy have also been put to good use. In Atlanta, in September 1989, he hosted peace talks in an effort to put an end to the civil war between the Marxist-Leninist government of Ethiopia and the Eritrean rebels to end three decades of civil war.

The public opinion polls reflect that in a remarkably short time, a lot of people around the world, many of them former critics, have changed their minds about Carter. They see that while he seeks opportunities to do good, former president Ronald Reagan peddles his time and talents to the highest bidder, Gerald Ford perfects his golfing style, and Richard Nixon struggles to refurbish his image for (it seems) the millionth time. A recent *Wall Street Journal*/NBC News Poll found that Americans, in retrospect, now approve of the way Carter handled his job, by 47 to 43 percent.[1] By comparison, Richard Nixon still has negative ratings and Ronald Reagan is barely even.

Many Americans of both parties who permitted Ronald Reagan to mesmerize them in 1980 have apparently now concluded that some Reagan administration failures make elements of the Carter record look good by comparison. Although Carter's Iran hostage ordeal was a national humiliation, he did get the hostages out alive. Reagan, when he left office, still had United States hostages in Lebanon and had lost 241 American servicemen in a futile peacekeeping mission there. Also, the Carter administration had nothing comparable to the Iran-Contra scandal, the HUD mess, or the savings and loan bailout.

Today, it would appear, that Jimmy Carter is in the process of redefining the meaning and purpose of the modern ex-presidency (and earning the title of "America's greatest ex-president" – not just a backhanded compliment). He is showing that the White House can be used as a stepping-stone to a greater and more important global role – that of world-class humanitarian. Says Carter: "As President, I wouldn't have had time to do all the things I'm doing now."

Carter is also gaining respect from some of the presidential scholars who made him a scapegoat for the problems of the late 1970s. It is true that, for the most part, his former detractors aren't calling Carter great or near-great. They still see him as someone who pitched, stubbornly and head-on, into too many of the toughest issues to face a modern president, refusing (despite advice) to postpone some of them to a second term — and, in consequence, emerging with only scattered triumphs. Naively, they say, he thought the presidency would be all good works — with no Ted Kennedys or Tip O'Neills or bureaucrats or special interests to frustrate his determination to make a difference. By promising always to do "right," he invited measurement against impossible standards. He was, in short, a classic example of a man using his independent judgment to try to do what he thought was right — despite what he must have known were the inevitable political perils of such a course.[2]

Ex-president Jimmy Carter now appears to be mellow and triumphant. Behind him now are the Iran hostage crisis, which helped deliver him into Ronald Reagan's eager hands; the scorn of various pundits and self-appointed guardians of Washington society; the *Playboy* interviews and the "malaise" speech. The "Man from Plains," who went to Washington to head the most politically frustrating nation in the world, appears to have discovered that there can be life after all that.

Notes

Prologue

1. Concerning the events which led to the scandal of Watergate and Nixon's resignation see *New York Times*, August 9, 1974. For full accounts of Watergate history, see Theodore H. White, *Breach of Faith* (New York: Atheneum, 1975); and the staff of the *New York Times*, "The End of a Presidency" (New York: Bantam, 1974); *New York Times*, March 24, 1974, p. 32.

2. An action since rescinded by Congress. For Ford's reasoning on the Nixon pardon see Gerald R. Ford, *A Time to Heal* (New York: Harper and Row, 1979).

3. President Ford had, in fact, inflicted a wound on his administration from which it would never recover. In response to the Gallup Poll question, "Do you approve of the way Ford is handling his job of President?" in August, 71 percent approved; after the pardon of Nixon only 50 percent approved. The drop of twenty-one points was the steepest decline in such a short time in the thirty-five years of poll surveys of presidents. See *Public Opinion*, 1 (March/April 1978), pp. 28–29; and "The Pardon That Brought No Peace," *Time*, CIV (September 16, 1974), p. 10.

Chapter 1: Jimmy Carter's Quest for the Presidency

1. Carter took the oath not as James Earl Carter, Jr., his given name, but as "Jimmy" Carter, which he had used as his official name from his first entry into politics and throughout his term as governor of Georgia. He continued to use the name during his presidency, making him the first President to use his colloquial name as his official name.

2. Micah 6:8.

3. Jimmy Carter, *Keeping Faith: Memoirs of a President* (New York: Bantam, 1982), p. 20.

4. For the text of Carter's inaugural address see Congressional Quarterly, Inc., *President Carter* (Washington, D.C.: Congressional Quarterly, 1977), p. 89. Also see Carter, *Keeping Faith*, p. 21.

5. Furthermore, during the 1969 inaugural of Richard Nixon the president's limousine was hit by stones thrown by anti–Vietnam demonstrators; in 1973, fruit and garbage were hurled at the president's car.

6. They were not called inaugural balls as in the past — further evidence of the spirit of egalitarianism.

7. Also a first in inauguration festivities, as several society editors were quick to point out.

8. Quoted from Robert Shogan, *Promises to Keep: Carter's First 100 Days* (New York: Crowell, 1977), p. 108.

9. Carter's sister reported that when Carter told his mother he was running for President, she asked, "President of what?" (Ruth Carter Stapleton, *Brother Billy* (New York: Harper & Row, 1978), p. 103.

10. Jules Witcover, *Marathon: The Pursuit of the Presidency, 1972-1976* (New York: Viking, 1977), p. 105. Carter later told Robert Shogan that in winning the governorship of Georgia he reckoned that he had given 1,800 speeches and shaken 600,000 hands. (Shogan, *Promises to Keep*, p. 22.)

11. Shogan, *Promises to Keep*, p. 30.

12. See Congressional Quarterly, Inc., *President Carter*, p. 8.

13. Shogan, *Promises to Keep*, p. 33.

14. Why did he have to be liberal or conservative, he asked, when most of the American people were not? (Witcover, *Marathon*, p. 207.)

15. George McGovern, the Democrats' 1972 liberal presidential candidate, said Carter didn't act like a liberal, and the conservative *Wall Street Journal* said he was no conservative. James T. Wooten, writing in the *New York Times*, summed it thusly: "He is not a liberal, not a conservative, not a racist, not a man of long governmental experience, not a religious zealot, not a Southerner of stereotypical dimensions," and from such negative deductions, many, he said, had concluded "that Jimmy Carter is not entirely unacceptable as a presidential candidate." (Quoted from T.R.B. in the *New Republic*, June 19, 1976.)

16. For accounts of how Carter overcame these obstacles to win the nomination and election see Witcover, *Marathon*; and Martin Schram, *Running for President 1976: A Journal of the Carter Campaign* (New York: Stein and Day, 1977).

17. For a discussion of Carter's ties to the Trilateral Commission see Thomas R. Dye, *Who's Running America? The Carter Years*, 2nd ed. (Englewood Cliffs, N.J.: Prentice-Hall, 1976), pp. 58-62.

18. Several prominent Republicans were members of the Trilateral Commission including George Bush, John Anderson, RNC William Brock, and Senator William Roth.

19. For an incisive discussion of Carter's links to the Trilateral Commission members in his 1976 campaign, see Laurence H. Shoup, *The Carter Presidency and Beyond: Power and Politics in the 1980s* (Palo Alto, Calif.: Ramparts, 1980).

20. Theodore H. White, *America in Search of Itself: The Making of the President 1956-1980* (New York: Harper & Row, 1982), p. 188.

21. Hamilton Jordan, *Crisis: The Last Year of the Carter Presidency* (New York: Putnam, 1982), p. 171. Also see Congressional Quarterly, Inc., *President Carter*, p. 64.

22. For more information on Carter's campaign team, see Shogan, *Promises to Keep*, and Jordan, *Crisis*.

23. For the contents of Jordan's memorandum see Schram, *Running for President 1976*, pp. 379-380. Also see Stephen J. Wayne, *The Road to the White House: The Politics of Presidential Elections*, Second Edition (New York: St. Martin's, 1984), p. 111.

24. Witcover, *Marathon*, p. 319.

25. John A. Crittenden, *Parties and Elections in the United States* (Englewood Cliffs, N.J.: Prentice Hall, 1982), p. 69.

26. Congressional Quarterly, Inc., *President Carter*, p. 3.

27. Crittenden, *Parties and Elections in the United States*, p. 67. Also see "The Impact of '74," *U. S. News and World Report*, November 18, 1974.
28. Wayne, *The Road to the White House*, p. 111.
29. Witcover, *Marathon*, p. 320.
30. For a discussion of the nomination and election strategy plan developed for Carter by Jordan see Witcover, *Marathon*, pp. 136–138.
31. Congressional Quarterly, Inc., *President Carter*, p. 4.
32. See Herbert S. Parmet, *The Democrats: The Years After F.D.R.* (New York: Macmillan, 1976), p. 293.
33. Theodore H. White, *The Making of the President 1972* (New York: Atheneum, 1973), p. 31.
34. A procedure under which, when a caucus was called, some local party leader might produce a list of absentee voters and cast enough votes to outweigh the concerned citizens gathered to vote.
35. *Mandate for Reform, Report of the Commission on Party Structure and Delegate Selection to the Democratic National Committee* (Washington, D.C.: Democratic National Committee, 1970), pp. 10–11.
36. For details of the commission's reform proposals see *Congressional Quarterly Weekly Report*, July 8, 1972, pp. 1650–1654.
37. The adoption of quotas resulted in a sharp increase in black, female and young delegates at the 1972 Democratic convention: 14 percent of the delegates were black, 23 percent under thirty and 36 percent women, up 8, 21, and 22 percent respectively from the 1968 figures. (Dennis G. Sullivan, Jeffrey L. Pressman, Benjamin I. Page, and John J. Lyons, *The Politics of Representation* [New York: St. Martin's, 1974], p. 23.). Hamilton Jordan eventually complained that "affirmative action" exploded to include the handicapped, Native Americans, gays, senior citizens, and so on. "It seemed," he wrote, "as though the only persons not guaranteed a voice in the party were the ordinary voter and elected officials who had to run on the Democratic ticket." (Jordan, *Crisis*, p. 329.)
38. See Donald Johnson, *The Politics of Delegate Selection* (New York: Robert A. Taft Institute of Government, 1976), p. 9. Also see Crittenden, *Parties and Elections in the United States*, p. 62.
39. After Carter was elected, the special interest groups spawned by these same reforms made it more difficult for him to govern effectively and, as we will see, to be reelected.
40. For a discussion of the effect of the Democratic reforms on the 1972 Democratic presidential primaries, see *Western Political Quarterly* 33 (March 1980), pp. 50–72.
41. The Republicans, of course, were not affected by the Democratic reforms. They did follow with their own reform commissions but avoided such sweeping changes. In 1969, the Republican national chairman appointed a Committee on Delegates and Organization (known as the "DO Committee"), which recommended objectives similar to the Democrats'. The 1972 convention made most of these effective for 1976. The changes tended to be advisory, rather than obligatory, to the state parties. The Republican Party, which was less affected by insurgent reform movements, had less reason (or willingness) to establish a "mass membership" party as the Democrats had done. They preferred a less centralized organization with considerable party authority at the lower levels. The DO Committee did make considerable progress, however, in making the Republican Party more a "party of the open door." See William J. Crotty, *Political Reform and the American Experiment* (New York: Crowell, 1977), pp. 255–260.

42. On the 1974 charter conference, see Jeffrey L. Pressman, Dennis G. Sullivan, and F. Christopher Arteron, "Cleavages, Decisions, and Legitimation: The Democrats' Midterm Conference, 1974," *Political Science Quarterly* (Spring 1976), pp. 89–107.

43. The text of the party charter can be found in *Congressional Quarterly Weekly Report* 32 (December 14, 1974).

44. Robert Strauss, the chairman of the Democratic National Committee, expressed the view that the charter was something the party had rather to survive than to achieve. Also, when he was asked why he permitted the party to go through the agony of public self-criticism in Kansas City in the first place, the wily Texan said: "Being chairman of the Democratic Party is like making love to a gorilla. You stop when *it* is ready." (Quoted in Garry Wills, *Lead Time: A Journalist's Education* [Garden City, N.Y.: Doubleday, 1983], p. 190.)

45. See *Congressional Quarterly Almanac 1975*, pp. 387, 410. Also see the chapter on "Reform" in Nelson W. Polsby and Aaron Wildavsky, *Presidential Elections: Strategies of American Electoral Politics*, 6th ed. (New York: Scribner's, 1984), pp. 208–266.

46. After Watergate, fifteen big corporations pleaded guilty to making illegal campaign contributions to the Nixon campaign.

47. On the impact of PACs on the political parties see Hedrick Smith, *The Power Game: How Washington Works* (New York: Ballantine, 1988), pp. 216, 217, 250.

48. It should also be noted that small contributions are encouraged by the federal income tax credit for campaign contributions. In 1976, a taxpayer could credit 50 percent of all campaign contributions up to a tax credit of $100 on a single return and $200 on a joint return. These tax incentives applied to money contributed at any level: national, state or local. (See Herbert Alexander, *Financing Politics* [Washington, D.C.: Congressional Quarterly, 1976].)

49. Crittenden, *Parties and Elections in the United States* (Englewood Cliffs, N.J.: Prentice-Hall, 1982), p. 132. Also see Nelson W. Polsby, *Consequences of Party Reform* (New York: Oxford University, 1983).

50. Shogan, *Promises to Keep*, p. 23.

51. *Congressional Quarterly Weekly Report*, November 30, 1974, p. 3214. Mondale's announcement that the price of the presidency was too high came as a shock to the American public, which had long assumed that no price was too high for the attainment of the highest elective office in the land. It would hurt Mondale in 1980.

52. Udall warmed up audiences by telling about the day he walked into a barbershop in Keene, New Hampshire, and shook hands with the man in the first chair. "I said, 'Hi, I'm Mo Udall, and I'm running for President.' And he said to me, 'Yeah, I know. We were just laughing about it.'" (Related from Witcover, *Marathon*, p. 139.) Actually Udall was probably too witty for his own good—his good humor created an impression of frivolity which hid his considerable substance.

53. The last member of the House of Representatives to go directly from the House to the White House was James A. Garfield.

54. Humphrey was widely considered to be the "talkiest" person ever elected to the Senate. It was said that he could "talk faster than most people could listen."

55. The Gallup Poll of December 1975 reported that Humphrey was the top choice of Democratic voters for the party's 1976 nomination, winning the support of 30 percent of the Democrats polled nationwide. He was followed by Wallace

with 20 percent, Senator George McGovern and Senator Henry Jackson each with 10 percent, Senator Birch Bayh with 5 percent, and Carter and all other candidates with less than 5 percent. (See Congressional Quarterly, Inc., *President Carter*, p. 82, and Eugene H. Roseboom and Alfred E. Eckes, *A History of Presidential Elections*, 4th ed. [New York: Macmillan, 1979], p. 318.)

56. Gerald Pomper with Colleagues, *The Election of 1976: Reports and Interpretations* (New York: McKay, 1977), p. 8.

57. Quoted in Wills, *Lead Time*, p. 168.

58. See Witcover, *Marathon*, pp. 145–147.

59. Witcover, *Marathon*, p. 162.

60. Witcover, *Marathon*, p. 148.

61. Witcover, *Marathon*, p. 190.

62. Pomper with Colleagues, *The Election of 1976*, p. 9.

63. That is, 13.5 percent of the popular vote and forty-six electoral votes. In 1968, Wallace carried Alabama, Mississippi, Georgia, Louisiana, and Arkansas (the only state carried by the Democrats was Texas). On the appeal of Wallace in 1968, see Theodore H. White, *The Making of the President 1968* (New York: Atheneum, 1969), p. 364; and Lewis Chester, Godfrey Hodgson, and Bruce Page, *An American Melodrama: The Presidential Campaign of 1968* (New York: Viking, 1969) On George C. Wallace's early years see Marshall Frady, *Wallace* (Cleveland, Ohio: World, 1968).

64. James Wooten, *Dasher: The Roots and Rising of Jimmy Carter* (New York: Summit, 1978), p. 114.

65. On the day the Democrats' 1974 mini-convention opened in Kansas City, Gallup released a poll that showed Wallace ahead of all other Democrats among independents, the very people that "reforms" of the sort promised at Kansas City were supposed to be attracting; among them he won 24 percent of the people's loyalty, to 12 percent for Jackson. (Wills, *Lead Time*, p. 187.)

66. Quoted in Wooten, *Dasher*, p. 113.

67. A Gallup Poll of Republicans and Independents in late June 1975 gave Ford 41 percent and Reagan 20 percent in a field of the prospective candidates. In a two man matchup, the results were: Ford 61 percent, Reagan 33 percent, undecided 6 percent. (Witcover, *Marathon*, p. 55n.) The result, Crittenden suggests, was that Ford may have benefited from a climate of diminished expectations following Watergate. (Crittenden, *Parties and Elections in the United States*, p. 70.)

68. Witcover, *Marathon*, p. 89.

69. Ironically, Ford was not Nixon's choice. Nixon preferred John Connally, but Congressman Melvin Laird convinced him that it would be difficult for Connally (or Rockefeller or Reagan) to be confirmed by the Senate, and he selected Ford as the "safest choice." (Ford, *A Time to Heal*, p. 106n.)

70. Pomper with Colleagues, *The Election of 1976*, p. 18.

71. Witcover, *Marathon*, p. 81.

72. Witcover, *Marathon*, pp. 83–84.

73. In 1972, Richard Nixon had run for president from the Oval Office, treating the nomination and election campaign as a bothersome intrusion. (Witcover, *Marathon*, p. 53.)

74. Witcover, *Marathon*, p. 86.

75. A *New York Times* poll of Republican county chairmen in early 1974 revealed that Reagan was heavily preferred over then Vice President Ford. (*New York Times*, March 24, 1974, p. 32.)

76. Lou Cannon, *Reagan* (New York: Putnam, 1982), p. 98.

77. When Reagan was asked if the casting was right for him to be the governor of California he replied: "I don't know. I've never played a governor." However, the Hollywood movie producer Jack Warner was sure that Reagan was wrong for the part. On hearing that Reagan might run for governor of California, he reportedly said: "No, Jimmy Stewart for governor, Ronald Reagan for best friend." (William E. Leuchtenberg, A Troubled Feast [Boston: Little, Brown, 1973], p. 282.)

78. Rowland Evans and Robert Novak, The Reagan Revolution (New York: Dutton, 1981), p. 31.

79. Evans and Novak suggest that Reagan was closer to the nomination than most people thought. They cite studies which suggest that a switch of only six votes in the unit rule (winner-take-all) states of Mississippi and Florida would have deadlocked the convention on the first ballot and led to Reagan's nomination on the third ballot. (Evans and Novak, The Reagan Revolution, p. 40.) One can only speculate on the future course of American political history if Reagan had been nominated in 1968 instead of Richard M. Nixon.

80. Roseboom and Eckes, A History of Presidential Elections, p. 327.

81. Quoted in Witcover, Marathon, p. 92.

82. F. Clifton White and William J. Gill, Why Reagan Won: The Conservative Movement 1964–1981 (Washington, D.C.: Regnery Gateway, 1981), p. 172.

83. Quoted in Witcover, Marathon, p. 91.

84. A participant describes the experience more graphically: "You drive miles through a cold winter night to the meeting place, sit through mind-numbing party business, then express your preference in front of your neighbors, take a position for a candidate rather than simply cast a ballot in the privacy of a polling booth. Then, if your candidate receives less than 15 percent of the initial vote, he or she will be declared nonviable and you are required to vote again for someone else. The whole process can take two to four hours."

85. Carter, Keeping Faith, p. 43.

86. Only 45,000 Democrats, or 10 percent of the eligible Democratic voters, attended the Iowa precinct caucuses. Even so, Iowa had one of the highest turnouts for caucus voting in 1976. The national average for caucus states in that year was just under 4 percent. (Elizabeth Drew, Portrait of an Election [New York: Simon and Schuster, 1981], p. 58.)

87. James David Barber, The Pulse of Politics: Electing Presidents in the Media Age (New York: Norton, 1980), p. 187.

88. Especially helpful to Carter in making him a front-runner was R. W. Apple's New York Times story on the 1976 Iowa caucuses. Carter was also helped by the 726 lines he received in Time and Newsweek, compared with an average of thirty lines for the other candidates. (See Wayne, The Road to the White House, p. 103.)

89. In 1976 there were only 118,000 registered Democrats in New Hampshire.

90. As Jules Witcover points out, New Hampshire had always been a pitfall for front-runners. In recent history primary setbacks in New Hampshire suffered by incumbents Harry Truman (1948) and Lyndon Johnson (1968) had helped to persuade them to withdraw. (Witcover, Marathon, p. 83.)

91. Witcover, Marathon, p. 191.

92. Roseboom and Eckes, A History of Presidential Elections, p. 321.

93. Carter, Keeping Faith, p. 22.

94. Witcover, Marathon, p. 193.

95. In 1972. Representative Barbara Jordan was elected from Texas the same year.

96. Quoted in Shogan, *Promises to Keep*, p. 44.

97. Quoted in Congressional Quarterly, Inc., *President Carter*, p. 4.

98. As Shogan points out, Philadelphia County, which Rizzo controlled, was the only one of sixty-seven counties in the state that Carter did not carry. That, as Carter was well aware, would be a problem in the general election if Rizzo could not be won over. (Shogan, *Promises to Keep*, p. 7.)

99. Ironically, Brown's Maryland triumph did not prevent Carter from receiving a majority of that state's delegates.

100. During the summer of 1975 Reagan had made a speech in Chicago saying that $90 billion could be carved from the federal budget by cutting federal programs and turning them over to the states along with the resources—i.e. tax base—to carry them out. The states could then decide for themselves whether they wanted to continue the programs or let them expire. The press concluded that it was a hideously complicated and patently unworkable scheme advocating unrealistic measures that could never be taken if he became president.

101. T.R.B. in the *New Republic*, February 7, 1976.

102. Ford, *A Time to Heal*, p. 367.

103. Cannon, *Reagan*, p. 214.

104. Under the Convention rules the North Carolina delegation was committed to split its vote between Reagan and Ford on the first ballot.

105. Ford's loss to Reagan in North Carolina was, as he put it in his memoirs, a "jolting experience." It was only the third time in United States history that a challenger had defeated an incumbent president in a primary state. Also, it was the first time in nearly thirty years that Ford had lost at the polls. (Ford, *A Time to Heal*, p. 375.)

106. Cannon, *Reagan*, p. 218.

107. Witcover, *Marathon*, p. 438.

108. Evans and Novak, *The Reagan Revolution*, p. 55. Also see White and Gill, *Why Reagan Won*, p. 179.

109. Quoted in Ford, *A Time to Heal*, p. 395.

110. Pomper with Colleagues, *The Election of 1976*, p. 29.

111. For a full account of the 1976 Democratic Convention see Sullivan, *et al.*, "Candidates, Caucuses, and Issues: The Democratic Convention, 1976," in Louis Maisel and Joseph Cooper (eds.), *The Impact of the Electoral Process* (Beverly Hills, Calif.: Sage Publications, 1977). Also see Sullivan, Denis, *et al.*, *Exploration in Convention Decision-Making* (San Francisco: Freeman, 1976).

112. However, because of the Democratic Party reform rules established in 1974, the percentage of minority delegates to the Democratic National Convention declined. A post-convention survey by the national committee indicated that 36 percent of the delegates in 1976 were women, compared with 38 percent in 1972; 7 percent were black, compared with 15 percent four years earlier; and 14 percent were youths, compared with 21 percent in 1972. (Congressional Quarterly, Inc., *National Party Conventions 1831–1876* [Washington, D.C.: Congressional Quarterly], p. 119.)

113. Garry Wills, the journalist, suggests that there was so little dissent aired at the convention that its critics—mainly journalists—were tempted to call it "rigged" by Carter. However, Wills also suggests that it was not necessary for Carter to "rig" the convention since his victory had been so overwhelming that his critics were left with little to say that was not silly. (Wills, *Lead Time*, pp. 196, 197.)

114. Quoted in Richard Reeves, *Convention* (Harcourt Brace Jovanovich, 1977), p. 75.

115. Quoted in Reeves, *Convention*, pp. 167–168.

116. In time, Mrs. McCormick met the eligibility requirement for federal funds and received almost $250,000 from the United States Treasury to espouse her anti-abortion views. (Wayne, *The Road to the White House*, p. 50.)

117. Stephen Wayne points out that Carter was the first candidate in some time not to use the traditional red, white and blue colors. His selection of deep green, Wayne suggests, was designed to convey the freshness and purity of a new day. (Wayne, *The Road to the White House*, p. 237n.)

118. Reeves, *Convention*, p. 168.

119. A barefoot Carter, surrounded by his family, watched the proceedings on TV in his hotel room. As Ohio put him over the top, he leaned forward and flashed his wide grin. The nation had just watched Carter watch himself on television as he "privately" savored his victory. (White, *America in Search of Itself*, p. 191.)

120. Reeves, *Convention*, p. 177

121. For Carter's procedure in selecting Mondale see Pomper with Colleagues, *The Election of 1976*, pp. 27–28. Also see Congressional Quarterly, Inc., *President Carter*, p. 5.

122. Carter, *Keeping Faith*, p. 36.

123. Carter, *Keeping Faith*, p. 35.

124. Pomper with Colleagues, *The Election of 1976*, p. 28.

125. Mondale thus became the first Korean War veteran to be nominated for national public office.

126. For the full text of the speech see Congressional Quarterly, Inc., *President Carter*, pp. 87–88.

127. Pomper with Colleagues, *The Election of 1976*, p. 32.

128. Cannon, *Reagan*, p. 225. This was almost the identical margin of Ford's victory on the Rule 16C vote.

129. Pomper with Colleagues, *The Election of 1976*, p. 27.

130. Quoted in Pomper with Colleagues, *The Election of 1976*, p. 27.

131. Quoted in White and Gill, *Why Reagan Won*, p. 190. Also see Denis Sullivan *et al.*, "Exploring the 1976 Republican Convention," *Political Science Quarterly* 92 (1977–1978), pp. 633–682.

132. Quoted in White and Gill, *Why Reagan Won*, p. 191.

133. Shogan notes that no candidate in modern times has sought the nomination from a place as remote as Plains, Georgia, a small town of 680 people in rural South Georgia served by no airline, railroad, or bus company. It was without any motel, hotel, or even a restraurant, except for a sandwich shop which, as a sign posted behind the counter informs its patrons, lacks a restroom. (Shogan, *Promises to Keep*, p. 82.)

134. Shogan, *Promises to Keep*, p. 50.

135. Shogan, *Promises to Keep*, p. 51.

136. Paul F. Boller, Jr., *Presidential Campaigns* (New York: Oxford University Press, 1984), p. 352.

137. Witcover, *Marathon*, p. 545.

138. Congressional Quarterly, Inc., *President Carter*, p. 63.

139. Witcover, *Marathon*, p. 526.

140. Witcover, *Marathon*, p. 540.

141. Shogan, *Promises to Keep*, p. 42. On Carter's attempts to deal with what Hamilton Jordan called the "weirdo factor" see various references in Witcover, *Marathon*, especially pp. 270–272, 330, 562–570.

142. Jimmy Carter interview, *Playboy*, November 1976, p. 86.

143. Shogan, *Promises to Keep*, p. 42. Subsequent polls revealed, however, that the *Playboy* interview apparently disturbed less than 10 percent of the voters sufficiently for them to vote against him.

144. An earlier version, the "Front Porch Campaign," was utilized with great effectiveness by William McKinley in his run for the presidency against William Jennings Bryan in 1896. It was used again by Warren Harding in 1920 because Harding's sponsors felt he would put his foot in his mouth every time he spoke.

145. Boller, *Presidential Campaigns*, p. 347.

146. Roseboom and Eckes, *A History of Presidential Elections*, p. 331.

147. Witcover, *Marathon*, p. 38.

148. Congressional Quarterly, Inc., *President Carter*, p. 63.

149. See Stephen Lesher with Patrick Caddell and Gerald Rafshoon, "Did the Debates Help Jimmy Carter," in Austin Ranney, ed., *The Past and Future of Presidential Debates* (Washington, D.C.: American Enterprise Institute, 1979).

150. It is estimated that the first Ford-Carter debate in 1976 attracted a viewing audience of ninety million to 100 million persons and was seen in thirty-five to forty million homes, in contrast to the estimated seventy-seven million who had watched the first Nixon-Kennedy debate in 1960. (Wayne, *The Road to the White House*, p. 225.)

151. Ford, *A Time to Heal*, pp. 422–425.

152. See Charles Mohr, "President Tells Polish-Americans He Regrets Remarks on East Europe," *New York Times*, October 9, 1976.

153. Congressional Quarterly, Inc., *President Carter*, p. 67. See also "Transcript of Presidential Debates," *New York Times*, October 16, 1976.

154. Congressional Quarterly, Inc., *President Carter*, p. 85. "It was the worst kind of thing he could have done," moaned Pat Caddell.

155. Shogan, *Promises to Keep*, p. 54.

156. T.R.B. in the *New Republic*, June 19, 1976, p. 452.

157. When the campaign was over, Carter, traveling in *Peanut One* and *Peanut Two*, had completed the most arduous campaign of any presidential candidate in American history. During the final eight weeks of the campaign alone, Carter and his entourage traveled nearly 50,000 miles and visited thirty-seven states. Since his declaration of his candidacy for the Democratic nomination twenty-two months before, Carter had covered about 500,000 miles and been everywhere that mattered politically. (Shogan, *Promises to Keep*, p. 2.)

158. Ford had moved from an incredible deficit of thirty-three percentage points in the opinion surveys to near victory. According to Gallup it was "the greatest comeback in the history of public opinion polling." (Boller, *Presidential Campaigns*, p. 348.)

159. Nearly eighty-two million Americans voted in 1976, some four million more than in 1972. Even so, voter participation continued to decline. Only 54 percent of those over eighteen went to the polls, a decrease from 55.4 percent in 1972 and a record 62.8 percent in 1960. (Roseboom and Eckes, *A History of Presidential Elections*, p. 336.)

160. Although it was a narrow victory, it was greater than JFK's in 1960 and Nixon's in 1968.

161. A *New York Times* survey indicated that 62 percent of votes from union households went to Carter.

162. Charles Jacob, "The Congressional Elections and Outlook," in Pomper with Colleagues, *The Election of 1976*, pp. 83–105.

163. Ford, *A Time to Heal*, p. 435.

164. Quoted in White, *America in Search of Itself*, p. 233.

165. Jimmy Carter was formally elected the thirty-ninth president of the United States at the traditional Joint Session of Congress held on January 6, 1977, to count the electoral vote. The final vote for the president was Carter 297, Ford 240, and Ronald Reagan one — cast by a "faithless" elector who, though pledged to Ford, bolted from his party's choice to cast a symbolic protest vote. In the separate tally for vice president, Mondale received 297 votes to 241 for Dole.

Chapter 2: President Carter and the Congress

1. Quoted in Shogan, *Promises to Keep*, pp. 83–84. Critics complained that the cabinet-level choices Carter made, for all their competence and experience, were not the new faces the country had been led to expect. (Shogan, *Promises to Keep*, p. 76.)

2. Which led some protectionist-minded conservatives to talk of a "conspiracy" backed by David Rockefeller and the Trilateral Commission to gain control of the American government. The generally conservative nature of Carter's cabinet appointments led Ralph Nader to characterize Carter's choices as "conservatives with high integrity," who, he predicted, would "follow the wrong policies straight instead of crooked." (Shogan, *Promises to Keep*, p. 88.)

3. Jordan, *Crisis*, p. 48.

4. Charles Schultze was subsequently named to chair the Council of Economic Advisers.

5. Carter ultimately named Paul Warnke to be chief arms negotiator and head of the disarmament agency.

6. Ironically, Bell had served as co-chairman of John F. Kennedy's presidential campaign in Georgia in 1960 and had been appointed to the federal bench by Kennedy when he became president.

7. Shogan, *Promises to Keep*, p. 89.

8. Shogan, *Promises to Keep*, p. 87.

9. Quoted in Shogan, *Promises to Keep*, p. 88.

10. Carter, *Keeping Faith*, p. 49.

11. White, *America in Search of Itself*, p. 223.

12. Quoted in Congressional Quarterly, Inc., *President Carter*, p. 35.

13. Carter, *Keeping the Faith*, p. 59.

14. Jordan, *Crisis*, p. 46.

15. Quoted in White, *America in Search of Itself*, p. 222. For Brzezinski's reflection on his role in the Carter administration see Zbigniew Brzezinski, *Power and Principle: Memoirs of the National Security Adviser, 1977–1981* (New York: Farrar, Straus, Giroux, 1983).

16. White, *America in Search of Itself*, p. 19. On the Brezinski-Vance conflict, see Smith, *The Power Game*, pp. 591–592.

17. Shogan, *Promises to Keep*, p. 91.

18. He had admitted that when he departed from the White House in 1964, he had taken with him sixty-three cartons of documents — including seven that were "classified" — to use in writing a book about the Kennedy administration, which was published in 1965.

19. Shogan, *Promises to Keep*, p. 92.

20. Shogan, *Promises to Keep*, p. 93. On the Sorenson nomination, see Norman Kempster, *Los Angeles Times*, January 28, 1977.

21. Jordan, *Crisis*, p. 68.

22. Carter, *Keeping Faith*, p. 32.

23. For a description of the first lady's relationship to the president see Rosalynn Carter, *First Lady from Plains* (Boston: Houghton Mifflin, 1984).

24. For Carter's views on cabinet government see Smith, *The Power Game*, p. 295.

25. For an incisive discussion of President Carter's philosophy of leadership see Erwin C. Hargrove, *Jimmy Carter as President: Leadership and the Politics of the Public Good* (Baton Rouge: Louisiana State University Press, 1988), pp. 13–32.

26. When the story went around Washington that the powerful House Ways and Means Committee was kept waiting because a White House official couldn't get a cab, the rule was changed. Carter also instituted a return to the playing of "Hail to the Chief" at official occasions. He later admitted that he found it impressive and that he liked it.

27. When Carter urged his Clinton audience (and anybody else who happened to be watching on television) to write to him personally about their concerns and ideas for programs, they took him at his word. The resulting tidal wave of mail and telephone calls necessitated an increase in White House staff, which Carter had promised to cut back as part of de-imperializing the presidency. (Austin Ranney, ed., *The American Elections of 1980* [Washington, D.C.: American Enterprise Institute, 1981], p. 6.)

28. It was estimated that more than nine million Americans tried to call their president at the toll-free number provided.

29. *Editor and Publisher* reported, "411 Dailies Support Ford: 80 for Carter," (October 29, 1976, pp. 5, 12–13).

30. See the section on Jimmy Carter in Sam Donaldson, *Hold on, Mr. President!* (New York, Random House, 1987), pp. 76–89. Jody Powell, Carter's press secretary, in his book *The Other Side of the Story*, suggests that Donaldson had it backward—that the ill feeling that existed between the president and the press was initially created by the media's unfair treatment of the president. See Jody Powell, *The Other Side of the Story* (New York: Morrow, 1984).

31. Donaldson, *Hold On, Mr. President!* p. 15. After the election, Carter humorously explained his lack of apparent humor: He said that he had told his staff that he wanted "to put on the image of a common man, someone who didn't have the accolades of the crowd and the homage paid to a strong and able leader. They said so far I have succeeded very well." (Reported in Shogan, *Promises to Keep*, p. 133.)

32. On Jimmy Carter's wit see Bill Adler, ed., *The Wit and Wisdom of Jimmy Carter* (Secaucus, NJ: Citadel, 1977); and Gerald Gardner, *All the President's Wit: The Power of Presidential Humor* (New York: Morrow, 1986), chapters 8–13.

33. Carter, *Keeping Faith*, p. 130. After Lance's resignation, the investigations continued, and in May 1979 he was indicted on thirty-three counts of conspiracy to obtain $20 million in loans for his personal benefit from forty-one different banks between 1970 and 1978. During the trial, most of the thirty-three counts were dropped, and in early April 1980, the trial jury acquitted Lance of nine counts of bank fraud. On one count of misapplying bank funds and two counts of making false financial statements, the jury deadlocked; the judge declared a mistrial, and the Justice Department decided not to retry Lance on these charges. Eventually, the judge dropped the remaining counts. The verdict was regarded by President Carter as a major victory for Lance and a personal vindication for himself; however, by that time very few people noticed or cared.

34. An incisive account of the Lance Affair is found in Haynes Johnson's *In the Absence of Power* (New York: Viking, 1980), pp. 198–214. Also see Clark R. Mollenhoff, *The President Who Failed* (New York: Macmillan, 1980), Chapter 6, and Austin Ranney, ed., *The American Elections of 1980*, pp. 22–23.

35. In 1979 Eilberg was found guilty of criminal conflict of interest charges.

36. In reality, as Carter and his advisers would quickly learn, the Ninety-fifth Congress was not exactly a Democratically controlled body. Although the Democrats had a majority of members in both houses, the Democratic Party was seriously divided at its base, and control of Congress really rested with a coalition of moderate Democrats, conservative Democrats, and conservative Republicans. (As Carter was essentially a moderate-to-conservative Democrat, this coalition should have helped him, but it did not.)

37. White, *America in Search of Itself*, p. 205.

38. For a survey of Carter's non-honeymoon with the Ninety-fifth Congress see Shogan, *Promises to Keep*. The Ninety-fifth Congress met from January 1977 to December 1978.

39. Their name was intended to suggest that they ate at the leaves of the Republican tree. (Smith, *The Power Game*, p. 466.)

40. For an excellent summary of President Carter's difficulties with Congress, see Johnson, *In the Absence of Power.*

41. According to *Congressional Quarterly*, in his first two years the Senate backed Carter on 84.4 percent of selected measures, the House on 69.4 percent—an unusually low level of support by congressional Democrats for their own president's programs. The success rate was comparable to President Nixon's, despite the fact that Democrats controlled Congress in each case. (*Congressional Quarterly Weekly Report*, December 9, 1978, pp. 3407–3408.) Hamilton Jordan suggests that 75 percent of the public criticism of President Carter in his first year in office came from Democrats. (Jordan, *Crisis*, p. 316.)

42. Jordan, *Crisis*, p. 171. Elizabeth Dole, conducting interviews during the Carter administration's first weeks in office, reported: "A man here said '[Carter] spent so much time in the campaign saying that he didn't owe anybody anything that nobody thinks they owe him anything.'" ("Our Far-Flung Correspondents: Settling In," *The New Yorker*, February 28, 1977, p. 87.)

43. Jordan, *Crisis*, p. 317.

44. It required a memorandum of 111 pages just to list all the promises, ranging from the economy and natural resources to foreign and defense policy, that Carter had made to the American people in his three-year-long campaign for the presidency. When the list became available to the press, reporters promptly dubbed it "Promises, Promises" and generally used it as a scorecard against which they could measure Carter's successes and failures as president.

45. Austin Ranney, ed., *The American Elections of 1980*, p. 19.

46. Smith, *The Power Game*, p. 454.

47. For which they had considerable justification. As Powell, Jordan, and Carter put it: "Where had they been, with all their sage advice, when the campaign was out of money and no one knew who Jimmy Carter was? What were they doing when Carter was drawing crowds of ten and twenty in tiny Iowa towns?" (James Fallows, "The Passionless Presidency," *Atlantic*, May 1979, page 46.)

48. *Wall Street Journal*, April 13, 1973, p. 10.

49. Quoted in Shogan, *Promises to Keep*, p. 207.

50. On the growing isolation of the president by Congress, see George Reedy, "On the Isolation of Presidents," in *The Presidency Reappraised*, edited by

Thomas E. Cronin and Rexford G. Tugwell (New York: Praeger, 1977). Also see
Walter Mondale, *The Accountability of Power: Toward a Responsible Presidency*
(New York: McKay, 1974).

51. A Harris Poll indicated that the public disapproved of the amnesty order
by a margin of about 46 to 42 percent. As Shogan reports, under Carter's executive
order some 10,000 young men, mostly white and middle class, who had either fled
the country or refused to be inducted into service, received relief. However, the
order was of no help to a much larger group, more than 400,000 Vietnam-era
veterans, many of them black and poor, who had received less than honorable
discharges for desertion and other violations of military law. Later, the president
approved a Pentagon program that made it possible for about 60,000 deserters to
have their discharges quickly upgraded and established a procedure for about
350,000 other Vietnam veterans to apply for upgrading of their discharges by
military review boards. (From Shogan, *Promises to Keep*, p. 120.)

52. Michael Tanzer provides useful background information in *The Energy
Crisis: World Struggle for Power and Wealth* (New York: Monthly Review Press,
[1975] c. 1974).

53. At the beginning of 1973 oil was selling on the world market at $3.41 a
barrel. It would go to $11.11 in 1974, to $15.54 in 1978, to $28.00 in the spring of
1980. Gasoline had cost $.37 a gallon at the pump in the summer of 1970; it cost
$.60 in 1975. It would go to $1.60 by the summer of 1980. And up with the price
of oil went the cost of living—and the tempers of Americans. (From White,
America in Search of Itself, pp. 152–153.)

54. Hargrove, *Jimmy Carter as President*, pp. 47–48.

55. Bob Rankin, "Carter's Energy Plan: A Plan of Leadership," *Congressional
Quarterly Weekly Report*, April 23, 1977, pp. 727–732.

56. Carter, *Keeping Faith*, p. 94.

57. Quoted from Congressional Quarterly, Inc., *President Carter 1978*, p. 31.

58. Carter, *Keeping Faith*, p. 98.

59. Carter was convinced that the nation's extremely low oil prices were encouraging waste and preventing exploration for new supplies of oil in the United
States. The low prices also meant that such competing energy sources as solar
power and synthetic fuels were underdeveloped. (Carter, *Keeping Faith*, pp. 104, 108.)

60. Congressional Quarterly, *President Carter 1978*, p. 30.

61. Hedrick Smith reported that President Carter expressed in his presence
his frustration over the entangling ways of Congress, citing the energy legislation,
which had to pass through twenty-two different congressional committees and
subcommittees—all of which were being pressured by special interests. In reality,
Smith says, the legislative process had passed being merely "frustrating" to the
president and had become an impossible legislative steeplechase. (Smith, *The
Power Game*, p. 27.)

62. As passed, the program's greatest impact would be inconveniences affecting only habit or lifestyle. And even those impositions could be overcome by
anyone willing and able to pay the extra price for big cars and central air-
conditioning. (Shogan, *Promises to Keep*, p. 238.)

63. Congressional Quarterly, Inc., *President Carter 1978*, p. 3.

64. The American Trucking Assocation spent $3 million in 1979 trying to
stave off deregulation of truck routes and rates. (Source: Smith, *The Power Game*,
p. 217.)

65. On the evolution of Carter's policy regarding the minimum wage, see
Hargrove, *Jimmy Carter as President*, pp. 81–83.

66. Business and right-to-work groups spent an estimated $5 million to kill the bill.

67. Carter, *Keeping Faith*, p. 101.

68. Shogan suggests that the significance of the president's attack on the water projects (which epitomize insider politics in Washington) went far beyond the dollar sums—that it was, in fact, his most tangible action in carrying out his determination to present himself as an outsider who intended to shake things up in Washington. See Shogan, *Promises to Keep*, p. 212–213.

69. Source: Shogan, *Promises to Keep*, p. 214.

70. The text of the president's veto message is printed in Congressional Quarterly, Inc., *President Carter 1978*, pp. 60A–61A.

71. Carter, *Keeping Faith*, p. 81.

72. As Hedrick Smith points out, the Rockwell Company, the prime contractor for the B-1 bomber, was able, with congressional support, to keep alive research and development for testing four prototype bombers, banking on a quick start-up of B-1 production if a Republican president were elected in 1980. To help out, Rockwell Company executives made large financial contributions to Ronald Reagan's 1980 campaign. When Reagan entered the White House, the B-1 was one of the first military projects revived.

73. Drew, *Portrait of an Election*, p. 15.

74. Three years later Gramm would lead a defection of southern conservative Democrats from Carter to support a Reaganite budget. In 1983 he switched parties, and he was elected to the Senate as a Republican in 1984. A year later, as a freshman senator, Gramm emerged as a prime architect (with another freshman senator, Warren Rudman of New Hampshire) of the highly controversial plan to balance the budget by 1991 through mandatory annual reductions in the deficit. (On Gramm, see Smith, *The Power Game*, p. 39.)

75. See Lawrence E. Lynn, Jr., and David Whitman, *The President as Policymaker: Jimmy Carter and Welfare Reform* (Philadephia: Temple University Press, 1981).

76. Shogan, *Promises to Keep*, p. 241. Also see Nick Kotz, "The Politics of Welfare Reform," *New Republic*, May 14, 1977.

77. Ninety-nine Democrats voted against the president.

78. The Kennedy proposal differed from Carter's in that it would make comprehensive health benefits available to the people in all income brackets. Employees would be offered a choice of private health plans by their employers, with premiums shared by employers and employees. Medical bills for the poor would continue to be paid by the government.

79. Congressional Quarterly, Inc., *President Carter 1979*, p. 71.

80. Although the word "malaise" was never uttered during the speech.

81. The text of the speech can be read in *Congressional Quarterly Weekly Report* 37 (July 21, 1979), pp. 1470–1472. (Carter's critics called his "failure of confidence speech" the "failure of competence speech.")

82. Smith, *The Power Game*, p. 304.

83. Jack Germond and Jules Witcover, *Blue Smoke and Mirrors: How Reagan Won and Why Carter Lost the Election of 1980* (New York: Viking, 1981), p. 39.

84. Quoted in *Time*, July 30, 1979, p. 11. Also see Johnson, *In the Absence of Power*, pp. 314–315.

85. Congressional Quarterly, Inc., *President Carter 1979*, p. 5. The president's poll ratings, which had risen nine points after his energy speech, soon returned once again to record low levels.

86. Congressional Quarterly, Inc., *President Carter 1979*, p. 6. Robert S. Strauss, the Democratic national chairman and the president's trade ambassador and Middle East envoy, said "not to worry." Jordan, he said, "had matured." Where he once wore blue jeans to work, now Jordan sported pinstriped suits. Where once he referred to Carter as "Jimmy," he had begun to call him "the president." However, Jordan denied this — insisting that he had not owned a pair of blue jeans in twenty years. (Jordan, *Crisis*, p. 173.)

87. See Powell, *The Other Side of the Story*, for a denial of these charges of cocaine use by Jordan.

88. Congressional Quarterly, Inc., *President Carter 1979*, p. 77.

89. For the evolution of Carter's economic policy, see Hargrove, *Jimmy Carter as President*, pp. 69–109.

90. Quoted in Shogan, *Promises to Keep*, p. 230.

91. Congressional Quarterly, Inc., *President Carter 1978*, p. 20.

92. By mid–1978 the unemployment rates were 18.5 percent for teenagers, and 34.4 percent for minority teenagers. For some of these groups, unemployment rates have been at depression levels for years; the unemployment rate for black teenagers has not been below 25 percent for more than twenty years.

93. By September, 57 percent of the Americans interviewed in a Gallup Poll thought inflation was the worst problem facing the nation.

94. Had it not been for OPEC, economists speculate, the 1979 inflation rate might have been contained at 8 or 9 percent instead of 12 or 13 percent. Administration policymakers did not regard this OPEC-induced inflation as a consequence of flawed economic policy. See Hargrove, *Jimmy Carter as President*, p. 101. Also see Bowman Cutter, "The Presidency and Economic Policy: A Tale of Two Budgets" in Michael Nelson, *The Presidency and the Political System* (Washington, D.C.: Congressional Quarterly Press, 1984), p. 482.

95. Congressional Quarterly, Inc., *President Carter 1979*, p. 4.

96. See Bowman Cutter, "The Presidency and Economic Policy: A Tale of Two Budgets."

97. Carter, *Keeping Faith*, p. 528.

98. Congressional Quarterly, Inc., *President Carter 1980*, p. 8. Domestic car sales ended the year (1980) down 24 percent from 1979.

99. For a fuller description of the theory see Jude Wanniski's *The Way the World Works* (New York: Simon and Schuster, 1978) and his "The Mundell-Laffer Hypothesis — A New View of the World Economy," *Public Interest*, Spring 1975. Also see Jack Brooks, "The Annals of Finance (Supply-Side Economics)," *New Yorker*, April 19, 1982, pp. 96–150. On supply-side economics also see Smith, *The Power Game*, pp. 45, 314, 344–345, and 354.

100. Evans and Novak, *The Reagan Revolution*, p. 65.

101. Quoted in Evans and Novak, *The Reagan Revolution*, p. 71.

102. Quoted in Carter, *Keeping Faith*, p. 144.

103. Ranney, *The American Elections of 1980*, p. 11.

104. Carter, *Keeping Faith*, p. 143.

105. Carter, *Keeping Faith*, p. 144. Delegates from the Helsinki nations met again in Belgrade in March 1978, but this time the Soviets flatly refused to sign a specific renewal of the Helsinki liberations.

106. Carter, *Keeping Faith*, p. 143.

107. Carter, *Keeping Faith*, p. 154.

108. Carter, *Keeping Faith*, p. 157.

109. At the time of signing of the treaties, Gallup Polls were still reporting

that only 39 percent of Americans were in favor of the treaties (with 46 percent in opposition). In contrast, the people of Panama overwhelmingly approved the treaties by a vote of 470,000 to 230,000.

110. Carter, *Keeping Faith*, p. 162.

111. For both sides of the debate on the Panama Canal treaties see Walter La Feber's *The Panama Canal: The Crisis in Historical Perspective* (New York: Oxford University Press, 1978), which supports United States withdrawal, and Paul B. Ryan's *The Panama Canal Controversy* (Stanford, Cal.: Hoover Institution Press, 1977), which opposes withdrawal.

112. A Gallup Poll in February 1978 found 45 percent of the respondents in favor and only 42 percent opposed — the first time a plurality in favor of ratification had been reported.

113. The ratification votes showed considerable partisan difference, with Republicans opposing the treaties by almost one and a half to one and Democrats supporting them by five to one.

114. Carter, *Keeping Faith*, p. 195.

115. Carter, *Keeping Faith*, p. 189.

116. Carter, *Keeping Faith*, p. 200.

117. Ranney, *The American Elections of 1980*, p. 27.

118. Powell, *The Other Side of the Story*, p. 58.

119. Ranney, *The American Elections of 1980*, p. 28.

120. Powell, *The Other Side of the Story*, p. 55.

121. See pages 115–116

122. Carter, *Keeping Faith*, p. 217.

123. Carter, *Keeping Faith*, p. 261.

124. Ironically, the shah had made no secret of his dislike for Carter, whose policies, the shah believed, had contributed to his downfall.

125. Jordan, *Crisis*, p. 55.

126. Germond and Witcover, *Blue Smoke and Mirrors*, p. 86.

127. Jordan, *Crisis*, p. 98.

128. Ranney, *The American Elections of 1980*, p. 45. Earlier presidents had also enjoyed substantial increases in popularity after similar crises. Truman's approval rating rose from 37 to 46 percent after the Berlin Airlift; Eisenhower's from 52 to 58 percent after the Marines' landing in Lebanon; Kennedy's from 78 to 83 percent after the Bay of Pigs and from 61 to 76 percent after the Cuban Missile Crisis; and Ford's from 40 to 50 percent after the *Mayaguez* incident. (From Karlyn Keene in *Public Opinion*, February/March 1980, pp. 28–29.)

129. Evans and Novak, *The Reagan Revolution*, p. 20.

130. Jordan, *Crisis*, p. 100.

131. Jordan, *Crisis*, p. 101.

132. Carter, *Keeping Faith*, p. 489.

133. Carter, *Keeping Faith*, p. 265.

Chapter 3: The Loss of Leadership

1. Germond and Witcover, *Blue Smoke and Mirrors*, p. 40.

2. See Congressional Quarterly, Inc., *Candidates '80* (Washington, D.C.: Congressional Quarterly, 1980).

3. The timing of the announcement of candidacy can be crucial. Once a candidate announces, he or she is barred by the so-called "Fairness Doctrine" from

appearing on the national television networks except as a news figure. The networks are bound by the Federal Communication Commission to give no special exposure to one candidate without offering equal time to all that candidate's rivals in the field.

4. White, *America in Search of Itself*, pp. 256, 279.

5. White, *America in Search of Itself*, p. 281.

6. Elizabeth Drew, *Portrait of an Election*, p. 35.

7. See T. R. Reid, "Kennedy," in Richard Harwood, ed., *The Pursuit of the Presidency* (New York: Berkley, 1981).

8. Germond and Witcover, *Blue Smoke and Mirrors*, p. 49.

9. Germond and Witcover, *Blue Smoke and Mirrors*, p. 48.

10. In Jonathan Moore, ed., *The Campaign for President: 1980 in Retrospect* (Cambridge, Mass.: Ballinger, 1981), p. 22.

11. Germond and Witcover, *Blue Smoke and Mirrors*, p. 52. Also see Hamilton Jordan, *Crisis*, p. 20.

12. Hedrick Smith, "Price for Kennedy's Quick Entry into Campaign Was a Ragged Start," *New York Times*, November 15, 1979. Later, Martin Schram reported in the *Washington Post* that when money was raised by Kennedy, it had been unwisely spent on high salaries and high living for the candidate and his aides (a private jet, etc.). From March to December 1979 the Carter campaign had spent $2.8 million; the Kennedy campaign had spent that amount in its first two months. (Martin Schram, "Making the Opponent the Issue," *Washington Post*, June 9, 1980, p. A-16.)

13. The audience did not know that the interview had been taped in August even before Kennedy had decided to run. However, once Kennedy had made the decision, the interview had to be used immediately or put on the shelf, because once he announced, CBS would be forbidden to offer such time to Kennedy without offering equal time to all. (White, *America in Search of Itself*, p. 13.)

14. The Mudd interview was aired at the same time as the first television showing of the movie *Jaws* on ABC. Afterwards, Senator Bob Dole observed that "seventy-five percent of the country watched *Jaws*, twenty-five percent watched Roger Mudd, and half of them couldn't tell the difference." (Germond and Witcover, *Blue Smoke and Mirrors*, p. 75.) However, many observers thought that more devastating to Kennedy than the Mudd interview was a *Reader's Digest* cover story entitled "Chappaquiddick, the *Still* Unanswered Questions," which savaged Kennedy just before the Iowa caucuses. The magazine then followed with a series of nationwide promotional broadcasts on television, designed to sear on the minds of the nation that Kennedy had not only left the scene of the accident, leaving a woman behind to die, but lied about it. (See White, *America in Search of Itself*, pp. 276–277.)

15. After his statement, the Iranians hailed Kennedy as "An American Prophet." The *Boston Globe* pictured crowds in Iran hanging signs saying, "Hurrah for Kennedy," and the *New York Post* reported his remarks with the headline "Teddy the Toast of Teheran."

16. See Congressional Quarterly, *Candidates '80*.

17. Hedrick Smith, "Ford Seems to Soften His Stand Against a 1980 Race," *New York Times*, November 20, 1979, p. B-12. Also: "An Ex-President Is Available," *Time*, February 18, 1980, p. 27.

18. Cannon, *Reagan*, p. 230.

19. Gerald Pomper with Colleagues, *The Election of 1980: Reports and Interpretations* (Chatham, N.J.: Chatham House, 1981), p. 10.

20. Spending for candidates accepting matching funds in 1980 was limited in nomination campaigns to no more than $14,720,000.

21. Some of Bush's critics suggested that he was the only presidential candidate in American political history who had held more political jobs than he had names.

22. Drew, *Portrait of an Election*, p. 30.

23. Adam Clymer, "Baker Joins Campaign for Presidential Nomination," *New York Times*, November 2, 1979, p. A-1.

24. Germond and Witcover, *Blue Smoke and Mirrors*, p. 117.

25. Germond and Witcover, *Blue Smoke and Mirrors*, p. 103.

26. Moore, *The Campaign for President*, p. 6.

27. Germond and Witcover, *Blue Smoke and Mirrors*, p. 94.

28. See the statement of Jo-Anne Coe, of the Office of Senator Robert Dole, in Moore, *The Campaign for President*, p. 5.

29. It should be noted that the Iowa Republican caucuses differ from the Democratic caucuses in several respects: (1) Republicans cast secret ballots, Democrats do not. (Technically, the Republican caucuses are straw votes.) (2) The actual vote total is announced for Republican candidates, but not for the Democrats (only the number of county convention delegates each candidate secures is announced by the Democrats).

30. "Beyond Debate in Iowa," *New York Times*, January 7, 1980, p. A-18.

31. A statewide poll showed that he dropped from 50 percent support in December 1979 to 26 percent support after the debate. (Ranney, *The American Elections of 1980*, p. 80.)

32. CBS Evening News, January 10, 1980. See Ranney, *The American Elections of 1980*, p. 204.

33. In 1979 Bush traveled something in the neighborhood of 350,000 miles. He spent 328 days on the road, dwarfing Jimmy Carter's record. (Moore, *The Campaign for President*, p. 93.)

34. Moore, *The Campaign for President*, pp. 12, 93. Also see Wayne, *The Road to the White House*, p. 112.

35. Cannon, *Reagan*, p. 247.

36. Nearly 120,000 Republicans (more than 20 percent of Iowa's enrolled Republicans) turned out to vote, which more closely resembles a primary election than a caucus turnout.

37. David Broder, "Iowa Vote: What Happened and Why," *Washington Post*, January 23, 1980, p. A-1.

38. James Herzog, "Iowa Caucus Puts Bush in Serious Contender's League," *Pittsburgh Press*, January 23, 1980, p. A-6.

39. The CBS/*New York Times* poll of February 1980 (p. 5) reported a jump in Bush's following among Republicans from 6 to 24 percent in less than a month.

40. Reagan's loss in Iowa was followed by public opinion polls showing that his early status as favorite among Republican voters had vanished in the wake of his defeat on the prairies. (Evans and Novak, *The Reagan Revolution*, p. 59.)

41. As we have seen, losing New Hampshire in 1976 had prevented Reagan's nomination.

42. The polls were now showing George Bush leading there by almost 10 percent (Bush 45 percent, Reagan 36).

43. Cannon, *Reagan*, p. 250.

44. For other examples of Reagan's effective use of wit to defuse the age and vitality issue see Gardner, *All the President's Wit*; Paul F. Boller, Jr., *Presidential*

Anecdotes (New York: Oxford University Press, 1981); and L. William Troxler, ed., *Along Wit's Way* (New York: Holt, Rinehart and Winston,1983).

45. While campaigning in New Hampshire, Reagan had told a joke involving a Pole, an Italian, a duck, and a cock fight, to a group of reporters, one of whom leaked it. It eventually was widely publicized.

46. Actually, Reagan's people probably initiated the idea of a two-man debate with the newspapers and had neatly mouse-trapped Bush.

47. The final tally was Reagan 50 percent, Bush 23 percent, Baker 13 percent, Anderson 10 percent, Connally and Crane 2 percent each, and Bob Dole less than one half of 1 percent (607 votes).

48. Although neither Reagan nor his opponents then realized it, Reagan's victory in New Hampshire effectively ended Bush's chances for the nomination.

49. Of the $18 million preconvention spending limit for each candidate, Reagan's campaign had used $12 million, and only the first primary was now finished. (Doug Weed and Bill Weed, *Reagan In Pursuit of the Presidency—1980* [Plainfield, N.J.: Haven, 1980].)

50. The vote was 124,226 (31.3 percent) for Bush to 123,076 (31 percent) for Anderson. Reagan ran a close third with 29 percent of the vote. Howard Baker with 5 percent of the ballots cast was a distant fourth. Non-Republicans provided two-fifths of the voters in the Republican primary.

51. Walter Cronkite on the CBS Evening News used Anderson's "strong Massachusetts finish" as his lead story. Although he mentioned that Anderson had finished second, the point was missed by many viewers.

52. The Massachusetts and Vermont primaries were also reported by the media as triumphs for Anderson—the "Underdog of the Month." (See "The Anderson Underdog Paradox," *New York Times*, March 6, 1980, p. A-22.)

53. The deadlines for filing in primaries which would select almost 40 percent of the convention delegates had passed.

54. James P. Herzog, "Reagan Win Expected in South Carolina," *Pittsburgh Press*, March 6, 1980, p. A-5.

55. Bush was third with 15 percent.

56. This bit of campaign history earned Connally an entry in *The Guiness Book of World Records*. The delegate, Ms. Mills, subsequently switched her support to Bush, which the media gleefully reported.

57. Anthony Lewis, "Anderson in Illinois," *New York Times*, March 13, 1980, p. A-23. Also see Pomper with Colleagues, *The Election of 1980*, p. 15.

58. Tom Wicker, "Getting Down to Cases," *New York Times*, March 16, 1980, p. E-19.

59. Garry Trudeau devoted two weeks of the "Doonesbury" comic strip to poking fun at Anderson's shoestring campaign and the kind of people it attracted. Also see Germond and Witcover, *Blue Smoke and Mirrors*, p. 231.

60. Thirty-six states would hold Republican primaries; in eighteen of these, crossover voting was allowed. Only four such "open" primaries had actually occurred prior to the Illinois contest.

61. *New York Times*, March 20, 1980, p. A-1. Also see Ted Knapp, "Reagan, Carter Win Big in Illinois," *Pittsburgh Press*, March 19, 1980, p. A-1.

62. Anthony Lewis, "The Reagan Prospect," *New York Times*, March 20, 1980, p. A-27.

63. On the CBS Evening News the day after the Illinois primary, a CBS political reporter put it: "John Anderson can go on, but he has to wonder...." (From Ranney, *The Election of 1980*, p. 208.)

64. Douglas E. Kneeland, "Bush Says He'll Quit Active Campaigning," *New York Times*, May 27, 1980, p. A-1.

65. The Carter strategy for 1980 was defined by Hamilton Jordan and outlined in a memorandum of January 17, 1979.

66. In the meantime the number of Democratic Party primaries had been increased to thirty-five.

67. See Martin Schram, "The President's Campaign," *Washington Post*, June 8, 1980, p. A-16.

68. Wayne, *The Road to the White House*, p. 115.

69. Martin Schram, "Carter's Campaign," *Washington Post*, June 8, 1980. Also see Martin Schram, "Carter," in Richard Harwood, ed., *The Pursuit of the Presidency 1980* (New York: Berkeley, 1980), pp. 83–120.

70. Drew, *Portrait of an Election*, p. 123. When the Florida primary was held on March 11, 1980, Carter annihilated Kennedy in the popular vote by 60.7 percent to 23.2 percent. Carter received seventy-six delegates and Kennedy twenty-three. (See Congressional Quarterly, Inc., *Congressional Elections Since 1789*, 3rd ed. [Washington, D.C.: Congressional Quarterly], pp. 56–62 for 1980 primary election results.)

71. Germond and Witcover, *Blue Smoke and Mirrors*, p. 90.

72. Drew, *Portrait of an Election*, p. 58.

73. Drew, *Portrait of an Election*, p. 56.

74. Drew, *Portrait of an Election*, p. 56.

75. Drew, *Portrait of an Election*, p. 63.

76. Paul R. Ambramson, John H. Aldrich, and David Rhode, *Change and Continuity in the 1980 Elections* (Washington, D.C.: Congressional Quarterly, 1982), p. 23.

77. Pomper with Colleagues, *The Election of 1980*, p. 23.

78. In 1980, the Iowa caucuses received extensive media attention. In 1972 the caucuses had merited only three items on the evening news; in 1976, half a dozen; in 1980, it would be a score. (Michael J. Robinson and Margaret A. Sheehan, *Over the Wire and on TV: CBS and UPI in Campaign '80* [New York: Russell Sage Foundation, 1983], p. 175.)

79. On Friday, January 25, 1980, the *Washington Post* carried the headline: "Fund Depleted, Kennedy Juggles Campaign Plans."

80. Drew, *Portrait of an Election*, p. 134.

81. An annual inflation rate of 18.2 percent would cut every pension or fixed salary to half its value in five years.

82. White, *America in Search of Itself*, p. 22.

83. White, *America in Search of Itself*, p. 298.

84. Drew, *Portrait of an Election*, p. 51.

85. George Will, *The New Season*, p. 138.

86. Carter couldn't know, of course, that Kennedy's own polls in Illinois showed that Carter was ahead 72 percent to 36 percent. (Source: White, *America in Search of Itself*, p. 297.)

87. Quoted in Jordan, *Crisis*, p. 58. Elizabeth Drew points out that Kennedy would soon find out that the support of Mayor Byrne also brought with it the animosity of the considerable number of political enemies she has acquired. (Drew, *Portrait of an Election*, p. 62.) Mayor Byrne would learn that it cost a bundle in lost federal funds to endorse Kennedy when Secretary of Transportation Neil Goldschmidt denied large sums of discretionary federal funds to Chicago.

88. Moore, *The Campaign for President*, p. 72.

89. Ten days before the primary Kennedy's in-house polls showed that Carter would carry the state by eighteen points. (See White, *America in Search of Itself*, p. 298. Also see Germond and Witcover, *Blue Smoke and Mirrors*, p. 152.)

90. See Jordan, *Crisis*, p. 228.

91. The CBS/*New York Times* exit poll of Wisconsin voters reported that most of those who cited Iran as having an effect on their vote went for Carter. The NBC/Associated Press poll indicated that the president received the vote of 48 percent of those who made up their minds on election day, compared with 28 percent for Senator Kennedy. (E. J. Dionne, Jr., "Iran and Wisconsin Primary," *New York Times*, April 3, 1980.)

92. Germond and Witcover, *Blue Smoke and Mirrors*, p. 20.

93. The Carter campaign frequently ran a thirty-second television ad that had Carter saying, "I don't think there's any way you can separate the responsibility of being a husband or a father or a basic human being from that of being a good President. . . . What I do in the White House is to maintain a good family life, which I consider crucial to being a good President." (From Drew, *Portrait of an Election*, p. 54.)

94. Jordan, *Crisis*, p. 229.

95. Although the Gallup/*Newsweek* Poll reported that 71 percent of those questioned approved of the effort.

96. Vance subsequently recorded his impression of American foreign policy in a memoir entitled *Hard Choices: Critical Years in America's Foreign Policy* (New York: Simon and Schuster, 1983).

97. Drew, *Portrait of an Election*, p. 187.

98. Cannon, *Reagan*, p. 264.

99. For the Republican platform see "The 1980 Republican Platform," *Congressional Quarterly Weekly Report* (July 18, 1980), p. 2045.

100. Lyn Nofziger, the press secretary of the Reagan-Bush committee, suggests that the Equal Rights Amendment (ERA) and abortion gave the Republicans a great deal of difficulty. For one thing, between them, the two issues projected the federal government more deeply into family life than anything the Democrats had ever dared propose. Also historically neither abortion nor ERA has been a "Republican" issue; both engender individual responses that cut across party lines and, within the party, across ideological lines. See Lyn Nofziger in Moore, *The Campaign for President*, p. 145.

101. An NBC poll at the opening of the convention showed Bush with 47 percent of the delegate preferences for vice president. The others were scattered behind Bush. (White, *America in Search of Itself*, p. 320.)

102. Consisting of William J. Casey, the campaign director; Edwin Meese III, Reagan's long-time assistant; and Richard Wirthlin, Reagan's chief pollster and a key adviser.

103. Consisting of former secretary of state Henry A. Kissinger, who, the conservatives concluded, was trying to set the stage for his own return to Washington as secretary of state (a frightening thought for them); Alan Greenspan, former chairman of the President's Council of Economic Advisers; and Ford aides Robert Barnett and John Marsh.

104. Quoted in Congressional Quarterly, Inc., *National Party Conventions 1831–1980*.

105. Others said that the most you could say for the office of vice president was that it was "inside work and no heavy lifting."

106. Probably, more importantly, Reagan was well aware that the day after

the inauguration he would still be "Mr. Reagan" and Ford would still be "Mr. President."

107. According to David Broder, the consensus of the press corps at the time was that a Reagan/Ford team was a politically "looney idea" to start with. Reporters and columnists would almost certainly point out that Reagan, in bartering away the powers of his presidency to get Ford on his ticket, did not understand the scope and magnitude of the job he wanted. In any case, the polls indicated that going with Bush instead of Ford did not cost Reagan any measurable support. (See David Broder in Moore, *The Campaign for President*, p. 157.)

108. Drew, *Portrait of an Election*, p. 217.

109. David Broder, "How Reagan's Bungling Helps Carter," *Pittsburgh Press*, July 19, 1980, p. B-2.

110. For a report of Reagan's acceptance speech see "Convention Texts, Acceptance Speeches, Reagan: 'Time to Recapture our Destiny,'" *Congressional Quarterly Weekly Report*, July 19, 1980. Also see *New York Times*, July 18, 1980, p. A-8.

111. Tom Shales, "Tailored to TV," *Washington Post*, July 18, 1980, p. C-6.

112. An NBC/Associated Press survey showed Reagan's convention had pushed him up to 55 percent over Carter's 24 percent. The Harris Poll reported Reagan 61 percent over Carter's 33 percent. (White, *America in Search of Itself*, p. 328.)

113. The Democrats ruled out Atlanta and Chicago because their states had not ratified the Equal Rights Amendment.

114. *Delegate Selection Rules for the 1980 Democratic National Convention* (Washington, D.C.: Democratic National Committee, June 9, 1978). Crittenden, *Parties and Elections in the United States*, p. 131, summarizes the goals of the reforms. Also see Polsby, *Consequences of Party Reform*.

115. For a breakdown of the delegates at the 1980 Democratic Convention see White, *America in Search of Itself*, p. 333. According to George Will, at the convention, Puerto Rico had more votes (41) than Oregon (39) or West Virginia (35). California's Democratic Party reserved 15 percent of its delegate slots for Hispanics — then counted Greeks as Hispanics. (Will, *The New Season*, p. 154.)

116. Recounted in Jordan, *Crisis*, p. 329.

117. See Thomas Ferguson and Joel Rogers, *The Hidden Election: Politics and Economics in the 1980 Presidential Campaign* (New York: Pantheon Books, 1981), p. 40.

118. Steven B. Roberts, "Democrats in Congress Fear Carter May Hurt the Ticket," *New York Times*, August 9, 1980.

119. A week before the convention, Gallup reported that 55 percent of polled Democrats approved of Carter releasing his delegates from their commitments and allowing them to vote for whomever they wished. (*Indianapolis Star*, August 7, 1980.) See Crittenden, *Parties and Elections in the United States*, p. 76.

120. In actuality, only 18 percent of the delegates present had ever had their names on a public ballot. In the overwhelming majority of state primaries delegates had been selected in caucuses and other party meetings.

121. See Edward Bennett Williams, "The Rule's a Bummer," *Washington Post*, August 7, 1980; and Hugh L. Carey, "An Open Convention," *New York Times*, May 21, 1980. For counter-arguments see Don Fowler, "The Kennedy Flip on Party Rules," *Washington Post*, July 16, 1980.

122. Congressional Quarterly, Inc., *National Party Conventions 1831–1980* (Washington, D.C.: Congressional Quarterly), p. 128.

123. Jordan, *Crisis*, p. 324.

124. Jordan, *Crisis*, pp. 326–327.

125. For the 1980 Democratic Platform see "1980 Democratic Platform Text," *Congressional Quarterly Weekly Report* 8 (August 16, 1980), p. 2405. Also see Christopher Buchanan, "Loser Kennedy Leaves Imprint on 1980 Platform," *Congressional Quarterly Weekly Report*, August 16, 1980, p. 2363.

126. Under Democratic Party rules, the nominee must indicate in writing any reservations he has about the party platform.

127. See Nelson W. Polsby, "The Democratic Nomination," in Ranney, *The American Elections of 1980*, pp. 37–60.

128. After Charlie stopped singing one-third of the crowd left.

129. Labor Day is the traditional starting date for general election campaigns. Working class whites make up more than one-third of the big industrial states whose large blocs of electoral votes swing presidential election outcomes.

130. Germond and Witcover, *Blue Smoke and Mirrors*, p. 220.

131. For a list of the "negatives" of Carter's candidacy as seen by his polling adviser, Patrick Caddell, see Drew, *Portrait of an Election*, p. 391.

132. Washingtonians joked that Carter was the first president with poll ratings lower than the prime interest rate.

133. James M. Perry and Albert R. Hunt, "Carter Plans to Win by Depicting Reagan as Shallow, Dangerous," *Wall Street Journal*, August 14, 1980.

134. Wayne, *The Road to the White House*, pp. 193–194.

135. Massachusetts and Arkansas ultimately went to Reagan.

136. Drew, *Portrait of an Election*, p. 287.

137. Jordan, *Crisis*, p. 318. The text of Carter's statement to the press may be read in Congressional Quarterly, Inc., *President Carter 1980*, p. 175.

138. Jordan, *Crisis*, p. 348.

139. See James M. Perry and Albert R. Hunt, "Reagan Plan Is to Make Carter the Issue, Stress Large Industrial States," *Wall Street Journal*, July 14, 1980. Also see Lou Cannon and David S. Broder, "Reagan to Attack 'Failed Presidency,'" *Washington Post*, July 19, 1980.

140. Ironically, Reagan could count Virginia, one of the most "Southern" of states, as a safe state in 1980. Carter had lost Virginia in 1976 and since then it had become a Republican state—some said as Republican as Vermont.

141. Wayne, *The Road to the White House*, pp. 191–193.

142. Cannon, *Reagan*, p. 272.

143. The American people generally agreed with Reagan. A poll conducted in 1980 by the University of Chicago's National Opinion Research Council revealed that 60 percent of those surveyed said that too little was being spent on the military. Only 12 percent said that too much was being spent. (Twenty-eight percent thought outlays were about right.)

144. Quoted in Jordan, *Crisis*, p. 352.

145. For an excellent discussion of Reagan's relations with the Moral Majority see Chapter 10 in Evans and Novak, *The Reagan Revolution*, p. 204.

146. A Democrat promptly suggested that Reagan's views no doubt grew out in playing second banana to a chimpanzee in the movie *Bedtime for Bonzo*. (Reagan's Dallas speech is reported in the *Dallas Times Herald* of August 23, 1980.)

147. Evans and Novak, *The Regan Revolution*, p. 213.

148. Quoted in Ranney, *The American Elections of 1980*, p. 150.

149. The September 15, 1980, ABC/Harris Poll revealed that 82 percent of the persons questioned agreed that Reagan "seems to make too many off-the-cuff remarks which he has trouble explaining or had had to apologize for making."

150. *New York Times,* October 19, 1980, p. 38.

151. On August 22 Defense Secretary Harold Brown had disclosed at a news conference the plans for the "Stealth" bomber.

152. It was not a debate really—merely a series of questions from a panel of journalists. NBC and CBS carried it live. ABC showed a movie.

153. The September 2–7 *Los Angeles Times* Poll put Reagan at 37 percent; Carter at 36 percent; and Anderson at 18 percent. The September 3–7 Lou Harris Poll reported Reagan at 41 percent; Carter at 37 percent; and Anderson at 17 percent.

154. Germond and Witcover, *Blue Smoke and Mirrors,* p. 227.

155. Germond and Witcover, *Blue Smoke and Mirrors,* p. 227.

156. Abramson, Aldrich, and Rhode, *Change and Continuity in the 1980 Elections,* p. 42.

157. Germond and Witcover, *Blue Smoke and Mirrors,* p. 250.

158. Quoted in Cannon, *Reagan,* p. 280. Also see Francis X. Clines, "Carter Suggests Turn to Racism in Reagan Views," *New York Times,* September 17, 1980, p. B-10.

159. Adam Clymer, "Carter Campaign Ad Attacked as a 'Smear,'" *New York Times,* September 21, 1980, p. 10.

160. Quoted in Cannon, *Reagan,* p. 283.

161. Curtis Wilkie, "Old Tricks of the Trail for Carter," *Boston Globe,* September 21, 1980.

162. Ranney, *The American Elections of 1980,* p. 156.

163. Germond and Witcover, *Blue Smoke and Mirrors,* p. 263.

164. Germond and Witcover, *Blue Smoke and Mirrors,* p. 234.

165. Even after Anderson declared as an Independent candidate, he remained on the Republican primary election ballot in a number of states and, in fact, got better than 10 percent of the Republican primary vote in the District of Columbia, Oregon, and New Mexico. (*Congressional Quarterly Weekly Report,* July 5, 1980, p. 1871.)

166. Drew, *Portrait of an Election,* p. 277.

167. See Abramson, Aldrich, and Rhode, *Change and Continuity in the 1980 Elections,* p. 36.

168. Drew, *Portrait of an Election,* p. 281.

169. Ironically, since Anderson qualified for federal funds in 1980, he was automatically eligible for funds as a third party in 1984, according to a 1983 Federal Election Commission ruling. (Wayne, *The Road to the White House,* p. 46.)

170. Generally speaking, Reagan had been willing to debate all along. Debates usually favor the challenger (the "Lincoln-Douglas rule"). Carter had been the unwilling one. Reagan later explained: "There's a lot of the Gipper in the governor. How could the Gipper not debate?"

171. Jordan, *Crisis,* p. 355.

172. Drew, *Portrait of an Election,* p. 323.

173. The reference to Amy infuriated President Carter and his advisers. The next day, a reporter for one of the television networks actually interviewed Amy in her schoolyard and she acknowledged that yes, she did think the spread of nuclear weapons was a big problem. Scores of "Amy" jokes soon began making the rounds. "Ask Amy" signs began appearing at Republican rallies, and reporters suggested a new campaign book, *Prospects for Nuclear Disarmament,* by Amy Carter. (Germond and Witcover, *Blue Smoke and Mirrors,* pp. 284–285; Cannon, *Reagan,* pp. 284, 295, 296, 300.)

174. The text of the debate can be found in *Congressional Quarterly Weekly Report* 38 (November 1, 1980), pp. 3279–3289.

175. Abramson, Aldrich, and Rhode, *Change and Continuity in the 1980 Elections*, p. 324.

176. Drew, *Portrait of an Election*, p. 324.

177. Evans and Novak, *The Reagan Revolution*, p. 83.

178. Quoted in Drew, *Portrait of an Election*, p. 320.

179. Drew, *Portrait of an Election*, p. 337.

180. At least the voters did not have to wait long to know the outcome. NBC reported Reagan's victory at 8:15 p.m. on the basis of their exit polling — the most rapid report in television history to that time.

181. The Republicans exulted that they even carried "the People's Republic of Massachusetts."

182. Taft in 1912, Hoover in 1932, Ford in 1976 (but he had not been elected to office), and Carter in 1980. Stephen Wayne suggests the lesson here is that incumbency is not necessarily an advantage in an age of high expectations, particularly if people believe that their standard of living has deteriorated over the course of an administration. (Wayne, *The Road to the White House*, p. 189.)

183. The voting results are from *Congressional Quarterly Weekly Report* 39 (January 17, 1981), p. 138. See William Schneider, "The November 4 Vote for President: What Did It Mean?" in Ranney, *The American Elections of 1980*, esp. pp. 225–227.

184. For an analysis of the spending in 1980 see Herbert E. Alexander, "Making Sense About Dollars in the 1980 Presidential Campaign," in Michael J. Malbin, ed., *Money and Politics in the United States: Financing Politics in the 1980s* (Washington, D.C.: American Enterprise Institute/Chatham House, 1984), p. 11.

185. In 1980, 2,551 PACs were registered with the Federal Election Commission. Of these, corporate PACs represented 1,204; labor, 297; trade/membership/health, 574; "non-connected," 378; corporations without stock, 56; and cooperatives, 42. From Malbin, *Money and Politics in the United States*, p. 295.

186. See Table 2.9 in Malbin, *Money and Politics in the United States*, p. 53.

187. Quoted in Drew, *Portrait of an Election*, p. 339.

188. However, Stephen J. Wayne suggests there is little evidence that Democrats behaved any differently from Republicans, who also stayed away from the polls. Hawaii, the last state to close its polls, voted for Carter. (Wayne, *The Road to the White House*, p. 253.)

189. On the flap created by the television networks' predictions of a Reagan victory before voting was completed on the West Coast, see Paul Wilson, "Election Night 1980 and the Controversy Over Early Projections," in William C. Adams, ed., *Television Coverage of the 1980 Presidential Campaign* (Norwood, N.J.: Ablex, 1983).

190. Quoted in Jordan, *Crisis*, p. 373.

191. See "What Went Wrong?" *Opinion Outlook*, November 17, 1980. Actually, the Democrats had more to grieve about than they realized. As George Will points out, in a span of five elections — 1968, 1972, 1976, 1980, and 1984 — Carter would be the only Democratic presidential candiate to win more than 43 percent of the vote. (Will, *The New Season*, p. 97.)

192. David S. Broder, "Is it a New Era?" *Washington Post* (November 19, 1980). Also see Douglas A. Hibbs, Jr., "President Reagan's Mandate from the 1980 Election: A Shift to the Right?" *American Political Quarterly* 10:4 (October 1982), pp. 387–420.

193. Carter suffered more from the decline in voter turnout than Reagan since it meant that a larger percentage of his supporters failed to cast ballots. It also meant that for every American who cast a ballot for Reagan, three did not.

194. A bumper sticker frequently seen in the East read: "Your candidate is even worse than my candidate." The cover of *Public Opinion* magazine depicted a man wearing four campaign badges on his lapel: one for Carter, one for Reagan, one for Anderson, and one reading "No Thanks." (Reported in Ranney, *The American Elections of 1980*, p. 305.)

195. Pomper with Colleagues, *The Elections of 1980*, p. 103.

196. Wayne refers to the CBS/New York Times Poll which estimated that approximately 20 percent of the electorate made up their minds in the final week of the campaign (many doing so on the final day). Since most of the public polls were completed by November 1, four days before the election, they did not detect the late surge to Reagan. (Wayne, *The Road to the White House*, p. 247; also see his Table 8-1 on the same page.)

197. The pre-election polls are discussed in Everett Carll Ladd and G. Donald Feree, "Were the Pollsters Really Wrong?" *Public Opinion* 3 (December/January 1981), pp. 13-17, 20. Also see John F. Stacks, *Watershed: The Campaign for the Presidency, 1980* (New York: Times Books, 1981), pp. 217-218.

198. Gerald Pomper suggests that the mood of the voters in 1980 is best illustrated by the close of a sermon given by a Massachusetts minister on the eve of the election: "Oh, thank God only one of them can be elected!" (Pomper with Colleagues, *The Election of 1980*, p. 113.)

199. See Adam Clymer, "Displeasure With Carter Turned Many to Reagan," *New York Times*, November 9, 1980. See also *Public Opinion* 3 (December/January 1981).

200. Quoted in White, *America in Search of Itself*, p. 21.

201. Barbara Honegger, in her book *October Surprise* (New York: Tudor, 1989), raises the possibility that the Reagan-Bush election campaign deliberately sabotaged President Carter's attempts to free the American hostages in Iran.

202. Congressional Quarterly, Inc., *President Reagan* (Washington, D.C.: Congressional Quarterly, 1981), p. 35.

203. Jimmy Carter, *Keeping Faith: Memoirs of a President* (New York: Bantam, 1982). He also wrote with Rosalynn *Everything to Gain: Making the Most of the Rest of Your Life* (New York: Fawcett, 1987).

204. Recounted in Jordan, *Crisis*, p. 7.

Epilogue

1. Dennis Farney in *Wall Street Journal*, June 24, 1988.

2. In his very perceptive book, *The Trusteeship Presidency: Jimmy Carter and the United States Congress* (Baton Rouge: Louisiana State University Press, 1988), Professor Charles O. Jones interprets the Carter years as the twentieth century attempt to govern by the principle of an eighteenth century statesman, Edmund Burke. According to that principle, what a politician most owes his constituents is his independent judgment—popular or not. "A trustee takes on the difficult issues first, not the easy ones," Jones says. "The Panama Canal treaty is a perfect example. And no pure trustee is going to want to be political. The notion that Jimmy Carter should have been like Lyndon Johnson is crazy." But a trustee, as Carter found out, is alone on a high wire.

Bibliography

Abramson, Paul R.; Aldrich, John H.; and Rhode, David. *Change and Continuity in the 1980 Elections.* Washington, D.C.: Congressional Quarterly, 1982.

Adams, William C. *Television Coverage of the 1980 Presidential Campaign.* Norwood, N.J.: Ablex, 1983.

Adler, Bill, ed. *The Wit and Wisdom of Jimmy Carter.* Secaucus, N.J.: Citadel, 1977.

Alexander, Herbert E. *Financing the 1976 Election.* Washington, D.C.: Congressional Quarterly, 1979.

Asher, Herbert. *Presidential Elections and American Politics: Voters, Candidates, and Campaigns Since 1952.* Homewood, Ill.: Dorsey, 1976.

Barber, James David. *The Pulse of Politics: Electing Presidents in the Media Age.* New York: Norton, 1980.

_____, ed. *Race for the Presidency: The Media and the Nominating Process.* Englewood Cliffs, N.J.: Prentice Hall, 1978.

Boller, Paul F., Jr. *Presidential Anecdotes.* New York: Oxford University Press, 1981.

_____. *Presidential Campaigns.* New York: Oxford University Press, 1984.

Brzezinski, Zbigniew. *Power and Principle: Memoirs of the National Security Adviser, 1977-1981.* New York: Farrar, Straus, Giroux, 1983.

Burns, James Macgregor. *The Power to Lead: The Crisis of the American Presidency.* New York: Simon & Schuster, 1984.

Caddell, Patrick H. "The Democratic Strategy and Its Electoral Consequences." In Seymour Martin Lipsit, ed. *Party Coalitions in the 1980s.* San Francisco, Calif.: Institute for Contemporary Studies, 1981.

Califano, Joseph A., Jr. *Governing America: An Insider's Report from the White House and the Cabinet.* New York: Simon & Schuster, 1981.

Cannon, Lou. *Reagan.* New York: Putnam, 1982.

Carter, Jimmy. *A Government as Good as Its People.* New York: Simon and Schuster, 1977.

_____. *Public Papers of the Presidents of the United States, Containing the Public Messages, Speeches, and Statements of the President.* Washington, D.C.: U.S. Government Printing Office, 1977-1980.

_____. *The Speeches of Governor Jimmy Carter, Presidential Campaign of 1976.* Washington, D.C.: U.S. Government Printing Office, 1981.

_____. *The Speeches of President Jimmy Carter, Presidential Campaign of 1980.* Washington, D.C.: U.S. Government Printing Office, 1981.

_____. *Why Not the Best?* New York: Bantam, 1976.

_____. *Keeping the Faith: Memoirs of a President.* New York: Bantam, 1982.

_____. *The Blood of Abraham: Insights into the Middle East.* Boston: Houghton Mifflin, 1986.

Chester, Lewis; Hodgson, Godfrey; and Page, Bruce. *An American Melodrama: The Presidential Campaign of 1968.* New York: Viking, 1969.

Congressional Quarterly, Inc. *Candidates '80.* Washington, D.C.: Congressional Quarterly, 1980.

_____. *President Carter.* Washington, D.C.: Congressional Quarterly, 1977.

_____. *President Carter 1977.* Washington, D.C.: Congressional Quarterly, 1978.

_____. *President Carter 1978.* Washington, D.C.: Congressional Quarterly, 1979.

_____. *President Carter 1979.* Washington, D.C.: Congressional Quarterly, 1980.

_____. *President Carter 1980.* Washington, D.C.: Congressional Quarterly, 1981.

_____. *President Reagan.* Washington, D.C.: Congressional Quarterly, 1981.

Crittenden, John A. *Parties and Elections in the United States.* Englewood Cliffs, N.J.: Prentice Hall, 1982.

Davis, James W. *National Conventions in an Age of Party Reform.* Westport, Conn.: Greenwood, 1983.

Drew, Elizabeth. *Portrait of an Election.* New York: Simon and Schuster, 1981.

Dugger, Ronnie. *On Reagan: The Man and His Presidency.* New York: McGraw-Hill, 1983.

Edwards, Lee. *Ronald Reagan: A Political Biography.* Ottawa, Ill.: Caroline House, 1981.

Evans, Rowland, and Novak, Robert. *The Reagan Revolution.* New York: Dutton, 1981.

Fallows, James. "The Passionless President." *Atlantic Monthly* 243 (May 1979).

Ferguson, Thomas, and Rogers, Joel. *The Decline of the Democrats and the Future of American Politics.* New York: Hill and Wang, 1986.

Fink, Gary. *Prelude to the Presidency: The Political Character and Legislative Leadership of Jimmy Carter.* Westport, Conn: Greenwood, 1980.

Fishel, Jeff, ed. *Parties and Elections in an Anti-Party Age.* Bloomington: Indiana University Press, 1978.

Ford, Gerald R. *A Time to Heal.* New York: Harper and Row, 1979.

Germond, Jack, and Witcover, Jules. *Blue Smoke and Mirrors: How Reagan Won and Why Carter Lost the Election of 1980.* New York: Viking, 1981.

Glad, Betty. *Jimmy Carter: In Search of the White House.* New York: Norton, 1980.

Goldman, Ralph M. *Search for Consensus: The Story of the Democratic Party.* Philadelphia: Temple University Press, 1979.

Greenstein, Fred I., ed. *The Reagan Presidency: An Early Assessment.* Baltimore: Johns Hopkins University Press, 1983.

Hargrove, Erwin C. *Jimmy Carter as President: Leadership and the Politics of the Public Good.* Baton Rouge: Louisiana State University Press, 1988.

Harwood, Richard, ed. *The Pursuit of the Presidency 1980.* New York: Berkley, 1980.

Johnson, Haynes. *In the Absence of Power: Governing America.* New York: Viking, 1980.

Jones, Charles O. *The Trusteeship Presidency: Jimmy Carter and the United States Congress.* Baton Rouge: Louisiana State University Press, 1988.

Jordan, Hamilton. *Crisis: The Last Year of the Carter Presidency.* New York: Putnam, 1982.

Keech, William R., and Matthews, Donald R. *The Party's Choice.* Washington, D.C.: Brookings Institution, 1976.

Kucharsky, David. *The Man from Plains: The Mind and Spirit of Jimmy Carter.* New York: Harper and Row, 1976.

Lasky, Victor. *Jimmy Carter: The Man and the Myth.* New York: Marek, 1979.

Lewis, Joseph. *What Makes Reagan Run: A Political Profile.* New York: McGraw-Hill, 1968.

Lynn, Lawrence F., Jr., and Whitman, David. *The President as Policy Maker: Jimmy Carter and Welfare Reform.* Philadelphia: Temple University Press, 1981.

Malbin, Michael, ed. *Money and Politics in the United States: Financing Elections in the 1980s.* Washington, D.C.: American Enterprise Institute/Chatham House, 1984.

Marshall, Thomas. *Presidential Nominations in a Reform Age.* New York: Praeger, 1981.

Mollenhoff, Clark. *The President Who Failed: Carter Out of Control.* New York: Macmillan, 1980.

Moore, Jonathan, and Fraser, Janet. *Campaign for President: The Managers Look at '76.* Cambridge, Mass.: Ballinger, 1977.

Moore, Raymond A. "The Carter Presidency and Foreign Policy." In Abernathy, M. Glenn, *et al.*, eds. *The Carter Years: The President and Policymaking.* New York: St. Martin's Press, 1984.

Page, Benjamin I. *Choices and Echoes in Presidential Elections.* Chicago: University of Chicago Press, 1978.

Patterson, Thomas E. *The Mass Media Elections: How Americans Choose Their President.* New York: Praeger, 1980.

Pomper, Gerald M., with Colleagues. *The Election of 1976: Reports and Interpretations.* New York: McKay, 1977.

————, with Colleagues. *The Election of 1980: Reports and Interpretations.* Chatham, N.J.: Chatham House, 1981.

Powell, Jody. *The Other Side of the Story.* New York: Morrow, 1984.

Quandt, William B. *Camp David: Peacemaking and Politics.* Washington, D.C.: Brookings Institution, 1986.

Ranney, Austin, ed. *The American Elections of 1980.* Washington, D.C.: American Enterprise Institute, 1981.

————. *Participation in American Presidential Nominations, 1976.* Washington, D.C.: American Enterprise Institute, 1977.

————, ed. *The Past and Present of Presidential Debates.* Washington, D.C.: American Enterprise Institute, 1979.

Reagan, Ronald. *The Speeches of Governor Ronald Reagan, Presidential Campaign of 1980.* Washington, D.C.: U.S. Government Printing Office, 1981.

Reeves, Richard. *Convention.* Harcourt Brace Jovanovich, 1977.

Roseboom, Eugene H., and Alfred E. Eckes, Jr. *A History of Presidential Elections.* New York: Macmillan, 1979.

Rutland, Robert A. *The Democrats: From Jefferson to Carter.* Baton Rouge: Louisiana State University Press, 1982.

Sandoz, Ellis, and Crabb, Cecil, Jr., eds. *A Tide of Discontent: The 1980 Elections and Their Meaning.* Washington, D.C.: Congressional Quarterly, 1981.

Schram, Martin. *The Great Video Game: Presidential Politics in the Television Age.* New York: Morrow, 1987.

————. *Running for President 1976: A Journal of the Carter Campaign.* New York: Stein and Day, 1977.

Shogan, Robert. *Promises to Keep: Carter's First Hundred Days.* New York: Crowell, 1977.

Sick, Gary. *All Fall Down: America's Tragic Encounter with Iran.* New York: Random House, 1985.

Smith, Gaddis. *Morality, Reasons and Power: American Diplomacy in the Carter Years.* New York: Hill and Wang, 1986.

Smith, Hedrick. *The Power Game: How Washington Works.* New York: Ballantine, 1988.

————, et al. *Reagan the Man, The President.* New York: Macmillan, 1980.

Stacks, John F. *Watershed: The Campaign for the Presidency 1980.* New York: Times, 1981.

Stroud, Kandy. *How Jimmy Carter Won.* New York: Morrow, 1977.

Sullivan, Denis, *et al.* "Candidates, Caucuses, and Issues: The Democratic Convention, 1976." In Maisel, Louis, and Cooper, Joseph, eds. *The Impact of the Electoral Process.* Beverly Hills, Calif: Sage, 1977.

————, et al. *Exploration in Convention Decision-Making.* San Francisco: Freeman, 1976.

————, et al. "Exploring the 1976 Republican Convention." *Political Science Quarterly* 92 (1977–1978), pp. 633–682.

Vance, Cyrus R. *Hard Choices: Critical Years in America's Foreign Policy.* New York: Simon & Schuster, 1983.

Wayne, Stephen J. *The Road to the White House: The Politics of Presidential Elections.* 2d ed. New York: St. Martin's, 1984.

White, Theodore H., *America in Search of Itself: The Making of the President 1956–1980.* New York: Harper & Row, 1982.

————. *The Making of the President 1968.* New York: Atheneum, 1969.

————. *The Making of the President 1972.* New York: Atheneum, 1973.

Wills, Garry. *Lead Time: A Journalist's Education.* Garden City, N.J.: Doubleday & Co., 1983.

Wirthlin, Richard B. "The Republican Strategy and Its Electoral Consequences." In Lipset, Seymour Martin, ed. *Party Coalitions in the 1980s.* San Francisco, Calif.: Institute for Contemporary Studies, 1981.

————, Vincent Breglio, and Richard Beal. "Campaign Chronicle." *Public Opinion* 4 (1981).

Witcover, Jules. *Marathon: The Pursuit of the Presidency, 1972–1976.* New York: Viking, 1977.

Wooten, James. *Dasher: The Roots and Rising of Jimmy Carter.* New York: Summit, 1978.

Index